Company image and reality

A critique of corporate communications

DAVID BERNSTEIN

ILLUSTRATED BY REX AUDLEY

HOLT, RINEHART AND WINSTON

THE ADVERTISING ASSOCIATION

Holt, Rinehart and Winston Ltd:
1 St Anne's Road, Eastbourne, East Sussex BN21 3UN

British Library Cataloguing in Publication Data

Bernstein, David
    Company image and reality.
    1. Corporations   2. Industrial design
    co-ordination
    I. Title
    659.2'85   HD38

    ISBN 0–03–910574–1

Text set in 10/13pt Linotron 202 Palatino, printed and bound in Great Britain at the
Pitman Press, Bath

To Jane, Lucy and Jonathan

Contents

Acknowledgements

Hans Nordenskjold of the Swedish advertising agency, Wennergren-Williams invited me to Gothenberg to give a speech on 'Company Image'. Anthony Wreford of the corporate communications consultants McAvoy Wreford invited me to Amsterdam to give a speech on Corporate Advertising. This book is a direct result of these two requests—plus some prompting from my publisher.

I am also indebted to Bob Worcester for providing material, contact and above all insights; to Gillian Hall of the *Financial Times* and Nick Winkfield of Research Services Limited for up-to-the-minute and confidential information not to mention guidance; to Tom Ryan of Marston, the New York public relations company, for invaluable background on crisis management; to *Advertising Age* for a long history of cooperation (Chapter 22 was born in their European magazine *Focus*); and to Wally Olins for showing all of us the way.

My debt to Time Inc is profound. They are publishers not only of *Time*, well known as commissioners of corporate advertising research, but also of *Fortune* without whose annual *Crosscurrents in Corporate Communications*, this book probably could not have been written.

I wish to thank my colleagues at The Creative Business, London, for their massive contribution (direct and indirect) to this book over the past dozen years; my colleagues at Le Creative Business, Paris, RSCG Paris and Colman RSCG London for both stimulus and suggestions. My thanks also to the many companies I have referred to, in particular to those clients of TCB London who gave of their time and ideas—especially Novo Industri Denmark, Shell and the Confederation of British Industry.

I have been helped more than I deserve by three personal assistants—Joanna Maxwell, Zoe Starkey and Lyndsey Crawford—who between them delved, annotated, filed, retrieved, typed, statted, word-processed, had a baby, retyped, kept tabs and their composure. Trevor Treen earns my gratitude for reading an early text and helping to reshape it. Susan, my wife, has both put up with me and directed my attention to authors I knew not of. Finally, my thanks to Rex Audley for both illustrating the text and illuminating it. Many of the ideas have been stimulated by his thinking and his researches.

As always, there are echoes from all over. Some I don't even recognise. The errors, responsibility, blame and the jokes, however, are mine alone.

David Bernstein.   London, July 1984

Preface

Image is reality.

It is the result of our actions.

If the image is false and our performance is good, it's our fault for being bad communicators.

If the image is true and reflects our bad performance, it's our fault for being bad managers.

Unless we know our image we can neither communicate nor manage. This is a book about the way companies manage their communications. And how they might do it better.

It draws upon UK, European and, disproportionately, US experience.

American business is more likely to take the subject seriously and less likely to be reticent about it.

1

What are you trying to tell me?

It was my second flight to New York. The first with this airline. I fixed my belt. The engines started. So did the muzak. As we lifted off the muzak played 'Something's gotta give'. Were they trying to tell me something? Perhaps not. Not consciously. But they were communicating nevertheless.

Companies communicate whether they want to or not. Deliberate reticence is itself a message. The public may interpret it as 'quiet assurance' or 'they've got something to hide'. Neither of these interpretations may be accurate. That does not make them any less valid. And if we exist in the world and need to do business, to progress and prosper in it, then the impressions we create are important. If they get it wrong it is not their fault but ours. Communication is the responsibility of the communicator. Misconceptions are the fault of the transmitter, not the receiver.

'Something's gotta give.' It's only a tune. Not as if they played the vocal. And anyway who knows the words? Does it matter? To me it mattered. I knew the words. Airlines don't show disaster movies. Airlines pay attention to detail.

The image of a company is made up of countless details. Some are more important than others. Our first impressions are generally sharper and harder to erase or substitute. Social psychologists debate whether the 'primacy effect' is stronger than the 'recency effect'. It depends of course upon the strength of the impression and the context. However, most investigators agree that we form opinions of people quickly, that we feel uneasy when we keep an open mind. Having formed our impression we are reluctant to change it radically, if at all, preferring to accommodate new information as fragments which contribute to the mosaic we have already constructed.

If a company chooses to transmit few messages of its own the public will choose to construct messages for it, utilising any generalisation, hearsay, fragment of 'information' to complete a pattern, no matter how distorted. Some companies choose not to communicate until there is little to say—except goodbye. A General Motors car worker in the US said, 'I guess I got laid off because I made poor quality cars. In 16 years not once was I ever asked for a suggestion as to how to do my job better. Not once.'[1] Some companies choose to communicate too much too late. Reticent victims of takeover attempts fill the quality press with lifelines of long copy. Bemused shareholders must wonder what kept them. Some companies are genuinely modest, believing that the public is not interested in their activities.

We make a modest profit as befits a modest organisation

Bob Worcester of MORI was told by a senior executive of a British food company: 'there's no reason why the general public should have heard of us'. In the next seven days Worcester drove past the company's headquarters building; then, in London, saw the company's van; then a recruitment ad, a financial statement in the quality press and the company logo in three different commercials. That senior executive was—and still is—in charge of public relations. Whereas another public relations executive—for a well-known high street chain—when asked how many people the company had in its PR department, replied 'forty-three thousand'.

It is easy for a company to communicate too little. It is virtually impossible for a company to communicate too much. Research on both sides of the Atlantic has shown that familiarity with a company is closely related to favourability.

> The best known industries are those to which the public is constantly exposed through advertising, product use, or everyday experiences . . . People are generally most favourable to the industries they know best.[2]

Companies find that their prospects' familiarity with the company name makes it easier for a salesman to get an appointment. Bob Worcester delineates three stages of corporate advertising:

1 This is who we are.
2 This is what we can do for you.
3 This is what we think.

Corporate advertising is only one means—and arguably not the most important—by which a company communicates. But anything a company does transmits a message. This book examines some of the means by which companies transmit messages—both internally and externally. Three themes coexist:

1 Company communication takes many forms and all forms must be coordinated.
2 'Communication Management' is as crucial as resource management and therefore needs to be the responsibility of the chairman or chief executive officer.
3 The ideal form of communication is person-to-person—i.e. face-to-face. Failures in communication occur when that model is lost sight of. Conversely, the more a company thinks of a consumer as a customer—i.e. a person, and of *itself* as a person, the better will it communicate.

The book takes the following path: We examine first the need of business to communicate and then the lack of genuine communication which exists among so-called communicators (e.g. the imprecision with which terms such as identity, image and personality are used).

We make a case for companies to regard themselves as people and analyse what happens when strangers meet. How do they learn from each other? We fix in aspic some key communication terms and attempt to draw up a model. What do we mean by 'The Company'? What is its 'Personality' and 'Identity'? Does it have a 'Philosophy' and a 'Message'? Whom does the company communicate with? How many audiences? And via how many channels? How many of those audiences does the company address and how many channels does the company use—consciously, unconsciously, in a planned way? How does it relate to and with the media?

We tackle the insubstantial chimera of 'image' (is it possible for a company to have only one?) and the need to integrate and co-ordinate all forms of company communication. We discuss 'corporate identity' and the use of corporate communications as a tool of management. Corporate advertising and research, both of which feature throughout, are then examined in detail.

We see what happens when companies are forced to communicate—i.e. in a crisis. We shall end with a prologue.

2

Communication in business

> Most management failures result from, or are accentuated by, a failure to communicate somewhere along the line. Recognition of this need to communicate ought to be written into the job specifications of every chief executive and senior manager.

So said Jacques Maisonrouge, chairman of IBM World Trade Corporation. The diagnosis is a truism—but no less true for that. The remedy he recommends is simple and largely ignored.

Communication is an overused word and an underused skill, particularly in business. A company communicates externally not only on its own behalf but on behalf of business in general. Historically, business has been notoriously bad at communication. It has preferred not to explain its actions, the system in which it operates, the contribution it makes to the common wealth, its reason for action.

If the general public—and especially the intellectual elements—are ignorant or misinformed, the fault is that of business itself. The onus is on the communicator. Always. The public's imperfect understanding of business generates further confusion. It chooses to interpret business's actions in a way which fits its previous impression, fitting the fragments into its mosaic. Says former *Fortune* editor, Max Ways:[1]

> The public needs to know more . . . about business—about its products, its processes, its performance, its profits, its motivations, its internal relations and the ways all these are changing.

Often today when a company communicates it is seen as having to respond to some request or order for information. The framework for debate has been set by the opponents of business, be they government, citizens' action or other pressure group. This results in company communication being reactive rather than proactive and different companies' communications appearing indistinguishable. We examine this aspect later when we look at corporate advertising which explicitly or implicitly answers criticism. The corporate response is inevitably defensive. With so many companies in the same boat, is it any wonder the public recognises the boat rather than the companies?

Once the public has cause for suspicion it ceases to take any paid-for message at face value. It looks for more 'meaningful' signals. When a company proclaims its part in UK wealth creation it suspects it of being foreign. When a foreign company asks in an ad 'do you have to be born in Britain to be British?' the public wonders how much of its real interest is in this country.

The gap between the customer and the company is wider than ever. Personal service has become the exception. Technology has traded places with trading. The further apart the transmitter and the receiver—physically, metaphorically—the greater the problem of communication. This distance, this lack of immediate feedback, may encourage the company to keep silent or at least limit communication to the necessary minimum executed by computer hardware.

But anonymity is no refuge. It transmits its own messages, no matter how depersonalised the process. The silent signal may be interpreted correctly or incorrectly. Either way, respondent perceptions will influence respondent actions—in the market place, local government, stock-market or wherever.

Research into companies which prefer to adopt a 'low profile' indicates that their action is often counter-productive.

> The low profile most usually associated such companies with words such as avoidant, uninvolved, passive, yielding and uninfluential. The high profile attributes were largely opposite, positive labels—visible, active, leader, pushy, vulnerable.[2]

The last two characteristics might confirm the cautious in their belief. The non-communicator is only too aware of the dangers of communicating. It makes life more complicated—and busier. If he communicates efficiently then respondents respond. He feels vulnerable.

In 1972 a London borough employed my company, The Creative Business, to analyse its communications. We devised a new format for its newsletter. We took the standard information and laid it out, not as an institutional leaflet, but in the form of a popular tabloid. After two months we had an annoyed client. Had the experiment failed? No. The reverse. The council offices had received more complaining letters than ever before. The reason? The information had been presented in a more effective way. Now the ratepayers knew more about their rights and, more especially, *whom* to contact if they had a problem.

The 'low profile' communicator has a relatively quiet life—in the short term. He knows, moreover, that communication is a difficult subject, that the more 'communicating' that goes on the less information seems to be getting through. He sympathises with Tom Lehrer:[3]

> It seems to me that if someone is having all that trouble communicating, the very least he can do is shut up!

He chooses to shut up even in the company of those who can do him the most good, namely business journalists. He responds with 'no comment' when asked a direct question, suspecting a skewed and selective report.

Worse, he refuses to give his own public relations department sufficient background information to make a release meaningful. He interprets a direct question about sales or market-share as an invasion of privacy, and then complains when a journalist's estimate is some way out. The journalist is human too. What he actually knows about a company would fill the back of a very small envelope. He has to fill a rather large article. Suppositions take the place of facts. The company executive omits to take the press into his confidence during the good days with the result that the ensuing bad days are worse than they need be. According to an article in the *Public Relations Journal*:[4]

> There is ample evidence that silence in the face of controversy implies guilt
> . . . continued silence moves growing numbers of the public to a stronger
> conviction of that guilt.

Companies who maintain that silence in the face of a customer enquiry or complaint, who don't listen to the public or seek their views can hardly complain when they themselves wish to speak up and find it difficult to get through, let alone accepted.

Attitudes to business in general greatly affect attitudes to a particular company. These attitudes have changed. Bob Worcester, who has been tracking public opinion of companies on a regular basis over fifteen years, confirms that the general public is now less concerned with what a company does, how it is structured and who runs it, and more concerned with how the company's actions and beliefs impinge upon the public.

In a recent MORI/*Sunday Times* poll business leaders came ninth out of thirteen in the credibility stakes. Of a representative quota sample of over 1000 adults only 25% trusted business leaders to tell the truth. (Mind you, that beat journalists [19%] and Government ministers [16%].) Social responsibility is not an optional extra, let alone a 'PR veneer', but an essential constituent of a company's personality. How well a company 'scores' may affect how well it succeeds with certain publics.

The general public by and large is not antagonistic to business. It believes business is necessary and shares Doctor Johnson's view that 'there are few ways in which a man can be more innocently employed than in getting money'. But it is realistic and cautious nevertheless. It regards some large companies as faceless (which is often no more than large companies deserve, since they in turn regard customers that way). It believes companies are inimical to individuality. It doubts their ability to nourish the imagination or foster creativity. Conformity is an inevitable by-product of mass production.

These are broad generalisations. But, as already indicated, impressions are the true counters in the game of communications and a company ignores that at its peril. Furthermore in the media, where good news is no news, stories of bribery, tax avoidance, cartel agreement, creative accounting, multinational sleight of hand and sundry misdemeanours, not to mention reports of surveys which reveal popular dissatisfaction with companies' indifference towards consumers, their inadequate communications and disregard for the environment—all these sharpen blunt generalisation with specific edge.

And the businessman cannot assume that the environment in which he operates is a permanent fixture. The capitalist system is—what?—two hundred years old? Longevity is no guarantee of eternal survival.

Business has to put its case collectively and individually. This is not to advocate a confrontation or adversarial pleading. What is needed is reasoned contribution to the debate rather than silence, yelps of pain, utterings of excuse or outbursts of outraged innocence. Collective statements, of course, are generally bland. The bodies (e.g. Confederation of British Industry (CBI), Institute of Directors, employers' federations) have to consider a variegated range of members. But they ought to endeavour to set up the appropriate context in which the debate can take place.

Meanwhile, each public communication of a company in the private sector is indirectly participating in that debate. Companies rarely give the broader issue much thought. Conversely, they are concerned with communicating on behalf of their products and/or company against specific target audiences to achieve specific objectives. Nevertheless, each message is part of the sum total of messages transmitted by business and helps create the impressions perceived by the various publics. And whereas it may be difficult for business collectively to construct the framework for the debate, it is surely not impossible for an individual company to establish a framework for its own activities. The onus is on the communicator.

Companies are reluctant to state publicly what their goals are. The void is filled from the respondent's rack of clichés. Power. Control. Manipulation. Profit. Kenneth Mason, former head of Quaker Oats, said:[5]

> Making a profit is no more the purpose of a corporation than getting enough
> to eat is the purpose of life. Getting enough to eat is a *requirement* of life.

The average company, alas, isn't that articulate. But presumably it has a company *philosophy*? Is it secret? If so, how are the aims of the company communicated to its staff, its suppliers? If they are told, then the 'secret' is out. Why shouldn't the general public be told? The successful companies seem to have a more relaxed attitude towards security. They are also far better at communication. They will have not simply a corporate philosophy, but a communications strategy.

> Try to find a communications strategy in any but the most sophisticated
> companies. It ought to be in a drawer next to the corporate strategy
> document, alongside the research and development file. But in all probability
> you will have to wander through the advertising, public relations and
> personnel departments before you can put together the various bits and
> pieces.[6]

Graham Kemp wrote that in 1972. The situation is little better today. Whereas communication may be more highly regarded, coordination is as loose as ever.

A company has a *duty* to communicate. A duty to its many publics and to *itself*, because non-communication is negative communication. Impressions will be made. The company had better have a hand in making them. There is also the broader duty—to society. But here again it is the company which benefits. Enlightened self-interest rather than pure social responsibility may prompt a company to agree with the following:

> Businesses . . . must in today's conditions have more to say for themselves.
> They must say it in comprehensible form to the people who want to know. In
> particular, they must say it in good time. If information is Power, to lack
> information will be considered by the people to be an infringement of civil
> rights and a crime against society.[7]

The sophisticated company doesn't question the need to communicate. There simply is no choice. It is not a question of whether but how, what, where, when, etc. Non-communication is negative communication. A company may elect not to appear in a television programme on industrial relations. But it has no comeback when the programme goes out and its reputation goes down. As the CBI reminds us:[8]

> Management has a duty to put its case and to put it with the kind of skill and
> professionalism it takes for granted in other important arms of its business
> such as finance, production and marketing.

Of course, these other disciplines require practice and timing. Communication is something we have been practising since childhood. The lessons we learned then need to be relearned in the adult business world. To communicate professionally—in whatever medium—requires application.

Businesses often complain that interviews are unfair, that selective editing gives a false picture. Media men on the other hand believe that businesses refuse to appear—or appear in a bad light—'not because it's impossible to make a case in 30 seconds but because it's damned difficult'.[9]

Writing an ad is difficult. Writing a corporate strategy is difficult. Writing a company's philosophy is difficult. Why should expressing it succinctly and in a motivating manner be any less difficult? Perhaps if the means of communication were not so readily available or so widely and popularly used, companies would regard communication as the tough discipline it really is. 'I've been speaking and writing most of my life, therefore I can communicate,' is as fallacious a supposition as 'I can swim ten lengths of the bath, therefore I'm Mark Spitz.'

Companies must communicate for their own sake and for the sake of the constituency they represent. But pious pleas for improved communication at gatherings of the mighty are useless unless communications are taken seriously and the nature of communication understood. Only then can the various estates of our society begin to understand each other. As I indicated, not via corporate bodies but by means of individual company communication.

Corporate advertising is one such example. As Ann Burdus said when she was Chairman of the Advertising Association:[10]

> The effect of corporate communications of this kind can be to take a debate into a wider arena, and get issues aired more fully, than otherwise would have happened . . . In our society today there is a need for corporate advocacy with several objectives—to educate the public, to communicate the interests of the company, and to engender a positive attitude about industry and production.

Max Ways dismisses those who regard communication as the 'grease that lubricates the social machine'. Rather it is the 'nuts and bolts and welds that hold the machine together'.[11] How well do *you* understand the machine? Do you have a manual? Are the terms clear? Come to that how do you define 'communication' . . . ?

3

Image, identity and other imprecisions

A 'There's nothing wrong with the company. We've just got a little image problem, that's all.'
B 'Our identity is out of line with our product performance.'
C 'We don't express a consistent personality.'
D 'I want each of our communications to convey the character of the corporation.'
E 'Is this statement conveying the impression we want?'

I have invented each of these corporate musings. They are, however, based upon actual comments. You probably recognise similar statements from direct or observed experience. No doubt you understand what each of the characters (*A–E*) is saying.

However, the language is far from precise. The key terms—image, identity, personality, character and impression—are used indiscriminately, interchangeably. Whereas, as we shall see in Chapter 5, they each have a discrete meaning.

Each of the statements is concerned with a mismatch of the actual and the perceived. Note the mismatch in all cases is itself a perception—in the mind of the transmitter. He is attempting to assess how his own signals are being received by the intended public. The signals may be printed messages (advertisements, reports, brochures, catalogues, press releases, etc.), or visual expressions (the company livery, trademark, notepaper, vans, uniforms), or the physical performance of the company's products or its staff in the course of its normal activities.

What the company actually does and how it is perceived are seen as two linked but *detachable* entities. It is this separation—this ability to treat image as detachable from reality—which has exacerbated the problems which business has with its publics. For all key words we enumerated above are used as synonyms for image—something regarded as *separable* from the real world of company action.

An image is powerful. It helps to determine how a person will behave towards a company. How that company is perceived: as weak or strong, open or devious, warm or cold, rigid or flexible, etc., will influence that person's disposition, his readiness to buy the company's products, give credence to what it says, commend its actions, purchase its stock, even to seek work there. If an image can do all that no wonder companies are tempted to concentrate upon 'image' at the expense of 'reality'. Social sciences confirm their actions. What is 'reality' after all? Man is but a bundle of senses. He can react only to what he experiences and perceives. This is his reality. As Carl Rogers[1] says:

> I do not react to some abstract reality but to my perception of this reality. It is this perception which for me *is* reality.

In 1953 the Cabinet discussed smog. There had been public pressure for action. Harold Macmillan doubted anything could be done but recommended setting up a committee. At least the Government will be seen to be busy. And that, he said, would be half the battle. (A smog to hide the smog? Eventually, of course, the committee deliberated, one thing led to another and the smog disappeared.)

Politicians try to create images during elections, hoping that the illusion can hold till polling day. They then have four or five years to make the reality fit the image, to adjust the mismatch. Politicians trade on illusions.

> The American voter . . . defends passionately the illusion that the men he chooses to lead him are of finer material than he. It has been traditional that the successful politician honour this illusion. To succeed today, he must embellish it. Particularly if he wants to be President.[2]

Political image-making and advertising techniques came together seriously in the 1950s. Politicians were allegedly 'packaged'. By which critics meant that a person was sold as a product. Today many advertisements endeavour to sell a product *as a person*, to invest the thing with a personality, with the traits of a lovable, strong or whatever human being. Indeed the intellectuals' criticism was never accurate. What the image-makers attempted was not so much a packaging exercise as an identity change (see Chapter 5). They adjusted certain outward manifestations of a candidate's personality in order to bring it into line with what their researches had shown an ideal perception of a candidate would resemble. With politicians—as with products—we, the public, are willing to accept some degree of illusion. Daniel Boorstin[3] insists:

> In the last half century we have misled ourselves . . . about men . . . and how much greatness can be found among them . . . We have become so accustomed to our illusions that we mistake them for reality. We demand them. And we demand that there always be more of them, bigger and better and more vivid.

More sanity and realism have, thank goodness, entered into our relations with both our leaders and products since those words were written. Nevertheless we must respect the basic truth of Boorstin's analysis. There is within us a willing acceptance of a degree of illusion.

Most of the battles between advertising and public relations on the one hand and their adversaries (educators and consumerists) on the other are fought on this ground. No advertisement is entirely dispassionate. It is, after all, advocacy. The most factual advertisement will employ emotional elements (e.g. the choice of typeface). For advertising's critics to demand that advertising merely inform is to imply and assume that all purchases are made on entirely rational grounds and that a product is a thing (i.e. its constituents) rather than a totality, a package of benefits.

The particular combination of benefits, the emphases, the way the totality is presented all contribute to a synthesis which we may choose to call in David Ogilvy's term the 'brand image'. The image can never be more important than the brand. But the brand may be nothing without its image—and can never be divorced from it.

When a consumer chooses brand *A* rather than brand *B*, he or she is identifying with that image, joining a club. The image is not a single entity and it is difficult to make tangible. It is an impression which the consumer perceives of the brand, a synthesis of many impressions as a direct or indirect result of a variety of signals transmitted by the brand (and perhaps the company) of which the advertising is one. The advertisement is part of the product. Which is to say that the image is part of the product.

Let us return from product advertising and political advertising to corporate advertising, which stands roughly midway between the two. It shares with product advertising a commercial purpose but, like political advertising, promotes not products but human beings (for a company is people).

Some writers would disagree with that. For example the International Advertising Association[4] defines corporate advertising this way:

> In essence, corporate image advertising takes the company as if it were a product, promoting it with care within its industry or industries, giving it a clear differentiation from others resembling it and basically 'selling' it to the audiences selected.

I, however, believe corporate advertising should treat the company as if it were a person. I'm stuck with this anthropomorphic view of companies. I can't help thinking of them as people.

One fundamental difference between corporate and product advertising (and one which incidentally has contributed to the imprecision of terminology) is the fact that 'image' can be built into a product whereas it can, at best, only be *adjusted* for a company. A product is artificial. A company is artificial only in the legal sense. It is natural in the sense that it consists of human beings. A product can be totally fabricated: one essential part of that fabrication is what is generally referred to as its 'image'. We can decide at the outset what impression we wish our particular audience to perceive of our product, what characteristics it has which differentiate it from the competition, how it should be 'positioned' in the mind of the public. Furthermore, it is relatively simple to ensure that the correct image signals are being sent—through packaging, display, point-of-sale and advertising. The image, we might say, is under control. Of course it must be related to the reality of the product. But in new product development we may decide to concentrate on the image first and construct a product to fit.

The situation is very different in corporate communications. The company precedes the image and the degree of control is minimal. Reality is in charge. Which is not to say that nothing can or should be done. Were that the case there would be no point in writing this book.

I have tried to suggest that whereas so-called product image is manipulable, company image is less easily controlled. Essentially, image is determined by performance. What the company does and believes determines how it is perceived. It is the job of the company's (internal or external) communications advisers to ensure that the thrust of the company's actions and beliefs is accurately communicated and that all messages and signals emanating from the company are consistent. The corporate communications manager is a guardian of the 'image' whereas his colleague in product advertising may well be the 'image-maker'.

I have used the term 'image' in this chapter in the loose and all-embracing way in which the public and most of the communications industry use it. The word, moreover, is also regarded as pejorative. Image is opposed to reality. There is often a dichotomy between what is and what is perceived. If the perception is unfavourable, so the myth goes, all we need to do is adjust our 'image'. Image is a false mask we can adopt to fool people into believing we are different from what we are—better, worthier, bigger, poorer, richer, more decentralised, more concerned. Whereas politicians have a few years to live up to their 'image' or get thrown out, corporations have little or no time to adjust their performance and/or get rejected.

Image in the popular vocabulary means falsehood. (If any word needs an 'image-job' it's image.) In *Key Concepts in Communication*[5] the authors refer to the original meaning of image as a 'visual representation of reality' but assert that:

> Now it commonly means a fabrication or public impression created to appeal to the audience rather than to reproduce reality: it implies a degree of falseness insofar as the reality rarely matches up to the image. In this sense we talk about the image of a consumer product or of a politician.

A company image is regarded as something manufactured rather than a true reflection of the company. One communicator[6] compares the situation with that of a new mother receiving compliments on the baby who says 'I know you think he's beautiful but wait till you see the pictures.'

But we—the public—*do* want to see the pictures. How often is the holiday more enjoyable once the photographs have synthesised and framed our enjoyment? A studio audience repeatedly peeks at the monitors in order to fix the transmitted picture. The screen is the true reality not this tangle of cables and studio floor personnel. But at least in the studio and with the holiday there is a definite causal relationship between the reality and the image. In corporate advertising there is often little connection, causal or otherwise. The image is artificial, a 'public relations exercise' (another term now almost wholly pejorative) or, in the current jargon, a 'media hype'.

The relationship between image and reality should be that of cream and milk. Real cream from one particular bottle of milk. However, image is commonly regarded as artificial cream. Max Ways chooses a different metaphor:[7]

> There's a well known difference between improving one's looks by cosmetics and improving them by better health.

Our image problem is no longer a cosmetics job — it needs plastic surgery

The fact that performance is more important than image should not lead us to concentrate upon performance *at the expense of image*. To eschew all concern with image because reality is more important, and image will reflect reality, is to believe that communication exists in some sort of ideal vacuum immune from the external realities of the market-place, the activities of competitors and, most importantly, the preoccupations of the audience. As we have said, for all their insubstantiality, perceptions are legal tender.

We must be concerned with image, not because we want to manufacture it but because we need to discern how our signals are being received (indeed *whether* they are being received), and how those perceptions square with our self-image.

And besides, in my book—which this is and which henceforth will be more rigorous in its terminology—it *cannot* be manufactured.

Image can only be perceived. What we can do something about is the company's identity. To point out the difference—and to end this chapter on a suitably *precise* note—here is an extract from an article on Tesco.[8]

> By the early 70s one of the problems Tesco was encountering was that of securing local authority consent to develop. *'This was not so much a conflict of image'*, commented Ian MacLaurin, 'as what might be referred to as the Catch 22 of retailing. Without establishing a new modern presence on the High Street, the company would remain *trapped within its old identity*, yet without a new identity it was becoming increasingly difficult to persuade local authorities that Tesco had a positive constructive role to play in their communities.'

Ian MacLaurin is aware that the existing perception of Tesco may be in conflict with the company's new thinking. However, he knows also that it is the physical structure and look of the company which he has to attend to. We deal with this in succeeding chapters. Meanwhile, notice how Ian MacLaurin personalises Tesco. *People* play roles.

Graham Kemp has a simple definition of business communication:[9] 'People talking to people and understanding each other.' The last point may sound more of a hope than a definition but the first part, though by no means comprehensive, reminds us of a fundamental truth: COMPANIES ARE PEOPLE.

4

Companies are people

'I can't help feeling wary,' said J B Priestley, 'when I hear anything said about the masses. First you take their faces from 'em by calling 'em the masses, and then you accuse them of not having any faces.'[1]

It suits a totalitarian leader to indulge in mass stereotypes. Social psychologists have proved in tests what ordinary folk have known from personal experience, namely that if you get to know an adversary as a person he ceases to be quite so adversarial. George Orwell, in the Spanish Civil War, refused to believe an enemy soldier holding up his trousers could be a fascist.

You can't give a Fascist salute AND hold your trousers up, that's for sure..

Most mistakes of business communication—both internal and external—occur when the target audience has no face. The word 'target' betrays a militaristic approach to communication. You don't enter into dialogue with targets. You hit them. Or try to.

The process of communication has *people at both ends*. This is easy enough to accept when discussing interpersonal communication but we have been conditioned to regard company communication as mass communication—i.e. the transmission of messages from an organisation to a faceless amalgam, a large and homogeneous public. This sort of communication is of course 'one way'. The only response required is the one predetermined—a purchase, a shift in attitude, a change in behaviour. No participation is invited, nor are there means of accommodating it. By the same token the other factor in this equation is equally depersonalised. The company too is faceless. Even within the organisation itself. It is easier for outsiders to give it a face—maybe that of the founder, chief executive, local representative, receptionist or spokesman in the company's television commercial. Within the organisation, on the other hand, the company may have a philosophy, a statement of corporate planning, but the visual projection of the company will almost certainly be an abstraction—a symbol, a trademark, a slogan or maybe the head office building.

This view is encouraged by much traditional corporate advertising which chooses to sell ideas rather than people or products—particularly if those ideas are divorced from human form and expression. What possible face do these abstractions suggest?

> A WORLD LEADER IN ELECTRONICS.
> WHERE IMAGINATION BECOMES REALITY.
> BETTER IDEAS BEAUTIFULLY MADE.
> TECHNOLOGY IS OUR STRENGTH.
> A TRADITION OF PROGRESS.

The limited palette which corporate artists use makes for images neither distinct in themselves nor distinct from other corporations. And though it may be difficult for us to perceive how the creators of such abstractions can see themselves, the public will receive *some* impression—a corporate image composed of countless messages it has received from the company direct or its advertisements or literature or representatives or intermediaries or neighbours. The receiver will, if need be, visualise the transmitter. He pieces together those fragments of corporate activity he knows about into a concept. This is what we know as a corporate image. This is what the receiver perceives simply as 'the company'. And—even if this does not happen—we must never forget that an impression of facelessness is nevertheless an impression. 'What's your impression of the XYZ Co?' 'They're a faceless lot.' Does *that* tell you something? I think so.

Undoubtedly, some companies appear faceless not because they have failed to communicate successfully but because they have decided not to show a corporate face. They regard it as unrealistic to treat a corporation as a person. *Which* person they ask? Why one and not another? And if they can't decide on one they are thrown back on a compromise, a neutered amalgam. A company is a fabrication, a machine for transforming resources by the addition of value, into goods and services. A company is a legal entity. But a company is made up of people, of individuals. This legal entity can do anything a person can do. The only difference between John Smith trading as John Smith and trading as John Smith Ltd is not the liability but the *amount* of liability. As an article in the *Harvard Business Review* makes clear:[2]

> Concepts and functions normally attributed to persons can also be attributed to organisations made up of persons. Goals, economic values, strategies and other such personal attributes are often . . . projected to the corporate level by managers and researchers.

Accompanying the article is an extract from Conoco's in-house booklet on moral standards. It refers to the judgement of Sir Edward Coke in the 17th Century who:

> . . . concluded that a corporation was but an impersonal creation of the law—not a being, just a product of written rules and government fiat.

Conoco comments that times have changed. Corporations employ thousands and are owned by millions.

> Although it may be true that Conoco remains an inanimate being for legalistic purposes the company has a very personal existence for its shareholders, employees and directors . . . Conoco's reputation considers their reputation as well . . . Perhaps it is then appropriate . . . to think of Conoco as a living corporation; a sensitive being whose conduct and personality are the collective effort and responsibility of its employees, officers, directors and shareholders.

('Reputation' is another term loosely trading places with image. It is less pejorative. A reputation is earned and harder to 'manage'. Though less 'visual', reputation like image is nevertheless *perceived*.)

If we treat companies as people then we apply to corporate communications the same principles and criteria which we apply to ordinary personal communication. This principle is adopted by major *product* advertisers. They regard their brands not as objects but as persons. The advantage is that this widens the possibilities of portraying the brand. The agency considers not simply what the brand can do for the consumer but what it *is* and how it lives.

My colleagues in Roux, Séguéla, Cayzac & Goudard (RSCG), France's second largest agency group, owe their success to a philosophy of regarding products as people and turning those people into stars. There are three main attributes for a star. The brand must have a 'physique': that is, what the product consists of and what it does; a 'character': the psychology of the brand; and a 'style': the permanent features of the communication—the clothes, manner and outward manifestation of the brand. If this works for brands then surely it must work for companies. Companies after all are only people.

The J.Walter Thompson agency have conducted considerable research in the UK and the US to prove that companies have personalities. If they do, then presumably in the words of chief executive Don Johnson, 'the average citizen ought to be able to describe companies as though they were people.' They did.

> People can relate to companies as personalities. Companies have rational attributes and human personalities and it is probably better to be liked than disliked! [3]

Companies, like people, have reputations. But—thanks to the earnest endeavours of corporate men—companies are nowhere near as idiosyncratic as people—or products come to that. There are few bright or garish shades on the limited palette. As Wally Olins says in his seminal book *The Corporate Personality*:[4]

> If companies share the idea of corporate omniscience, it is also inevitable that they tend to look similar. To allow humour or whimsy to play a part in the way they look or behave would be to imply that the company had human as opposed to superhuman characteristics, that it could laugh, cry, lose its temper, make mistakes, forget things or even go mad.

Perhaps putting this demi-god into a face-to-face situation would bring him down to earth? And isn't face-to-face the supreme form of communication whether on the shop floor, in the investment manager's office, at the annual general meeting or at the point of sale? And are not all other channels of communication substitutes for person-to-person? If a company could find a means of speaking personally one at a time to each of its potential, existing and lapsed customers at a cost equivalent to that of its advertising budget would it not do so?

The advantage of true person-to-person dialogue is *relationship*—the story can be related to the respondent and dialogue can ensue. (It's another of commercial communication's quirks that it uses the word respondent but rarely asks for *response*.) Communications people within companies denied contact with actual consumers suffer withdrawal symptoms. Their remedy is to visit outlets with the salesman, sell in a store or attend a research group.

All channels of company communication should attempt to achieve the condition of face-to-face. By ceasing to treat an audience as a grey, impersonal mass, by noting the distinguishing features of the faces in the crowd, by turning the 'corporate philosophy statement' into a colloquial language, by transferring abstract reality into a bloke with a face and an accent, by such conscious humanisation of our otherwise depersonalised encounter we can make each channel—product advertising, annual report, public announcement, presentation, corporate advertisement or even corporate identity—understandable, motivating and distinctive.

There is one other incidental but important advantage in a company attempting to treat all its communication channels as surrogate personal encounters. Coordination of communications is easier.

5

People make impressions

In this chapter we examine the personal encounter. It will serve as the basis for a model of company communication and provide illustrations of the terms we now employ with greater exactitude.

Two men meet at a cocktail party. They have not been introduced. What do they say to each other? How else do they communicate? The scene could be played something like this:

> *A*: Crowded.
> *B*: Yes.
> *A*: Julia's parties always are.
> *B*: Yes.
> *A*: Haven't seen you at one before.
> *B*: Oh, about a year ago.
> *A*: Friend?
> *B*: Of Robert's.
> *A*: Work with him do you?
> *B*: Yes.
> *A*: Insurance?
> *B*: London and General.
> *A*: They're all the same to me.
> *B*: What do you do?
> *A*: Export.
> *B*: Export?
> *A*: What they used to call a merchant adventurer.

Let us imagine that we are *B*. What do we know about *A*? And how do we know it? *A* seems aggressive, knowledgeable, almost proprietorial. This is partly *what* he says ('Julia's parties always are') and the *way* he says it ('Work with him do you?' rather than 'Do you work with Robert by any chance?'). *B* might not like it assumed that a working association constitutes his only right to be at the party. *B* might interpret *A*'s never having seen him at one of Julia's parties before as dismissive. Clearly he had not made an impression. The remark about insurance companies being all the same is also dismissive. Neither *B* nor his firm, it appears, has left its mark. Can all this be conveyed in 50 words of dialogue? Easily.

Of course there are other cues. Other signals are being transmitted by *A*.

There is the *negative communication*. What *A* hasn't said—e.g. 'Hello' 'How are you?' 'My name is . . . ' (Non-communication, remember, is negative communication.) There is the *accent*. Public school? Oxbridge? Perhaps the delivery is clipped. The *tone* alone, can convey indecision or concern or indifference or arrogance. The *choice of words* can exclude *B* rather than involve him. They may be appropriate to the subject but not to the listener. The speaker may have made no effort to adapt his language (e.g. specialised technical jargon). The pitch and strength of voice, and speed of delivery can also convey significance beyond the literal meaning of what is said.

His body language will also send signals. In fact non-verbal signals can totally dominate a face-to-face encounter. *B*'s impression of *A* will be affected if *A* does any of the following:

. Nods a greeting
. Touches him
. Moves closer (or further away)
. Stands at an angle
. Puts his hands on his hips
. Yawns
. Nods an agreement
. Remains impassive
. Points a finger at him
. Looks at him while talking
. Looks at him while listening
. Perspires
. etc. etc.

Appearance (which is also body language) conveys signals and significantly modifies the effect of others. *A*'s jacket, shirt and tie will themselves communicate (the adjective 'loud' is very appropriate here). *B* doesn't have to play Sherlock Holmes to discover clues to *A*'s character. The tie: the way it's knotted, its size, the colour coordination with the suit; the handkerchief in the pocket; the buttonhole; the appropriateness of the suit to the occasion (morning suit because he is coming from, or dinner jacket because he is going to, somewhere important); etc., etc.

Neither yet knows the other's name. Perhaps they will exchange cards. Further clues. But by this time *B* can probably imagine what *A*'s card looks like. *B* has quickly summed him up. Everything seems to fit his early mental picture. The 'primacy effect' is at work—did *B* but know it. The gestures, appearance and subsequent comments are further proof of a first impression. Of course he *would* be in 'export'. Export of all things. And wouldn't you guess he'd use an expression like 'merchant adventurer'?

The dominant impression may not occur first but some way into the encounter. Earlier impressions would then be reinterpreted. But wherever it occurs it affects all other messages. Otherwise, quite neutral signals are taken as reinforcements of a core attitude. This phenomenon is known as the 'halo effect'. The one dominant impression casts its strong light over the total picture.

In all the foregoing we have regarded *B* solely as a receiver, a receiver of signals, which has enabled him to become a *perceiver* of impressions. The *interpretation* of signals has created these perceptions. However, in all this *B* has been far from passive. He is not a clean sheet of paper on which *A* projects his personality. Interpretation of a signal demands participation and is, of course, affected by the receiver's own personality (his beliefs, value system, immediate context, state of the bowels, etc.).

B may also be totally mistaken in his perception. What he interprets as arrogance may in fact be acute shyness. Hostility in *A* may be a pre-emptive strike at a supposedly hostile *B*. *B* may be paying more attention to the non-verbal signals than they warrant. He may be judging *A*'s behaviour, assessing his character or even comparing him with himself. He may, of course, be doing none of these things. He may be bored out of his skull, looking for an unaccompanied woman, or hoping to get to the bathroom. He could give *A* the benefit of the doubt. Vocal communication is mostly natural, unpremeditated and spontaneous. The non-verbal communication, similarly, is a true expression of the speaker's character.

An actor on the other hand selects pieces of reality and arranges them in a planned way in order to arouse the emotions of the audience, to elicit sympathy or identification or persuade to a point of view—i.e. to alter the behaviour of the receiver. The actor is not spontaneous.

> The element of choice, the variable of the unknown, is diminished, if not removed: and rehearsal with some foreknowledge of what is to occur takes place. The *how* of communicating is considered as well as the *what*.[1]

If any roles are to be played then *we* must allocate them. That is why we try to determine early on in an encounter who our opposite number is, what he does and whether he has an 'angle'. We try to establish a relationship. For any communication to take place the two participants must have things in common. *A* and *B* share a common language (though their uses and versions of it may differ significantly). They may share some social activities and have friends in common. They will seek out areas of mutual interest or concern. This is popularly known as breaking the ice. In fact what is going on is research—into each other's knowledge and attitudes—the better to understand each other. Though we may not wish for complete understanding. Just sufficient background to help us determine the other's role. Once that role is delineated we can play our own role better.

Now neither of these roles may necessarily be 'true'. Just as we may be mistaken in our impression of the other person (through his own role-playing or our misinterpretation of cues), so he may choose to select from our own repertoire of gestures, language, style and behaviour a package of signals to fit the situation.

There are further complexities. *B* may be influenced by cues he does not know are there. The angle of a lamp may cast shadows which add a dimension to *A*'s appearance which in turn modifies or reinforces what he says. *B* may interpret a frown to mean displeasure or disagreement, a smile to represent honesty. *B* may base an intellectual judgement on purely emotional factors. He *likes* something and therefore perceives it as *correct*. He may give credence to an opinion if he has previously decided that he respects the speaker. He may be affected by the location in which the impression is made. The same opinion expressed by the same person in a totally different environment could meet with a different response. Moreover, the location may not permit the speaker or the listener to give full rein to the views expressed. The party context may be emotionally or physically inhibiting. *B* will generalise about *A*'s character from a limited sample of *A*'s behaviour.

What have we learned from this party piece? We'll end this chapter by constructing a very simple model of the encounter. The terms we use we have already met—and will meet again. *A* has a *personality*. Personality is 'the sum total of the characteristics of the individual'.[2] Those characteristics —behavioural and intellectual—serve to distinguish one individual from another.

Personality   Identity   Image

A person has a personality. That is inevitable. Equally inevitable, he projects it. The means by which he projects it we call his *identity*. Some elements (or cues) of his identity are planned—e.g. his clothes, his visiting card, his manner of speech. Other elements are unplanned—e.g. his unconscious mannerisms, his height, the shape of his face.

The sum of the cues equals his identity. Note we are now using this word in a restricted sense—a complex of formal and informal cues. The more usual, one might say non-commercial, meaning of the term barely distinguishes it from personality. Our terminology clearly separates the two: identity provides the information from which the receiver (*B*) gauges the personality of the transmitter (*A*). The impression formed by these cues is what we call the 'image'.

Hence, our model at its most basic reveals character *A* with a distinctive personal make-up (*personality*) sending, consciously or unconsciously, a set of signals or cues (*identity*) which form the basis for a perception by *B* of *A* (*image*).

6

People pass messages

Simplistic it may be, but the model of personality, identity and image will serve us very well in the pages to come as we examine commercial communication in all its forms.

The starting point for our enquiry has been 'image'—how the public perceive the company, how the company can 'improve its image'. In this chapter we are concerned somewhat less with image and more with planned as opposed to incidental communication of messages. We concentrate on formal communication, though obviously the received signal is accompanied by a perception of the sender and the two signals affect each other.

By 'formal' I mean deliberate communication undertaken with a firm intention. It is spoken or written (rather than sung or danced). It may be accompanied by illustrations, diagrams, maps or symbols. Its purpose is to influence the behaviour of the receiver. Not too difficult you might think. Then heed the words of Goethe:[1]

> No one would talk much in society if only he knew how often *he* misunderstands others.

The truth is we delude ourselves into believing we are communicating. We don't know. Too often, alas, we don't bother to find out. Worse, many of us don't even care. We are content with 'one-way' communication. In companies executives may prefer to send messages by means of memos. These invite no response other than action. I term this the pea-shooter model of communication.

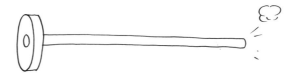

The transmitter shoots pellets of information (or probably of demand) to the receiver's brain, thereby conditioning him to respond in a desired way. A better model of communication is Newton's Balls.

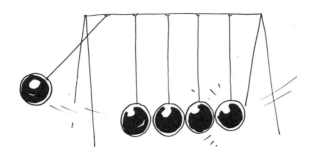

As has been said, the onus in communication, whether as image or message, is on the communicator. If the receiver misunderstands it is rarely his unaided mistake. It is not easy either to assemble a message or to guarantee that the message has been correctly understood. The fact that *you* understand what you are saying, fully appreciate the context in which you are using these words, can read the text before you transmit it vocally, counts for nothing. Try this test. 'Patio door'. You know what it is? Right. Speak it aloud. Can you understand how a listener might think it is the name of an Irish singer?

Style has been defined as the right words in the right order. The hardest part of speech writing and playwriting in my experience is structure— organising the beginning, middle and end. In commercial communication, which is nearly always persuasive in intention, it is not simply an aesthetic question of style but a vital matter of effectiveness. And perfect structure can, of course, be ruined by inadequate delivery, by the wrong emphasis or tone of voice.

Communication has been variously defined. 'The art of expressing ideas,'[2] and 'the science of transmitting information,'[3] seem to ignore the role of the receiver. Whereas this: 'process by which information is exchanged between individuals through a common system of signals, signs or behaviour,'[4] not only recognises the receiver and the act of *exchange* but also the importance of a common language or code. Our friends *A* and *B*, you remember, sought common ground.

We'll pause there to consider the *content* of communication. In a commercial context, where we wish to affect the behaviour of the recipient, then clearly we must transmit *information*. Information, as the theorists tell us, is 'anything that reduces uncertainty'.[5] Information *changes* knowledge. It may add to it or diminish it (by removing a previously held belief) but it should always sharpen its focus in order to modify the behaviour of the recipient. Information may be transmitted in order to reinforce or change an attitude. It may of course fail to reach the recipient let alone modify his behaviour, but there is always a *purpose*.

Purpose so far has not appeared in our array of definitions of communication. For its comprehensive brevity therefore I commend to you the definition of political scientist Harold D Lasswell in the *Encyclopaedia Britannica*:

Who says what to whom via what channels and with what effect.

It's not complete but it will help us draw another model:[6]

Transmitter   Receiver

As before we have a transmitter and a receiver. Now, however, we are concerned with the transference, *not* of a personality with identity cues into a perceived impression or image, but of a thought (or 'piece of information') from one mind to another.

The first decision the transmitter makes is channel. Choice will depend upon the whereabouts of the receiver, the particular needs of the transmitter, the availability of channels and the ability of the channel accurately to convey the message. Next, the transmitter has to 'encode' the message.

Transmitter   Receiver

This sounds arcane. Actually it is second nature. We use codes all the time. Speech is a code. The sounds we utter to indicate an object or feeling are a code. We see a four-legged fouler of pavements and exclaim 'dog'. The sound signifies the thing. It is a code, a verbal symbol for the object. We then wish to convey the idea via written language. We write the letters *d—o—g*. This is another code, a symbol for the spoken symbol. A double code. Other codes are far more complex. Mathematical, chemical and electrical symbols, technical drawings, foreign languages, specialist languages, 'secret' writing, esoteric signs, etc.

The receiver's first job therefore is to 'decode' the signal.

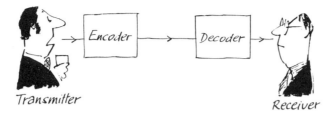

Accurate decoding in our example is not too difficult! Though even here other factors may have modified the message or, as the information theorists say, 'diminished the integrity of the signal'. This we call 'noise'. There are three types.

1. Channel Noise

This is static on the line, physical interference. A hoarse voice, a squeaky blackboard, a radio next door, a dirty slide, too much (or too little) illumination, etc. There was probably a lot of it going on at our cocktail party.

In television advertising, Rosser Reeves coined the term 'video vampire' to represent any visual element which detracted from the selling thrust of the commercial. I created a video vampire in a commercial for a disinfectant. It showed a toddler on a floor. The voice-over spoke of the danger areas where germs lurk. Each of the areas was numbered. To emphasise these we had numbers painted on large kiddies' building bricks. Viewers contacted the television station to ask where they could buy—not the disinfectant—the numbered bricks. That's channel noise.

2. Psychological Noise

A corporate message intimidates when it should inform, a public notice invites graffiti, at the cocktail party *A*'s tone of voice, display of superiority and dismissive language and gestures irritate *B*. These are all examples of psychological noise. The nature of the message is affected by the feelings of the recipient, by the relationship established between the two participants. President Nixon, at a Watergate press conference, stumbled on the word 'integrity'.

Body language, of course, is psychological noise when it counteracts the message. On the other hand it may reinforce the message. In which case it is 'sound' rather than noise. Though we may not hear it. We may simply accept it, intuitively interpreting a non-verbal code. Gestures similarly can be either sound or noise. A nod may reinforce what is being said or may contradict it. Judge the effect of saying 'I thought it was a great idea' whilst holding your nose. Or observe a speaker who gestures to emphasise a point but whose timing is slow. Do you believe what he says?

Communication experts tell us that 'the spoken word is never neutral'. It is always affected by the nature of our delivery. These non-verbal factors then constitute *paralanguage*.

3. Language Noise

Language noise is the result of a mismatch of code between transmitter and receiver. *A*'s signals may not be understood or, more likely, misunderstood by *B*. Remember Patty O'Dore? How do you interpret this headline?

8TH ARMY PUSH BOTTLES UP GERMANS

And do you have sympathy for the Canadian motorist who thought the sign 'FINE FOR PARKING' was encouragement rather than a warning? I heard a radio news item on international banking. I thought it referred to 'detonations'. The announcer had actually said 'debtor nations'. Mixed metaphors, also, can contribute noise, the meaning becoming submerged in incongruous imagery.

When *A* uses a foreign phrase which *B* doesn't understand we have an example of both *psychological* and *language* noise. Of course, if he speaks with a code id his doze, we have all three.

In *The Languages of Communication* Gordon calls all the external factors 'psychologics'.[7] He contrasts them with the 'logics' of communication, i.e. 'a man with an idea (one) speaks through an instrument (two) and acts upon an individual or group (three).' Against that, and 'attacking the communication at all points are the "psychologics"'. Gordon quotes I A Richards' well-known description of communication:

> Communication takes place when one mind so acts upon its environment that another mind is influenced and in that other mind an experience occurs which is like the experience of the first mind, and is caused in part by that experience.

'This description', says Gordon, 'is primarily a psychological statement.'

Another element of language noise is *redundancy*. Redundancy is an overkill of information. Strictly speaking, it may be redundant to say 'A for apple' when either 'A' or 'apple' will do. But redundancy aids accurate decoding and helps to overcome noise on the channel. We can decipher bad handwriting because sufficient information remains in the words and characters we *can* recognise to enable us to decipher the words and characters we cannot read. You can check redundancy for yourself by hiding the top and then the bottom half of a row of type (e.g on this page), and seeing how well you can 'read' the line. It could be regarded as inefficient since the extra information could be unnecessary. However, if it helps us to transmit the message, it is in reality very efficient. Redundancy is a tool of presenters. The speaker knows the audience can't stop and re-read the text, so he structures his spoken text with short sentences and is careful to repeat key words. Examine the text of a good radio commercial and compare it with a press ad. Ideally he will also employ visual aids, reinforcing his message with a complementary illustration or simply duplicating the information by screening the key word The transmitter who uses redundancy is a good communicator because he is *conscious of the needs of the receiver*.

The speaker who knows his audience will employ redundancy if he believes the audience needs to be motivated or does not share the depth of his own background knowledge. The sophisticated audience resents redundancy because it believes it doesn't need it. Certainly, addresses to intellectual gatherings contain less redundancy than those at popular meetings.

Orators employ redundancy. How much of this 1940 speech by Winston Churchill is necessary to understanding?

> We shall not flag or fail. We shall fight in France, we shall fight on the seas and oceans, we shall fight with growing confidence and growing strength in the air, we shall defend our island, whatever the cost may be, we shall fight on the beaches, we shall fight on the landing grounds, we shall fight in the fields and in the streets, we shall fight in the hills; we shall never surrender.[8]

Delete the repetitions. Meaning is not lost. But the power of the speech to persuade and motivate has almost totally disappeared. 'Hello', 'please' and 'thank you' may be redundant. They don't add information but they do communicate respect for, and interest in, the receiver and may then aid the reception of the information.

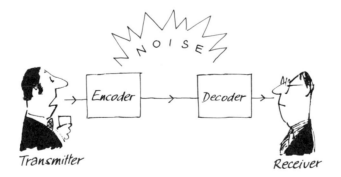

Here then is the model of the communication process we have discussed so far. One element is missing. What is missing? Whatever you reply is in a way the answer: Feedback.

Feedback is evidence of communication. Or, to be more exact, evidence of the signal having been received. The decoding of the feedback, in turn, tells us whether the signal has been correctly interpreted (always assuming that we, for our part, have correctly interpreted the feedback signal). The possibilities for misunderstanding are enormous—and the happy hunting ground of comedy writers.

Without feedback there is no communication. Feedback is the contribution of the receiver but it has to be *earned*; if necessary, invited. If we in English popular conversation employed an equivalent of the French 'n'est-ce pas?' instead of the bland, unquestioning 'you know' maybe we would understand each other better.

Have you ever had a conversation with someone who gave you no indication that he follows what you are saying? No words or grunts or looks? It is the death of communication. Looks, especially. Since we all tend to look more at people we like, how disconcerting it is not to be looked at. And try conversing with somebody wearing opaque sunglasses. How do you know he is reacting—*if* he is reacting?

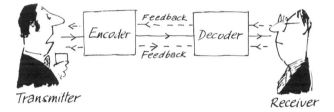

We have now drawn two very simple models of people communicating —making impressions and passing messages. Now we need to consider the communication process in somewhat less mechanistic terms.

7

Components of communication

The second of our two models has served communication theorists and practitioners very well. However, it does beg a few questions. By being concerned with signals to the exclusion of impressions, it does not by itself serve our purposes as we examine the many ways companies communicate.

We need to take into account certain key aspects of the communication process. First, social psychologists regard communication as:

> . . . a shared social system . . . two or more people are involved, both with their own expectations and interpretations.[1]

As communications theorists have begun to put more and more emphasis on the role of the receiver so, coincidentally, companies—firmly guided by public opinion, government and consumer group pressure, legislation and the growth of an articulate citizenry—have put more emphasis on consumer involvement. Consumer 'participation' has been extended from the point of purchase. Consumers serve on panels, are regularly researched, are instrumental in product improvements, modifications and withdrawal. All this is common knowledge.

Less well known is the advertising industry's changing attitude towards how advertising works. We are revising our traditional linear models—inevitably one-way—of advertising 'doing things' to people. Now, encouraged by the work of Judie Lannon, Peter Cooper and others, we are asking 'what do people *do with* advertising?' People are changing, are 'more sophisticated in enjoying doing things with advertising and rejecting the patronising conventional advertisements'.[2] Qualitative research methods show advertisers how consumers experience the world not as totally rational beings, but as totally *human* beings —with fantasies, fears, desires and an imagination which not only feeds on brands but uses those brands as part of its own being. Consumers are not passive partakers of products but active choosers of, *identifiers* with, brands.

Compare that recent view of advertising with this view of communication, also stimulated by research.

> Communication is a 'transaction' between the perceiver and the perceived, a process of negotiation in which the perceptual end product is a result of both influences within the perceiver and of characteristics of the perceived.[3]

When B meets A, the yardstick he uses is the one channel to hand—B. We regard ourselves as the norm by which we perceive or judge others. If we have a definite picture of ourselves then we find judging others relatively easy, and our characteristics affect the characteristics we are likely to recognise in others. Secure people are more likely 'to see others as warm rather than cold'[4] whereas insecure people detect problems in others. Unless the transmitter understands the receiver he runs the risk of having his (to him) simple signal totally misunderstood. As social psychologists Krech and Cruchfield[5] note:

> The true intent of the communication may be of little or no significance to our audience, while the *perceived* intention is or may be critical . . . the *objective* of the stranger at our front door is the first concern, and our interpretation of *it* will modify our response to *him*.

If we see him as a public opinion pollster we react one way, an evangelist another, a salesman a third, a detective a fourth and so on. If he chooses to say nothing about his objectives our reaction may be decidedly different. Even though the opening statement by the visitor is in each case identical.

The second key aspect is the need to regard communication as an ongoing, dynamic system. The problem with models, particularly linear ones, is that they seem so leisurely and once-and-for-all, whereas signals go from A to B and from B to A. They are frequent, consecutive *and* concurrent. They change in intensity and meaning and purpose. A signal rarely dies when it reaches the receiver. It breeds. Another signal returns. The signal, as well as changing his knowledge, affects the impression the receiver holds of the transmitter. This impression is in turn transmitted in suitably coded form from the receiver to the transmitter (along with further knowledge). The return signal affects the transmitter's impression and so on.

In social situations people are continually projecting images and learning from the return signals how acceptable they are. Social psychologists refer to this as 'impression management'. Taken to extremes this can lead to the contrived posturing of the 'actor' who projects a public self quite distinct from his private personality, possibly even taking in himself in the process.

In the cut and thrust of image projection our attitudes change. The signal stays alive. A feigns interest in B, who accepts it at face value and shows genuine interest in A, who starts to reconsider his original perception of B. What is appearance? What is reality? And which has created which?

Obviously a company does not engage in such rapid exchanges as this and it suits both the company and the consumer for the latter to have a fairly consistent attitude towards the company and/or its products. (As Kotler[6] reminds us: 'attitudes economise on energy and thought'.) Nevertheless, it is a delusion for a company to believe that signals travel single or even day-return. They have season tickets.

The third key factor, already noted, is that verbal and non-verbal communications are part of the same system—and the whole is bigger than those two parts. This leads us into tricky territory. It is not that the complexities of non-verbal communication (symbols, 'psychologics', entropy and the like) are difficult to grasp, but the emphasis they put on noise makes us doubt if we can ever construct any model of communication which bears relation to reality.

Nevertheless: entropy is loss of information. It is not the same as noise. Noise is any interference which results in a signal being diminished. Noise therefore causes entropy. Entropy varies from medium to medium and according to the effort and understanding put in by the transmitter and receiver. There is less entropy in a read text than a heard speech—all other things being equal. There is less entropy in a love letter than a tax form.

Gordon admits that it is difficult to diagnose accurately the 'degree of psychological entropy involved in any communication'.[7] Shannon and Weaver's model[8] does not take it into account. If communications are regarded as entirely logical and concerned essentially with the transmission of verbal messages then a mathematical—even linear—model may be regarded as significant. Gordon believes that without admitting 'psychologics' into the equation, a mathematical model is 'as useless as a photograph of a man would be giving us an idea of his behaviour'.[9]

Symbols help us to communicate. Man is a natural user of analogy and metaphor. Unfortunately analogy and metaphor, because they describe object X in terms of object Y, inevitably add to the signal *elements of Y* which may distract. Symbols make noise. (To avoid entropy re-read the last sentence aloud.)

But symbols are fundamental to human thought. No communicator can or should avoid their use. But he should remember that a symbol is never itself. It is a:

> sign, object or act that stands for something other than itself, by virtue of agreement among the members of the culture that use it.[10]

Sometimes a sign resembles the object (e.g. the weather chart graphics). Sometimes a sign bears no resemblance (e.g. ♀ signifying female). Images (in the sense not of perceived impressions as we are using the word throughout this book, but of transmitted visual ideas) are also symbols. These again are metaphors and carry parasitical impressions.

The use of emotive, image-rich language can aid comprehension but risks causing distraction. If I say someone is 'aggressive' you may consider the argument. When, however, I describe him as an 'aggressor' you may begin to see pictures. If I call him 'an Attila' your pictures are in focus.

'One picture may be worth a thousand words.' The trouble is one picture can represent a thousand *different* words. Each listener may have a slightly different impression. No two received 'pictures' may be the same. The picturesque route is rarely the direct one—in life, on maps, or models of the communication process.

One final factor affecting our view of the communication process is the *relationship* between the transmitter and the receiver. Communication is a people process. So far we have concentrated upon content. Certainly, more time in companies is spent on what is being said as opposed to what effect that message has upon the relationship between the transmitter and the receiver.

Often of course the message (written or spoken) *establishes* the relationship. It—e.g. a corporate advertisement—could be the first item of communication between a company and a reader. Companies have to be reminded that every time is a first time for somebody. Some people are coming into a market just as some people are going out. So in effect each commercial communication is addressing different people at different stages of a relationship and obviously, in certain cases, establishing those relationships at the outset. Not that it will remain fixed for ever. As we know, relationships change. However, the primacy effect (first impression) is crucial.

The lesson for corporate communications is obvious. The initial question is not 'what do we want to say?' or even 'what do we want the reader (viewer, passer-by, etc.) to believe?' Important as that latter question is, it is not the first. We must instead ask 'what relationship do we want to establish?' or, subsequently, 'do we need to change our relationship or reinforce it?' Relationships are determined as much—if not more—by the approach, as by the content of the message.

> If by expression, manner of speech, tone of voice or verbal content the sender seems to be evaluating or judging the listener, then the receiver goes on guard.[11]

In recorded social encounters, experiments have proved that 'speech used to control the listener evokes resistance'.[12] It should need no ghost from Harvard to tell us this. But we all need reminding. People in marketing and advertising spend much of their time trying to change attitudes or influence behaviour. Yet from their own personal—e.g. family—experience they know that any attempt to influence someone else's behaviour 'evokes resistance'. The attempt to alter a person implies criticism. There is an assumption that the person to be changed is inadequate. On the other hand when the transmitter *seeks help* from the receiver and wants to collaborate with him in finding a solution, he more readily secures cooperation since no predetermined solution is (apparently) about to be imposed. The word 'apparently' warns us that bluff in this context could be worse than direct persuasion, since people react even more vigorously to attempts to manipulate them or use them as guinea pigs. Spontaneous behaviour reduces tension and defensiveness, particularly if it reveals empathy for the receiver's feelings and an awareness of—even an identification with—the receiver's problems.

Intimations of superiority and expressions of deprecation are counter-productive. 'Why should I help *him*? He knows the answer anyway.' Conversely, the transmitter who appears to be weighing up the situation, taking provisional attitudes rather than taking sides, is more likely to win over the receiver. Note that these conclusions are based upon experiments conducted on people in social encounters, not companies in commercial communication situations. It is much harder for a company to act as spontaneously as a person or to weigh up the issues dispassionately without seeming disingenuous. However, it needs to understand how people respond to a *manner* of communication—as much as to the *matter*.

If the complexities attending person-to-person communication haven't discouraged you altogether we shall return to companies communicating and take a closer look at its terminology. But, since you're probably ready for a drink, we'll stop off first at our cocktail party.

8

Some terminology

Back at the party we are on first name terms. Instead of *A* and *B* our participants are called—what? Alf and Bertram? Hardly, you say. Why not? The things they said indicated otherwise? Perhaps *you* are contributing more than you know? Do you have images of 'Alf' which fit unhappily with the behaviour of *A*? Aren't you bringing a few preconceptions to the party? But, you say, perception is the true reality. Right. Anthony and Brian . . .

We left Anthony transmitting messages to Brian. Some only Anthony knew about. Some Anthony and Brian both knew about. Some only Brian knew about. The first didn't get through (at least in the way intended). The second succeeded in getting through. The third were received even though Anthony didn't know they were being sent.

During the opening exchanges Brian's picture of Anthony was coming into focus. Anthony was establishing a relationship of superior to inferior. Admittedly, Anthony asked questions, but in a manner that invited verification rather than amplification. In social science terminology Anthony was eliciting defensive rather than supportive responses from Brian.

Anthony clearly is trying to exert power.[1] In other words he is seeking to modify Brian's conduct in the way he wants without allowing Brian in any way to modify his. Power we might infer is a dominant trait, a key part of a 'total pattern of motivation, intellectual and social characteristics' which distinguishes Anthony from other people. We need not pause to contemplate how he 'grew' his personality save to say that influences on his character, conscious and unconscious, had probably done their work well before he was out of his teens. The idea of Brian changing that is ludicrous. All Brian can do, should he wish to pursue communication, is to *allow for* the personality.

Is a company personality 'grown' in the same way? Hardly, for two good reasons. Firstly, it is a *corporate* personality. Even in the case of a company dominated by a single entrepreneurial figure, other influences are at work—colleagues, customers, suppliers, the market-place, etc.— considerably modifying the unique personality. Secondly, there is far greater *control* of a corporate than a human personality. Even the entrepreneur can regard his company as an alter ego. Corporate personalities can be determined before the company starts trading. In this sense (as in the legal sense), a company is an artificial construct. It starts with a ready-made personality. Its parents can choose rather than wait to see what life and inherited genes reveal.

Despite its artificial birth a corporate personality develops normally. It is equally prone to external influence (including parental influence of course). Wally Olins describes corporate personality in human terms:[2]

> It is the soul, the persona, the spirit, the culture of the organisation manifested in some way.

Elsewhere he expands on culture:[3]

> Individual organisations, as they get more complex, have to develop a culture that enables people working within them to understand one another. This culture is often best projected visually . . .

Anthony projected himself visually by means of his suit, shirt, tie, visiting card, hairstyle and so on. Visual identity is a complex of cues. Most people find it quite easy to adopt a consistent identity. They don't think about it. 'Be yourself' is their motto. Other people work at it—some very successfully —though you are usually conscious of the effort that has gone into it. A third category veer between the two—'being themselves' one day and practising 'impression management' the next.

Most *companies* are in the third category, resorting to a 'corporate identity scheme' to put some order into the random idiosyncratic cues they naturally transmit. And identity—it is hoped—will put an end to this disorder. Identity, says the *Shorter Oxford English Dictionary*, is 'the quality or condition of being the same; absolute or essential sameness; oneness'. Companies crave that. Particularly company accountants and others with a tidy mind. But identity (of course), also means individuality (which takes us, for our purposes, too close to personality). More general is the sense of *identification*. And identity 'serves to identify the holder' and, by implication, *no one else*. Olins says:[4]

> Visual identity . . . is a part of the deeper identity of the group, the outward sign of the inward commitment, serving to remind it of its real purpose.'

Though this may be hard to square with the proliferation of seemingly trivial and interchangeable house styles and identity schemes, the definition is useful since it links identity firmly to reality. Identity must come from within.

When a company asserts that a corporate identity scheme can 'solve' a corporate problem such as a merger of disparate units, it is applying identity *from without*—and will almost certainly fail unless the design consultants can penetrate the 'soul' of the merged company and show the company to itself. It may not much like what it sees, particularly:

if the reality is unclear and if a company is not sensitive to its consumer needs, attitudes and particularly ethos.[5]

In which case corporate identity schemes are 'doomed to failure'.[6]

Anthony's cues equal his identity. They are of two sorts. I choose to categorise them as *physical* and *behavioural*.

By physical I mean the way he dresses and grooms himself, his accoutrements, his 'graphics' (Olins' outward sign). By behavioural I refer to the way he acts—the *non-verbal* messages he sends, e.g. his gestures, stance, physical proximity. It is the sum total of these cues which, interacting with the verbal content of the spoken messages, form the basis of Brian's image of Anthony. How far Brian's image is a true reflection of Anthony, Anthony might question.

Strictly speaking, image means 'likeness'. The company must try to ensure that the perceived image bears a strong relationship to the reality of the personality. Attempts to do otherwise will be found out. Note that 'like' is not the same as 'identical to'. Absolute exactness is neither possible nor essential. But the image we hope is received via the identity we convey must be credible. The parts must be consistent. The image must be consonant with the impressions already perceived. Reality is the basis.

A better definition of image is 'a representation in the mind'. What the audience *perceives* is paramount. If we are to learn —about ourselves, how our company is perceived—we need to get inside the mind of the perceiver and find ways of transmitting that image from the film of the mind on to the sensitised paper of, say, a research report. (See Chapters 31 and 32.)

Chambers Twentieth Century Dictionary defines *public image* as 'the picture in the minds of most people of what, e.g. a political party stands for'. And the *Pan Dictionary of Management* brings us nearer home (and the office) with 'mental picture that someone, or people in general, have of a person, company, organisation, product, etc.' Bob Worcester recommends this definition of corporate image:[7]

> Corporate image is the *net* result of the interaction of all the experiences, beliefs, feelings, knowledge and impressions that people have about a company.

Some of these are correct, some are misconceptions—and frequently more likely to be subjective than objective.

He reminds us also that there are other image influences at work. One of these we met in an earlier chapter—the image of the product class as a whole. An oil company's image is affected by the genus 'oil companies'. The image of a domestic company communicating abroad is modified by the image of the exporting country in the importing country. Brian's image is influenced by Anthony's image of insurance people.

Which brings us to stereotypes. Walter Lippman first used this term in 1929 in reference to the perceptions we have of others.[8]

> In the great, blooming, buzzing confusion of the outer world we pick out what our culture has already defined for us, and we tend to perceive that which we have picked out in the form stereotyped for us by our culture.

Stereotyping is, alas, inevitable in commercial communication, particularly television commercials where time constraints do not allow for character development and force advertisers into comic strip characterisations. There is, however, less excuse for a corporate advertisement to depict stereotypes. Yet corporate advertising is full of them. The pressures here are very different. The need to adopt a defensive posture makes everybody look the same. And the traits of character which Company X wishes to project are very similiar to those which Company Y wishes to project. The result too often is stereotype people in stereotype situations beneath cliché headlines.

Back at the party, Anthony and Brian were in a stereotype situation and making stereotype judgements. Each of them (more obviously Anthony) was anxious to fit the other and his behaviour into a familiar contextual setting. Man is emotionally disturbed (often enjoyably) when information cannot be accommodated into a handy pigeon-hole. Clichés slip in without effort. Novelty brings its own shining new pigeon-hole. Anthony doesn't accept that one insurance company is any different from any other. He is, however, anxious to distinguish himself from all other export agents by calling himself a merchant adventurer.

In the next chapter we shall attempt to combine elements of our two communication models, look at some related factors, begin to discuss the implications for company communication and to lay down a few guidelines.

9

A model

What then are the main factors we need to consider in our basic model? Communication is 'who says what to whom along what channels with what effect'. Communication is a complex, dynamic and continuous activity. There are several return journeys. The freight of communication is information. But information we know is not received as discrete items of abstract fact. What we receive are thoughts consciously transmitted and impressions consciously and unconsciously transmitted.

Our normal yardstick for measuring communications is cognitive. 'What did he say?' But cognition is related to emotion, style and motive. How he said it, how I felt about him at the time and why he said it (or why I *think* he said it) affect not only my impression of him but my perception of what he said. Style is manner rather than matter. But the distinction appears abstract when we try to analyse it in examples. What is the difference between 'open the palace gates' and 'set wide the palace gates'? The matter is the same. But hasn't the manner of the second made the *act* of opening somewhat more grand, more *palatial*? Is 'set wide' more 'poetic'? More *'emotionally charged'*? Emotions change our cognition. And vice versa. As Gordon reminds us, emotions 'are often mediated to us or changed in quality by cognition'.[1]

Herein lies our difficulty in attempting to construct a communication model, when the emotional quotient is not only high but often indistinguishable from the rational. Can poetry be conveyed by algebra? A communication model has to accommodate both verbal and non-verbal communication, i.e. formal messages (thoughts and ideas) to which the mind of A gives articulated form, and informal messages (expressions of character via dress and gesture) which are transmitted without the use of the spoken or written word.

The formal message undergoes coding. The thought is transformed into appropriate language—i.e. a code which B understands, and can therefore decode and interpret. Perfect reception occurs when the received thought in mind B corresponds to the original thought in mind A.

Informal messages are more complex—because they are non-articulated, because they are often unconscious and because they are harder to monitor by means of feedback. The content of an informal message is—partly or wholly—the personality of the transmitter. This is expressed by means of his identity. The perceived impression of these cues represents the image. However, the less attention the transmitter pays to his identity the more likely is the image to correspond with the personality. An 'image-conscious' transmitter may attempt to transmit a different personality and regard communication as successful if this is the image perceived by the receiver irrespective of reality.

The formal and informal messages are being transmitted simultaneously. And they react upon each other. Suppose *A* is anxious to transmit a thought to *B*. The informal messages transmitted, say, by the tie he happens to be wearing may severely modify the strength of his important formal message. Conversely, *A* may wish to create an impression rather than convey an idea but the formal message can undermine this, e.g. the topic of conversation may be inappropriate to his chosen identity.

Formal messages transmit thoughts and impressions. Informal messages transmit impressions only. Formal messages are conscious. Informal messages are conscious and unconscious. Formal messages and informal messages interact. They can reinforce each other or they can undermine each other. In the latter case the dissonant message is a form of noise.

A has a personality which he transmits in informal messages via his identity. The resulting perceived impression is his image. However, *A*'s personality is also transmitted in his formal messages. The thought cannot be divorced from the personality and the personality cannot be divorced from the thought. *B* transmits messages by return. This is feedback. These again are both formal and informal. The same interactions apply. *A* interprets *B*'s feedback as proof (or denial) of his message having been received and understood.

The exchange of messages of one or other sort is continuous. Communication is dynamic. As it changes the knowledge of the participant, so it affects the relationship between them. Any complete model of the communication process would therefore have to accommodate:

1. THOUGHTS AND IMPRESSIONS.
2. PERSONALITY—IDENTITY—IMAGE.
3. TRANSMITTER—ENCODER—DECODER—RECEIVER.
4. FORMAL AND INFORMAL MESSAGES (AND THEIR INTERACTION).
5. NOISE.
6. FEEDBACK.
7. DYNAMISM (REPEATED EXCHANGE OF MESSAGES).
8. RELATIONSHIP OF PARTICIPANTS.

10

The company, what and who?

The company—what is it? How realistic is it to consider corporate communication as a person-to-person exercise when clearly a company is more than one person? Furthermore, if it was agreed *one* person should represent the company, there would be difficulty deciding who. Finally, the persona perceived by the different publics would be different.

The task is easier the smaller the company, the more coordinated its activities, the more centripetal its structure. This is not to suggest that a company's development should be determined by its communication policy. However, it has to be appreciated that each decision within the company (e.g. change of structure, new product, acquisition, refinancing) may possibly affect how the company is perceived, not simply whether the image is 'better' or 'worse' but whether the image is more in focus or less, whether the persona can be clearly distinguished.

What then is a company?

> A corporation [which is the word Americans prefer] formed for a limited and specific purpose according to simple procedures set out in the laws of the country of incorporation.[1]

So much for the business definition. The *Chambers Twentieth Century Dictionary* on the other hand says:

> A person or persons associating with one; any assembly of persons . . . persons associated for trade.

This serves our purposes better than the previous, dehumanised, version. Moreover, it reminds us of the unifying nature of the enterprise. People are coming together for a purpose.

One person starts a company. There may be more than one founding partner but the idea began in one mind. The begetter believes he sees a solution to a marketing problem which is new and/or different, the pursuit of which will create profit. The idea may be a product or a service. The idea satisfies a human need presently unsatisfied or satisfied in a different way or possibly never recognised.

In the early days of the company two forces are acting centripetally: the inspiration of the founder and the creation of the product or service. The single-minded relationship of the company and the original idea will act as a unifying force. When that idea is presented to its public the perceived image of the company may be faint but it will not be ambiguous. Furthermore, company and product (or service) will be linked. At this stage it would be impossible to distinguish corporate from product advertising. Corporate advertising suffers from many definitions. It seems sufficient, however, to call 'corporate' an advertisement which 'sells' the company rather than the company's product(s). In the beginning, the company will obviously need to sell itself as much as the product. Indeed the name of the product may be so closely tied to that of the company that the two become indistinguishable. Guinness and extra stout. Horlicks and malted milk. Cinzano and vermouth. Hoover and vacuum cleaner. In these and countless other cases the company name became the product name, or rather, since the adoption of the individual's name affords it greater distinctiveness, it would be more correct to call it *brand* name.

In those early days of a company's existence, it is impossible to contemplate that the image of the company was either faint or ambiguous. That is, provided the company chose to declare parenthood.

A company's perceived need today for corporate advertising may well result from a decision some fifty years ago whether or not to declare parenthood. Heinz is Heinz is Heinz. Its name is on everything it makes, and everything it makes is called Heinz. The name Procter and Gamble is on everything it makes (but generally on the back of the pack in small type adjacent to an arcane symbol) and the things it makes are known by the public as Ariel, Fairy Liquid, Bold, etc.

It is clearly easier to imagine (i.e. form an image of) Heinz than Procter and Gamble. Always assuming the latter wants you to perceive them—which is arguable. But the majority of the cases are not that black and white.

Most companies inhabit a twilight zone. Wally Olins[2] calls this category 'endorsed'—in contradistinction to 'monolithic' and 'branded'. The company name extends over some brands whereas other brands seem to bear the company's imprint without actually carrying the name. Other brands seem totally detached. And though it is possible that some consumer-goods' companies see little point in any corporate communication since their names are closely and overtly associated with their brands, it should be borne in mind, as Thomas Garbett[3] stresses in his comprehensive book on corporate advertising, that corporate association is

> . . . far less strong than management suspects. More important, products and their advertising may not be conveying as acceptable a picture of the corporation as it would like.

The problem grows as the company grows. Naming policies become more complex. They diversify, acquire other companies, find new brand names harder to think of and, particularly, to register, and therefore use existing brand or family names in areas for which they were not originally intended and/or are not appropriate.

When the American Charles William Post introduced a cereal beverage for people who preferred not to drink tea or coffee at night and called it Postum, the association of brand and company was obvious. In 1929 General Foods, then recently formed, took over the company. General Foods also took over the Birds Custard company in the UK. Until very recently you could still buy Birds Instant Postum.

The case of Cadbury's is even more complex. Whereas GF in the UK hide behind their sub-company names (e.g. Birds, Maxwell House), Cadbury's use both their company name and sub-company names (e.g. Typhoo and Schweppes). Furthermore, the primacy effect is at work here: to the vast majority of the UK public Cadbury's means initially and primarily chocolate. Thus the message 'got any Cadbury's?' is almost certain to be understood by the recipient. Cadbury's also make Smash. The packaging of this instant potato, and its advertising, in no way serve to diminish the integrity of the 'got any Cadbury's?' message. However, to look at it the reverse way, the name Cadbury's on the Smash packet does constitute noise.

Unilever—who spend not one penny on corporate advertising (unless you count their annual statement)—are another who operate a sub-company policy. Each Unilever company (e.g. Lever Brothers, Van den Berghs, Elida Gibbs) is a corporate entity as far as external communication is concerned. However, where they differ from Cadbury's (or as they are now known Cadbury Schweppes) is that few of these sub-company names are corporately promoted. Certainly there is no corporate advertising. The names of the companies are known, if at all, individually via their use in brand names, e.g. Birds Eye Fish Fingers (from Birds Eye Walls) or Gibbs SR (from Elida Gibbs) or Knights Castile from the now defunct Hudson and Knight. But these are exceptions. Lever Brothers is almost as hidden from popular gaze as Procter and Gamble. The name 'Lever Brothers' appears on the back of packets of Surf, Lux, Drive, Comfort, etc. On the front of Persil you will see the word 'Lever' to distinguish it in Germany (where it is sold to British troops in the Naafi) from the local Persil, a name which is owned by the competitive firm of Henkel.

Procter and Gamble and Lever Brothers operate a brand policy. The company name —or sub-company name—is not promoted *per se*. They also operate a sub-brand policy, i.e. a brand name is capable of generating other related brands. The qualities associated with the brand and seen as part of its character are deemed appropriate to a new product. For example Fairy Soap begat Fairy Snow begat Fairy Liquid begat Fairy Toilet. (In the last case, should one assume that the historic brand name associations make the sub-brand's message powerful enough to counteract the contemporary language noise in the name 'Fairy Toilet'?)

If the brand is hermetically sealed from the parent company it can in no way affect the company image. A brand image may be potent, but unless identified with the company it lives a life of its own. And of course by *not* identifying with it, the company can, if it wishes, avoid corporate association if and when the brand hits trouble. Conversely, it is harder for a company's image to benefit in times of brand success. And individual brands which don't advertise get no spin-off (via a shared name) from other brands which do. A brand in this discrete form merits the following description from Wally Olins:[4]

> (It) is a figment of the marketing man's imagination. It is the ventriloquist's dummy, the corporate marketing people pick it up and put it down again whenever they feel like it. The consumer may react to the dummy, but the dummy cannot respond by itself: it is manipulated by the company.

But how discrete is discrete? What sort of image do you have of the name 'Nestlé'? or 'Nestles'? Is the image affected by the logo depicting birds in a nest? The name Nestlé is that of the founder. To ask for a bar of this gentleman's chocolate in the original accent might cause grave, or rather, acute, embarrassment. 'Nest' and 'nestle' originally had nothing to do with it. But the noise persisted and has now become part of the message. Nevertheless, Nestlé make chocolate and Nestles make cream. Ask the public who makes Nescafé and very few will be able to tell you. The corporate image of Nestlé to the general public is coloured light brown—a mixture of chocolate, cream and Milky Bar. To the *Financial Times* reader the image is more exact, though whether it is any more focused is another matter since he or she will have to accommodate several more cues: Findus, baby foods, L'Oréal, Vittel and the other possessions and productions of the Swiss multinational.

What then *is* a company? We can make one quick and easy distinction. It differs from a brand by virtue of the fact that, as Olins points out:[5]

> A brand identity is aimed at one audience—the final consumer—but the company identity is aimed at many.

We could also say that the company is everybody who works there. If the PR department is 43,000 people then the company is the workpeople. But when the workpeople aren't communicating to customers, friends and relatives how good the company is, they are doing a wide variety of jobs at various levels in various circumstances. Can all of that variety be grasped in a single image? And how realistic is it to imagine that the individual images perceived by the various publics in any way coalesce, that the multiplicity of cues can form a cohesive image? Just consider the number of conscious and unconscious informal messages, the variety of channels, sources of noise, and the relationship, or lack of it, of the various receivers with the various transmitters. Quite apart from the planned communications of the advertising department and the public relations department, formal messages are being transmitted from the sales force (to the individual buyer), the finance department (to the financial community), the personnel department (to the community and the employees) and the board of management (to the stockholders).

Of course, a company might regard the last of these audiences as not simply the most important but the only one worth bothering about since it is the only audience—apart from staff and government—to whom the company is legally accountable. But who, Milton Friedman apart, today believes that a company's accountability begins and ends with its stockholders? As Robert P Zabel,[6] president of N W Ayer, elaborated at a *Fortune* Seminar, management has a greater responsibility:

> . . . to the accepted standards of moral conduct . . . Top management is accountable to itself, not just in terms of growth and profits, but in terms of searching out the truth about itself, deciding who it really is, *who it wants to be and when*, and then taking great care to impress that honest image on itself, first on its employees and stockholders, and then on its external audience.

Notice—'*who* it wants to be'. Not *what*. Though 'what' will inevitably come into it. After people ask your name, they need to know what you do. If your company name is Guinness they know. If it's Fiat they know. If it's Tampax, Volkswagen, Heinz or Goodyear they know. If it's Shell they probably know. If it's Thorn-EMI they possibly know. If it's Van den Berghs they are unlikely to know. If it's Wander they probably don't know. And if it's SSIH (UK) Ltd[7] they won't know.

The only thing the public knows we make is money . . .

If it's a conglomerate it has special problems. As Olins says:[8]

> If a company is involved in a lot of different things it needs some kind of standard to explain to people what it does, because nobody takes the time and trouble to listen for very long. In the absence of any clear and consistent

explanation it will generally be assumed that the company still does what it has always done.

Spillers means flour to one generation, canned pet food to a slightly younger generation but dog biscuits to an older generation who dimly recollect shapes—Spillers Shapes. But Spillers is more than all of these. 'Metal Box is more than metal boxes.' That was the baseline of their corporate advertisement some years ago as they ventured into plastics. Cementa is another company trapped by its own name. The Rank Corporation grew from a cinema chain to embrace other communications industries, expanding now into holiday tour operations. It endeavours to keep its identity on all its divisions. This results in some contrived baselines and commercial end shots generally featuring the well-known trademark from the immediate post-war cinema, e.g. 'The man with the gong. A man of many skills.'

I always thought Ranks were gong manufacturers...

There could hardly be a better illustration or a better line to symbolise the problem we are discussing, the complexity on the one hand of trying to convey diversity and the desire on the other hand, for unification and personalisation.

11

The company, social animal

However, not only is the company 'a man of many skills', each person within it is a person of many parts. The company representative who communicates externally or internally is unlikely to speak with the voice of the company unless of course he is obsessively loyal, subservient or brain-washed. Even the most rigidly controlled organisation would regard it as counter-productive for its representatives to act as automata of the party line. Companies may still exist who employ hands rather than what Peter Drucker[1] calls 'the whole man'. But even hands communicate both internally and externally. And companies who employ the whole man accept the fact that they don't control the totality.

I am indebted for the following scenario to an article in *The Guardian*[2] on OPUS, the Organisation for Promoting Understanding in Society.

A manager in a large company is called upon to recommend the introduction of new technologies. He has acquired a word processor on trial loan. The choice facing him is between two typists or one typist and a processor. The rental is the same as the salary. But typists are getting more expensive and machines cheaper.

If you are the manager, what guides you? The question is far from straightforward. You are not playing one role but several:

1 A citizen (increasing the competitiveness of the country).
2 A stockholder (attending to profitability).
3 An efficiency expert (concerned with productivity).
4 A manager (keeping within budget).
5 An employee (pleasing the people at the top).
6 A parent of a teenage daughter (helping to secure future jobs for children).
7 A 'citizen of the company' (securing employment).
8 A union official (avoiding job losses).

All these role considerations could come into play before even the interview begins. We need to add a final role.

9 An ordinary human being, responding to the thoughts and impressions which he receives as the interview proceeds and as the relationships between the two establish themselves, adjust and form.

And how do you empathise with the girl? How much job satisfaction will she get? What is the alternative for her—is it that job or no job? Does she regard herself as interchangeable with a machine—and therefore as an *object?*

This scenario demonstrates the complexity of issues facing one person (how many then for a company?). It also takes us on to higher territory, to Zabel's 'accepted standards of morality'.[3] Social responsibility in the last twenty years has moved from the status of optional extra to a built-in component. Mind you, like some recent automobile components, social responsibility has been the result of external pressure rather than corporate initiative.

However, companies are adept at turning necessity into virtue and claiming the innovation as their own. (In a related area, who today regards Square Deal Surf as a Labour Government inspired development?) Or they can reassure themselves by combining rectitude with hard-nosed business practice, preach that honesty is still the best policy and wave a banner with that strange device 'enlightened self-interest'.

Of course there's truth in it. Unless companies attend to their communities there may be no customer for their products. If big companies can germinate small companies then the substructure of the economy will be healthy. If a company can create jobs for school leavers then skills may be learned for use later in life whilst in the short term relieving the dole queue, enlightening the gloom, and setting goals for others. And improving its image.

Sainsbury recruit one thousand school leavers under the Government's new Youth Training Scheme 'and it eventually hopes to offer them all employment,' chairman Sir John Sainsbury revealed at the company's annual general meeting. (Where else?) The National Westminster Bank is giving away £1,000,000 to help the jobless in run-down city centres. British American Tobacco joins forces with the Merseyside Development Corporation to turn a derelict warehouse into workshops for small companies. Success is measured by the turnover of companies as they grow out of the premises. Tesco gives a £5,000 boost to a community centre project at West Durrington in Sussex as part of the company's public relations programme to help develop and improve community life. Marks and Spencer allocate £5,000 to each store manager to spend as he sees fit on local causes: this to celebrate the M&S centenary.

Business acts corporately too. At the first weekend conference of Business in the Community in April 1983, Sir Hector Laing, chairman of United Biscuits, urged British companies:

> . . . to follow the lead of the Americans and put one per cent of their pre-tax profits to be used for community projects.[3]

There is greater pressure today on the corporation to be seen as a 'good guy'. The forces at work on companies to defend their activities in reactive advertisements are precisely those which impel social responsibility, and active and pre-emptive good works:

> . . . heightened social awareness . . . participation of special interests, segmentation within society, media which are responsive to social change.[4]

Of course, it is not sufficient to be seen as only a 'good guy'. In the business race—if not the human race—don't good guys finish last? And we want our business leaders to be successful managers and thus ensure employment. So there must be a balance of goodness and efficiency. Can they go together? Can the public mind comprehend a self-centred aggregate such as a business corporation being truly altruistic? The answer is yes—with difficulty. To the sceptic the dissonance is resolved by regarding the social concern as whitewash, 'public relations', or a 'tax dodge'. To the moderate such dissonance as exists is soon eradicated. It doesn't matter if the action is inspired by enlightenment or self interest. The two forces are fused in a rationalisation which inextricably links the company and society. There is a community of interest.

Dichotomy, however, is part of Anglo Saxon culture. The adversarial process is sanctified in our legal, parliamentary and educational systems. Conditioned to either/or, black/white, pro/con, winner/loser, the sceptic finds it difficult to accept community of interest or any game which isn't zero sum. How, he asks, can a company believe that consumer satisfaction is the criterion of a successful business? How can a supermarket chain expect anybody to believe its slogan 'We're on your side'?

Business—individually and corporately—has failed to explain how it works and who benefits. 'We sincerely believe,' said a Texaco spokesman in the oil crisis of 1974, 'the facts are on our side, but we failed to bring those facts home to the public.'[5]

The situation is better today—but only marginally. Antagonism has been replaced by doubt, particularly among young intellectuals. The majority of graduates prefer 'service' to 'manufacturing'. There is a duality in their attitude towards business. They appreciate that business creates wealth for the community at large, a wealth in which they share. But they do not appreciate that the *work of business* provides intellectual stimulus or challenge. Comments the CBI:[6]

> We need to create a climate in which business is recognised as the place where those with initiative and drive and, with standards of excellence, find a proper outlet for their energies and aspirations.

The company therefore has to be a good guy, a bright guy, energetic and efficient. He must make worthwhile products which serve a worthwhile purpose and promote them in an honest manner. And of course he must be a good neighbour.

So a company can construct a painting-by-numbers composite portrait from this amalgam of characteristics. The trouble is that so can every other company. Examples abound—bland generalisations, corporate philosophies processed into anaemic slogans such as 'we're involved' or 'we have connections'. Reading many of these corporate advertisements you get an impression of companies in a trance. They seem ill at ease and adopt language and postures which are unnatural to them but which some consultant Svengali has convinced them will make them well—and loved.

A company may have two problems when it starts corporate advertising. First, it may find it difficult to write a philosophy. Goals, objectives, missions and all the rest of the business consultant paraphernalia are at best abstract, at worst balderdash. Second, though it can happily tell you about what it makes, it gets tongue-tied when asked to talk about who makes it, namely itself. Knowing oneself is hard enough. Articulating that knowledge is tougher. And being able to relate one's beliefs and aspirations to society, particularly a society in ferment, makes the task quite daunting. Wally Olins accurately sums up the dilemma:[7]

> If young people and perhaps other parts of society are alienated from corporations, there are also plenty of corporations that are isolated from many currents in society. Some companies today are utterly bewildered, they really aren't sure what is expected from them. What are they supposed to be doing? If they don't make enough money they are inefficient. If they do make a lot of money they are greedy. If they are only concerned with their own affairs they are isolating themselves from the country and society as a whole.

The questions a company faces then are:

1 WHO IS IT?
2 WHAT IS IT?
3 HOW SHOULD IT COMMUNICATE?

Notice it should not question the *need* to communicate. Non-communication today is negative communication. It communicates even if it thinks it doesn't, even if it doesn't want to. It is transmitting messages which are creating images. It had better have some control of what those images look like.

And there is another reason to communicate. Doing the preliminaries will tell the company a lot about itself—and that could be worth the cost of the whole exercise.

12

Personality

The company. Who is it? First, is it a 'who' at all? Could the company save itself bother and embarrassment by ignoring the question altogether?

Possibly. However, the dialogue between the company-person and audience-person would continue because whether the company likes it or not, works at it or not, the public perceives the company in human terms. Though the company may consider itself an abstraction or too complex to personify, the customer chooses to make abstractions tangible and to simplify. The customer deals with people—even if he or she never meets them. British Gas perhaps is a typical bureaucrat, an image culled from a television programme maybe. Asked to draw him in a qualitative research interview he/she would have no hesitation. Of course he may have a featureless face. (But that communicates something: I doubt if the Gas Board would be very pleased.) A prompt call from a friendly repairman would add some features.

If a company thinks of each of its audiences as a single person, and of itself as a single person, relationships become far simpler to understand and plan. After all, each sale takes place between two entities. Mass communication is no more than the multiplication of single messages. A good broadcaster focuses on the individual viewer not the viewing figures. Also, of course, he remembers that messages go both ways.

Company performance, whether by staff or by product, affects the perceived image of the company. So do the formal and informal messages its various representatives transmit. Strictly speaking a company cannot *create* an image. Only a public can 'create' an image in that it consciously or unconsciously selects the thoughts and impressions on which that image is based.

The image is not what the company believes, but what the customer believes—or feels—about the company (and its brands and services) from his experience and observation; from what he knows about product performance, price, availability, delivery, after-sales service; what the company has to say about its products and service and what the company has to say about itself; what other people say; his own experience not simply with the products, but with the company via the telephone, letters, the receptionist's greeting and the people he does business with.

These fragments of information are part of what we have referred to as a mosaic. The picture is that of an individual, a corporate portrait of a 'Mr Cadbury' or 'Mr Shell' or 'Ms Avon'. What happens when you open an envelope from the company—or pick up the phone? Do you have a person in mind, a composite or maybe a dominant image of a particular person? Whom do people think of when your company contacts another company?

When a customer buys a product or service he is also 'buying' the company. In other words the company is promoting not simply a particular product, but a totality of which the company name—and therefore personality—is part. Everything the customer believes, knows, feels about the company is etched on the company face. It is a real face since reality—i.e. experience, both direct and indirect—created it. It is real too, despite the fact that the customer may have misunderstood the cues, misinterpreted the messages.

And the effects are real too. Would you buy a used car from a company with this face? Does the image which such-and-such a company or brand name conjures up fill you with trust, respect, confidence or other emotions? Would the character of the company which you interpret from the image convince you to pay a premium for the company's product?

The company cannot create the image. It *can* create the elements of the identity for the company (and all of the identity for the brand). It can also, if not create, at least determine what the personality should be.

But what if the company is *not* starting out? What can it do about its personality then? Clearly, the first thing it must do is find out what personality it has. Research among its audiences will show how the company is regarded, what it does and what it's like. It would be interesting simultaneously to ask management and staff the same questions. Better still, to ask them what *they* think and what they think about the public(s) they come into contact with think.

Some questions can be answered totally from within. What is the organisation structure? What is its growth pattern? What products does it make? What service does it provide? How does its performance rate on industry and government indicators? Other questions can be *asked* though the answers won't be as clear cut. (And perhaps the help of a qualified psychology-trained interviewer or moderator will be needed.) These are concerned with how the company operates as a social unit.

What makes CompanyX Company X? Management will say some things. Employees will say others. Long-term staff will quote less important factors than staff recently joined from *other* companies. If the company is old enough it will have developed, by design and by chance, 'patterns of relationships and interaction that are highly predictable and highly repetitive'.[1] Some of these frequently-occurring situations will be unique to that organisation. (Some incidentally will not have been recognised by management till they were pointed out.)

Uniqueness is the key. This book is using the following definition of personality:

> The sum total of the characteristics of the individual.[2]

Managerial psychologists write:[3]

> It is this uniqueness that is referred to when one speaks of the 'personality' of a company. This is what a management has in mind when it selects a new member with an eye to how he will 'fit in'.

Uniqueness then is what the investigation—internal, external, by research company and the company itself—is seeking to find. A company *is* unique. Every company is unique. No two fingerprints are identical. No two people are identical. No two companies are identical. (Though you would find that hard to believe after a surfeit of corporate advertisements.)

Should the investigation reveal surprises (and the real surprise is if it doesn't), then the company has to decide whether it should live with what it has discovered, 'be itself' and hang the consequences or whether it should make certain adjustments. Adjustments are all it can make. It can't radically change its personality without starting again.

The major determinant is consistency. How integrated is the perceived image? Where is the dissonance? Who (or which department) is responsible? Which product? Which message? Which element of its identity? Is one audience perceiving a clear image and another a faint impression? Is one audience receiving one image and another a contradictory image? (And if so, can the company do something about it? Indeed, should it?)

What is the company's response? It depends, of course, on how it sees the problem.

1 As an *image* problem.
2 As an *identity* problem.
3 As a *personality* problem.

If it believes it has an image problem then 'tinkering with the image' or changing it is no solution. Because strictly speaking, the company cannot directly change its image. As we know, an image is a perception belonging to the *receiver*. Companies who talk about 'image changing' generally suffer the delusion that minor external alterations will effect a change in the way the company is seen, which in turn will favourably affect sales, as if powder, beauty spot and rouge will help Cinderella's sister get her foot into the slipper.

What the company *can* do is adjust the identity and seriously question what it is doing, what it believes in, how it operates —factors which constitute its personality. Identity changes need to be profoundly considered. They are the outward manifestation of an inner set of beliefs, a company persona. A new logo won't do it. It may help—if the logo is part of, and wholly expresses or reinforces, a genuine change of heart and direction in the company itself. There's not much point in changing the signboard on a London Transport 73 bus to read 'Monte Carlo' (and make the upper deck roofless) if it still goes to Stoke Newington.

Advertising, public relations, a new glossy annual report—none of these will do it. An identity can only be founded in reality.

> If not supported by reality, the image advertising will merely aggravate distrust and cynicism.[4]

One American advertising critic commented at the start of the 1970s:[5]

> The gap between corporate claims and performance is at least as sizeable as the generation gap.

A couple of years later a practising US communicator was able to report progress:[6]

> More and more corporations are communicating with their publics not through the traditional verbal maneuvering and eye-pleasing graphics but through their actual deeds—actions they take, which are a reflection of how they think, how they feel towards society, the world and them.

Deeds, though understandably more important than words, still need to be noised abroad. They need to be put in context and packaged for consumption by busy publics. Verbal felicity (if not manoeuvring) and eye-pleasing graphics should not be regarded as a substitute for deeds but as the means by which those deeds are communicated, in the right way to the right audience. They are the clothes in which the deeds tread the earth—and by which the deed-maker can be identified.

Identification is easier if the 'identity' is consistent. Inconsistencies in identity betray either bad coordination of company communication or inconsistency in corporate character. Probably both. The airline incident quoted at the beginning of the book is an example. The 'choice' of a corporate identity should not be difficult if the company has a clear idea of itself. The parameters should be narrow. The company is not choosing among several fancy dress outfits. It is deciding which particular combination of clothes best expresses its personality.

'Style' is the man himself. The *Shorter Oxford English Dictionary* defines style as:

> The manner of expression characteristic of a particular writer . . . a particular mode or form of skilled construction, execution or production . . . a person's characteristic bearing, demeanour or manner.

If this seems to make it difficult to extricate the style from the personality, so be it. They are separable purely for purposes of analysis. They are as interwoven as manner and matter.

If style is an expression of personality so is life-style. The latter has a great advantage over the former, however, in communicating a company's personality in that it is far easier to analyse. Life-style goes beyond man's basic characteristics into his:

> . . . activities: how he spends his time at work and leisure; interests: what's important to him in his own immediate world and . . . opinions: how he feels about himself in light of the world in which he lives.[7]

Research into consumers' life-styles keeps all four aspects in balance—characteristics, activities, interests and opinions. Can these dimensions be used to help determine the life-style and ultimately the personality (of which the life-style is an expression) of the company? I believe so. They are currently being used to determine the character of brands. Why not determine the personality of companies who are, as I hope we are coming to believe, people already? Despite this fact—coupled with the probable inconvenience of an already established personality—the techniques by which the French agency RSCG investigate the personal verities of a brand seem most appropriate to the investigation of corporate character.

One technique they call the 'Chinese Portrait'. This is an analogy game. The brand is thought of as something—or someone—else. The company and the agency work together. A joint team of about six answer questions such as:

> 'If it were a car what car would it be?'
> 'If it were a magazine, an animal, a writer, a TV personality . . . ?'
> 'And which car would it most certainly *not* be?' etc., etc.

There seems to be no reason whatsoever not to apply this technique to companies. The Creative Business's experience with this technique has been illuminating. Seeing companies (or brands) as cartoon characters or film stars or football teams does provide insights into the way our clients see themselves—and, almost as important, how they see their competition. We did our best work for Dresdner Bank when the communications director said Deutsche Bank were Mercedes and Dresdner, BMW.

Corporate statements are often difficult—full of abstract qualities and platitudes. But equate your bank with BMW and its positioning is clear. Which bank is the more solid? Which is the more imaginative? Which would you go to for a safe, steady return of capital? And which would be the more likely to listen to an entrepreneurial idea?

There are many questions to be asked of a brand and of a competitor which are direct, factual and statistical. Sex? Age? Profession? Number of children? Conversely, a sociologist might wish to ask questions which might take longer to answer. Where does he (or she) go on vacation? What is his favourite entertainment? . . . favourite hobby? . . . favourite atmosphere? And least favourite atmosphere, hobby, entertainment and so on? Picture making and role playing, whether in the form of the Chinese portrait, or in role-reversal situations, or qualitative research exercises where respondents draw their answers, are particularly suitable for determining company personalities. They involve metaphor which, by making the familiar strange or the strange familiar, illuminate the dark landscapes of personality and reveal the distinguishing features. (Have you ever needed a visitor to your house to make you see something for the first time—as if through his eyes?) And of course by putting the imagination to work we are in the relevant territory.

Personality made manifest by identity is perceived as image. And it dwells where imagination dwells. It is appropriate that imagination should be called in to diagnose personality. It could help avoid a subsequent mismatch of personality and image.

We have not ended our exploration of corporate personality. But we have done enough to see the necessity to base it upon reality whilst enlisting the support of the imagination to help us find and express the eternal uniqueness. This is the true reality. And, as Bob Worcester says:[8]

> The degree perception and reality match are a measure of how accurate a company has been in projecting its corporate personality.

13

Identity

From the *Morning Advertiser*, daily paper of the drinks trade, 25 September 1982:

> Watneys London admitted yesterday that beer sales in its 1500 pubs are hampered by the company's poor image. On Monday, in a bid to sell one million barrels per year, the company is to change its name, livery and identity.
> Following the trend towards pub tradition and local heritage, the company is reviving its original title of Watney Combe Reid & Co. The red barrel logo, introduced in the 1930s is to be scrapped and will be replaced by a stag—Watneys' first ever trademark.

This is a textbook example: the process is correct (image research, analysis, identity change) and so is the terminology. The company is perceived to have a poor image. The company decides to change its *identity*. Marketing communication language is specialised.

> Identity means the sum of all the ways a company chooses to identify itself to all its publics . . . Image on the other hand is the perception of the company by these publics.[1]

There is another, narrower, sense in which the term is used in marketing communications. The two senses are related: the broader sense, naturally, embraces the narrower one. Identity, particularly in advertising, means *identification* inextricably linking the name of the brand and/or company to the promise of the advertisement.

Branding the name was a preoccupation of early marketers and advertisers. It was a guarantee to the customer of consistency and a sign to look for. It also said to the competition 'what's mine is mine'. The term is thought to originate from the practice of branding cattle with hot irons. A certain ranch owner called Maverick refused to brand his cattle. He was then able to claim that all unbranded cattle belonged to him. Hence the term.

Early advertisements may seem naive today but they rarely omitted the obvious. As a boy I remember seeing part of the Watney company mentioned above advertise at Chelsea football ground. The hoarding read: 'REID THE

DAILY STOUT'. There was another slogan in the programme 'BOVRIL FEEDS THE INSIDE RIGHT'. On the way home we passed 'MY GOODNESS! MY GUINNESS! '

Advertising is now more sophisticated. Often at the expense of branding. Viewers remember the commercial but not the name of the product. Indeed advertising people, whose job it is, often find it hard to identify which beer 'I'm only here for', 'your right arm's for' or which is 'the thinking man's lager.'

On the other hand, ask them which building society says 'We're with the Woolwich' or which oil company says 'You can be sure of Shell' and you might get a funny look—as if you had asked 'who wrote Beethoven's Fifth?'. Of course there are ways of branding other than using the name in the slogan or headline, other visual and verbal techniques.[2] Failing to brand is like writing a letter and forgetting to sign it. Often it's writing a letter and signing it with the name of someone else. One of the more regrettable consequences of advertising awards is the growth of mimicry. A prize advertisement, no doubt deserving its accolade, will twelve months later have spawned a dozen imitators. An original solution to one product problem becomes a not wholly suitable device for different products. Yesterday's idea becomes today's technique becomes tomorrow's cliché.

Unless an advertiser is the brand leader it is an act of criminal folly not to identify. Kodak could till recently promote the joys of photography and guarantee to reap the benefit. None of its competitors could dare to do that—they would be benefitting Kodak. In the world of double glazing Zenith is a small company. Their need to brand is proportionately more crucial. Whilst their competitors choose television personalities or the three wise monkeys as spokesmen, Zenith portray the confident peace of mind their product ensures by showing contented, sleeping customers at home, a constant stream of letter Zs emanating from their heads.

The Z is an advertising technique. Its job is to lock in the brand name with the benefit. It might—and should—echo the corporate identity of the Zenith company (e.g. the typeface) and the style of the commercial should be in keeping with the style of the company.

This is where we move from the narrower to the broader meaning of identity, from the tactical identification of brand name to the strategic establishment of a company personality by means of external signs and behaviour. As we mentioned, the latter embraces the former. If the corporate identity of the company is consistent and coordinated then locking in the brand name to the promise of the advertisement should be easy for the advertising agency since it will be second nature to the company's marketing executive who briefs them.

To explore the broader sense of identity we must return to the dictionary because there are three concepts we need to consider:

1 The quality or condition of being the same; absolute or essential sameness.
2 Individuality.
3 (A sign) that serves to identify the holder.

Branding an advertisement is part 3 of our meaning. Unless the advertisement 'identifies' the brand or company the effort is wasted.

Part 2 reminds us of the association with personality. (Indeed, the dictionary treats 'personality' as one definition of 'identity'.) Our identity— what we choose to do *with* what we have and *to* what we have—is a means by which we prove our individuality.

Part 1 reminds us of the need for consistency. 'The quality or condition of being the same.' The word *identity* comes from the latin *idem*: 'the same'. It is probably associated with *identidem*: 'over and over again'. Products were branded primarily in order to guarantee consumer satisfaction *every time*. Consumers were encouraged to look for a name or symbol so that they could *repeat the experience* of satisfaction. Slogans which reinforced this thought remain today: 'You can be sure of Shell', 'Dewars never varies'.

Identity is fundamental to communication—the identity of *who* is talking to *whom*. My identity is partly what I was born with (e.g. brown hair), partly what I have become (e.g. short-sighted and therefore wearing glasses), but chiefly *what I choose to present*. My identity is largely my concept and image of myself. *Your* image of me will be determined by what you learn second-hand but chiefly what you see and hear when we meet—the way I dress, talk, cut my hair. So I will choose my barber, my suit, my glasses in order to present the image of myself I want you to have. When a lady puts on a scent she is packaging herself, managing the impression she wishes to create and cosmetics, soap, clothes and accessories are part of the identity.

We all employ design consultants—our hairdresser, high-street tailor, chemist. But ultimately it is our choice. To wear a tie or not. To wear a bow tie to distinguish us from our fellows or a school tie to identify with them. The sum of our choices is our identity. Whether the result of that identity equates with our self-image remains to be perceived.

The cues which a person (or company) transmits can be classified in two main categories. I have chosen to call them, somewhat arbitrarily, physical and behavioural. By 'physical' I mean the look, the graphics, the 'clothes'. By 'behavioural' I mean the performance of the communicator, not what he says but the *way* he says it. Style obviously can be both physical and behavioural.

Identity in our specialised sense is always external. Corporate identity (which we examine in Chapter 25) is a planned assembly of visual cues by which the audience can recognise the company and discriminate one company from another and which may be used to represent or symbolise the company. Recognition comes from consistency. The same identity must be transmitted time and time again. And the constituent parts of the identity (the cues) must be consistent with each other.

Recognition breeds familiarity and as we know familiarity breeds —favourability. John O'Toole, President of Foote, Cone & Belding, said of corporate communications:[3]

> The programme should clearly communicate, through subject matter, copy style and graphics a unique, credible and personal identity for the company. People listen to, and buy from, someone they know and like and can recognise.

This is relevant for an idea, for a company, for a brand. A brand's identity, insists Jacques Séguéla of RSCG, is perceived through Physique (its physical make-up), its Character (its 'psychological universe' or personality—the unseen part which advertising unveils) and through its Style (execution constants which make it instantly recognisable).

Style is the creative person's province—language, production and above all 'signs'. To believe in a message, more important, to relate to a product, Séguéla believes, the public needs signs. Hollywood created stars out of bit players by careful grooming and strict attention to consistency. The 'signs' were crucial—Gable's moustache, Monroe's pout, Chevalier's straw hat, Chaplin's cane, Astaire's top hat and tails, etc. In advertising, too, consistency of style is essential to establish and maintain a brand. The Marlboro cowboy may change in detail but he is essentially always the same—serene, lean, weather-beaten, the outward manifestation of an inner spirit (in Olins' phrase) reflecting a brand personality—mature, contemplative and wise. We interpret all this from the external evidence, from the attention to detail—the face, the landscape, the language of the Western. It is recognisably the same. Without consistency there is no recognition and without recognition there is no identity. *Time* magazine covers have changed considerably in 60 years but they are recognisably the same. Persil has gone through several changes of formula and packaging but Granny recognises today's Persil as the one she used to use.

As a brand wishes to be recognised, so may a company. And the same constraints apply. After all, the visual identity which a company chooses encapsulates the essential *raison d'être* of the organisation. If the cues aren't consistent—over time and to each other—then the *raison d'être* is being neither expressed nor understood. (But inconsistency abounds. Generally because nobody's minding the store.)

Perhaps groups which comprise several companies find it easier to appreciate the need for continued and consistent identities? They need to keep the entities separate, not for the sake of administrative tidiness, but in order to exploit discrete sections of the market. Burton's revival has been due, says chief executive Ralph Halpern, to:

> . . . the implementation of what has been referred to as the multi-strategy market personality, which simply means that the Burton group operates several companies with clear identities which are perceived to appeal to specific segments of the market.[4]

The consumer knows where he/she is, what to expect, when the character of the store is communicated via a recognisable style. Consistency is important too in *internal* communications. A supervisor who changes his style, who adopts different modes of expression instead of his natural manner, finds his communication is less effective.

> Once a manager's true personality and style are perceived by his subordinates, they know what to expect. If he changes all his signals the result will be confusion and a less effective organisation.[5]

Sir Terence Conran rarely gets his signals mixed. Habitat was so sharply focused that the store name graduated to that of an entire lifestyle. Heals will be transformed into a 'chain of stores catering for the over–30s who've graduated from Habitat and have nowhere to go'.[6] Whereas Now speaks to teenagers interested in fashion. Conran is adjusting the identity of Mothercare.

> The clothes have become more fashionable. We've put carpets into the stores and made the lighting less supermarket and hard. The prices are still very good, but our customers are getting added value by design—both in the products and the environment.[7]

The changes are important but Mothercare's existing consumer franchise is even more important. And Mothercare is recognisably the same. The Conran Group is inevitably identified with Terence Conran. A corporate personality is far easier to convey when there is a single entrepreneur, extrovert and identifiable, at the helm: at Tesco, Jack Cohen; Lotus, Colin Chapman; Thorn, Sir Jules; IBM, Thomas Watson; Texas Instruments, Pat Haggerty; and at Mars, Forrest Mars.

In the world of finance, investors identify certain companies with their guiding lights—James Hanson (Hanson Trust), James Gulliver (Argyll Foods), Bernard Audley (AGB). The personality of the company is inevitably linked with the personality in charge.

Some companies take the brave step of having the chief executive represent them in advertisements. Being interviewed is one thing. Projecting yourself and acting as a presenter is something else. In the latter category you have chosen alien ground rules and will be judged as a professional communicator. You will also, almost certainly, have subsumed the personality of the brand into your own, as Victor Kiam has now subsumed Remington. If you are the eponymous owner then 'it' has become 'you' (Laker, Barratts Liquor Mart or, in the US, Purdue's Chicken). It can work and is undoubtedly potent. But it is probably short term—and very hard to follow.

*I am the company
chief executive —
which accounts
for my halting
delivery, lousy
acting and
unattractive mien...*

Sir Terence Conran would be the first to warn of the dangers of total identification. Does the company die with the individual? Again it is easier when a company becomes a group. In the case of the Conran Group the amount of 'Terence' in each of the member companies is sufficient to work some magic but the identity of each company is carefully controlled, the image is a totality of cues of which 'Conran' represents a minority.

Companies can adopt 'personalities' using the ready-made identities of celebrities to enhance their own or those of their products. Ronald Reagan means Lucky Strike; Jimmy Young, Ariel; John Alderton, Maxwell House, etc. Research in the US conducted by *Ad Age* revealed that most celebrities 'make little impression on consumers and those who do aren't considered very believable'.[8] (At least you can believe the chairman believes in the company.)

Celebrities are chosen because the company can bestow some favourable characteristics though, by definition, one personality will not exactly match another and the company has to consider whether the non-matching traits are irrelevant or constitute 'noise'. The danger has been well expressed by Joe McGinniss in *The Selling of the President*.[9] He compares the presenter to gift-wrapping:

> We respond like the child on Christmas morning who ignores the gift to play with the wrapping paper.

It also assumes that celebrities generate awareness. Here again the *Ad Age* research is cautious. McDonalds used the veteran actor John Houseman as their first ever corporate spokesman. He is a respected professional known for playing respected professionals. More than half the adult respondents did not recall having seen the TV commercial.

Of those who did nearly half (45%) said their reaction to the spot was neither favourable nor unfavourable.[10]

When the sample was asked to mention celebrities they had seen in commercials, comedian Bill Cosby was named by 103 out of 1,250 adults as the first to come to mind. Interestingly, next with 56 mentions was Lee Iacocca, chairman of Chrysler. He was the only chief executive to receive more than one mention. And I bet all of his 56 nominators remembered the product he was endorsing. Mention of Chrysler leads us to instance a good example of identity at three levels: company, division and brand.

Iacocca's chairmanship of Chrysler has been aggressive and gruff. He took over the company on the edge of bankruptcy and has led it back to viability. The character of the Chrysler Corporation is that of its chairman. Chrysler Corporation looks and talks like Iacocca. But each division tries to have its own identity. This was the chief concern of their new vice-president for sales and marketing who joined Chrysler in July 1983. The new arrangement he said 'baked in marketing organisationally'[11] (*sic*). Research indicated that:

> Dodge had almost no market identity, while Plymouth had upscale demographics but no matching image.[12]

Roughly translated this means that Dodge projected a very faint image whilst Plymouth, though it had a more wealthy clientele, appeared not to do so.

> To carve out an identity for Dodge, the division is using the theme 'Dodge, an American Revolution!'[13]

Meanwhile, in the Chrysler *division* they are trying to portray the Chrysler *brands*:

> In 1982 the Chrysler New Yorker was a rear-drive model. In the 1983 model year, the new front-wheel drive version was called the New Yorker and the rear-drive became the New Yorker Fifth Avenue. For the 1984 year, the front-drive version is called the New Yorker and the other the Fifth Avenue.[14]

Maybe they should call them Iacocca Marks I and II?

There is no quick solution to an identity problem and to attempt to impose a solution from above with 'a few nice graphics and a name change', without thoroughly considering the marketing implications throughout the organisation, is courting disaster.

Each year more and more of these half-thought-through identity schemes appear. The graphics are chosen not because the identity fits the company's personality but because *it looks like a corporate identity*. It distinguishes the company, not from other companies, but from those companies who can't afford a corporate identity. It says 'we've made it'—the smug boast of the nouveau-riche.

Simultaneously corporate advertisements appear parading platitudes, acknowledging society's ills and prescribing placebos. Says Stephen King of JWT:

> Real marketing requires a link between the customer and the corporate
> personality . . . There is no real reason why large companies shouldn't have a
> clear-cut corporate personality too, and the best do. Think of ICI, IBM,
> Kellogg's, Sainsbury, Marks & Spencer, Sony, Ford, Guinness. It requires a
> clear sense of direction, adhered to over a long period of time and it seems to
> me an essential fact of real marketing.[15]

The identities of those companies are clearly defined, single-mindedly
pursued, strictly monitored and consistently projected. Those companies are
in a different league from those who by arbitrarily choosing a fashionable
graphic and a cute turn of phrase succeed, in their search for identity, in
making themselves indistinguishable from a hundred others, thus losing
whatever identity they might originally have had.

14

Company philosophy

Business—and particularly the communication business—is rightly accused of abusing the English language. Ordinary thoughts are dressed in terms not meant for them with the result that, to part of the community, these words then take on a new and lesser meaning. When someone wishes to use one of these terms in its original sense he has to redefine it or apologise for using it or find some other word altogether. The richness of English enables him to adopt the last course. This, instead of clearing the confusion, merely adds to it. More terms are then seen as overlapping in meaning (connotation if not denotation) and subsequently treated as synonyms. 'Identity', 'image', 'personality', 'character' as we have seen are examples of this. 'Philosophy' is another.

Philosophy originally meant the 'pursuit of wisdom and knowledge'.[1] It also means 'knowledge of the causes and principles of things'.[2] This seems an awesome and somewhat unnecessary endeavour for a management committee of a paint company or an underwear manfacturer to undertake. Like putting on white tie and tails to fix the boiler.

On the other hand reverting to the original meaning (and it's often the case) does remind us of the ultimate duty of management—to know what it's doing. To know the causes and laws, to determine the 'principles underlying any department of knowledge'—that is in the context of the company—is fundamental. Management's related duty is to find the expression for that knowledge and then to disseminate it.

The encapsulation is called many things. Religion is a potent model. 'Creed', 'Holy Writ', 'Gospel' are some of the commoner terms. And 'bible'—with a small *b*—is a popular term for a codification of company practices inches thick. 'Commandments' is probably too authoritarian —to the doubters as well as the devout.

Company meetings—particularly sales conferences—become evangelical at times. Billy Graham and the sales manager seem to have effected a trade off. God's salesman has adopted the piety that goes with the passion. The cause is all. I once heard Charles Revson tell his company's international sales conference that Revlon were leading the Lanolin market by divine right.

The first deal I ever clinched was selling my soul to the devil

Nevertheless, biblical terminology is adopted also for worthier reasons. After all, a creed is something to live by. It should guide the disciple's daily life and prove a source of strength in times of trouble. It will, in the more liberal assemblages, attract the unenforced agreement of its followers, rather than compel unquestioning acceptance. It will, above all, serve to *unite* them.

In this context the word 'philosophy' seems wholly appropriate, especially in its specific sense of 'a particular philosophical system'. Management's job is to know what it's doing, find expression of that knowledge and communicate it. Important in this—and it is as relevant to religion as to philosophy—is the concept of 'particularity'. We choose to believe in God (or not) in one of a number of group ways. Philosophers group themselves into 'schools'.

A company statement of 'philosophy' must endeavour to be specific to that company. It will rarely entirely succeed but to be aware of the dangers of bland generalisation is at least healthier than blithely donning the off-the-peg platitudes of corporate language. When René McPherson became chief executive of the Dana Corporation he discovered policy manuals with a total thickness of 22½ inches. He 'substituted a simple one-page statement of philosophy'. It begins:

> Nothing more effectively involves people, sustains credibility or generates enthusiasm than face-to-face communication. It is critical to provide and discuss all organisation performance figures with all of our people.[3]

Digital's philosophy can fit on a single large sheet. There are fifteen short paragraphs with headings such as *honesty, profit, quality, society, customers* and *personnel development*. Under *'simplicity and clarity'*:

> We want all aspects of DEC to be clear and simple and we want simple products, proposals, organisations, literature that is easy to read and understand, and advertisements that have a simple obvious message.

The philosophy ends with a *'FIRST RULE'*:

> When dealing with a customer, a vendor or an employee, do what is 'right' to do in each situation.

IBM over thirty years ago expressed the company's shared beliefs as follows:

1 All employees should be respected and treated with dignity.
2 The company should aim to accomplish every task in a superior way.
3 The customer should be given the best service possible.

The success of the Mars company is invariably attributed to the five principles enunciated by Forrest Mars.

1 QUALITY
The Consumer is our boss, quality is our work and value for money is our goal.
2 RESPONSIBILITY
As individuals we demand total responsibility for ourselves: as associates we support the responsibility of others.
3 MUTUALITY
A mutual benefit is a shared benefit—a shared benefit will endure.
4 EFFICIENCY
We use resources to the full, waste nothing and do only what we can do best.
5 FREEDOM
We need freedom to shape our future: we need profit to remain free.

British Airports Authority is unusual in having its philosophy spelled out for it by Act of Parliament. BAA was established in 1965 following recommendations by a Select Committee appointed to find a way of making the nation's major airports pay their own way. This 'mission' permeates management's thinking and, because it is single-mindedly pursued and proclaimed, has the effect of integrating all their communication. Being successful is BAA's reason for being. It finds expression in staff literature, passenger information, advertisements etc.

> In 1966, we came to a decision. Not only would we make a profit, but we'd plough every penny we made back into the business.

The baseline reads: 'The World's Most Successful International Airport System.' Their brochure is sub-headed 'A British Success Story'. It emphasises 'where the money comes from' and 'taking care of our passengers'. The public relations director, Peter Sanguinetti, helped launch a 'please the passenger' campaign. It was aimed at the front-line staff—porters, baggage-handlers, security officers and police. Yet though Parliament gave BAA its philosophy, it seemed remarkably ignorant of its content. Accordingly, Sanguinetti made sure the House of Commons' own house magazine featured on the media schedule of its advertising campaign. The ad listed statements about airport funding beneath a headline 'True or False?' and elicited over 60 replies from members.

Most companies in my experience do not have a written corporate philosophy. They will tell you they have never seen the need for it or they regard the exercise as so much pretentious nonsense or that they tried it and were embarrassed at the outcome. (Not unlike some people's attitude to sex.)

Certainly, getting company management to be articulate about the essential *raison d'être* of the company is one of the most difficult tasks a communication executive (insider or consultant) has to face. Determining a company statement is like drawing teeth. Reticence, reluctance, modesty, fear of stating the obvious—whatever the reasons, the result is a hole where a corporate policy should be. And publics, like nature, abhorring vacuums, fill them with any scraps of evidence, hearsay and detritus they have to hand. One of these publics is the staff of the company itself. It has a need to know as employees, and a right to know as human beings what the company is about, that management knows what it's doing and what the company stands for.

The question is how to convince the chief executive that it needs doing—and that he must be heavily involved in its doing. There is a very simple answer: he gets other people to do it first. He chooses six executives representing different aspects of the company's activities and different functions within the firm and asks each to state in no more than 100 words what the company stands for, what its objectives are, and its main criteria for assessing its success. He should not be *too* specific. At this stage of the exercise he wants input in terms both of content and form. Their sense of priorities, what they feel should be in the philosophy, must not be inhibited by the format, let alone the subjects the chief executive has chosen. There are two possible outcomes to this exercise: reasonable unanimity or chaos. Either way the boss wins. If the executives display a unity of understanding and of purpose then the task of articulating the philosophy is far easier. Not only will the chief executive find writing it simpler, he will know that getting agreement is virtually assured. He may of course use the unanimity as evidence of a lack of need for a written philosophy. However, having gone this far, he is unlikely to stop the activity. Moreover, there are bound to be differences of degree, emphasis and style which he particularly wishes to adjust. And, of course, he is unlikely not to want to endorse his own personal stamp on the communication.

If, conversely, the results are chaotic, the need for a philosophy is self-evident. If there is no agreement concerning the firm's aims, beliefs and purpose then there are questions to be asked of management itself. Is it single-minded? Is it resolute? Is it communicating? In a sentence, 'Does it know what it's doing?' (Which is, remember, what we believe philosophy is all about.)

Writing a philosophy and getting it agreed then takes on a far greater significance. It could be argued that in the context of a disorganised leadership a written philosophy is an irrelevant luxury. The ship's off course. It's not the time to paint the figurehead. Only it's not a figurehead but a set of maps.

Some companies do have a set of maps. But they could be out of date. A statement of philosophy needs to be examined continuously. Do the guidelines of the 1970s equip us for the 1990s? Are the fashionable management school beliefs of our youth as relevant in the society of today? For example which (if any) of these general truths do we hold self-evident?

1 A company's first job is to stay in business.
2 The name of the game is profit.
3 Our central task is to get and secure a customer.

Is profit a goal in itself—or a measure of some other achievement? If so, what? To whom are we responsible? Shareholders, staff, ourselves, our customers? Is there a bigger responsibility? Have we social aims? Can we put these in a specific form, remembering that the philosophy should if possible relate to us and us alone? What do our products do for our customers and for society in general? What are the goals of our research and development achieving? Who will benefit from their achievements? And are our staff more than merely paid employees? What do we do for them?

A lot of questions. There will be lots more. In this self analysis there will be more material than can or should be accommodated in one philosophy statement. Nevertheless, that should not inhibit the group from assembling. all the material it considers relevant, that helps it in defining how it sees the company in order for it to communicate that insight. For communicate it must. Not only because society today requires it or because government legislation demands it but because a company needs to make itself known and its views heard in order to survive. Companies who complain that their views are ignored are justified if, and only if, their views have been cogently and distinctively phrased, well and frequently communicated. Individuals are more likely to be ignored if their individuality has not impinged upon the public consciousness, whichever public we may be talking about—government, media, trade, customer, staff, etc.

How is the company seen? How correct is that perception? Is it known only by its products? Should it not also be known by the values the company represents? And the goals it intends to achieve? But what are they?

> If there are no concepts worth developing, if the company has nothing to say to its audience, its commercial survival is probably in jeopardy. If there is nothing to say, there may be nothing to buy.[4]

But, as Kemp warns, trying to determine if it has something to say and then what constitutes that something, is where the trouble starts. We have examined some of the difficulties—complexity, disagreement, lack of individuality—which inhibit the exercise. There is another determinant. Guts.

> It takes courage to decide what kind of corporation you are and what kind you want to be. Then it takes courage to strip away the non-essentials that get in the way and face the issues of your real subject . . . it takes courage to be yourself, unique, to stand up before the public and especially before your peers . . . and say 'This is us. This is an expression of what our company is and what we stand for.'[5]

I have suggested earlier in this chapter a practical solution to the problem. But implementing the outcome of that solution will still take courage. Another technique is to throw the ball squarely at the chief executive and ask him to make the first move in the game by defining the 'corporate mission'. This is different from a philosophy. Or rather it represents only a part, the important part, of the philosophy. It is a succinct expression of company purpose, ideally setting it apart from all other companies. If the chief executive can get that right then the rest of the philosophy should not be too difficult to write. Furthermore once the 'mission' has been defined then the task of co-ordinating the various activities, not to mention the communications activities, of the company can confidently be tackled.

Theodore Levitt[6] originated this use of the word mission. However, the word has lost the concentration upon distinctiveness which Levitt gave it. 'An effective mission statement', says Kotler,[7] 'will be market oriented, feasible, motivating, and specific.' To aspire to 'leadership in food processing technology' is not a mission, though it might form part of a philosophy statement. However to 'help housewives become creative cooks without spending too much time' would be considered by Kotler to be a mission since it concentrates upon satisfying customer need rather than proclaiming manufacturer ability—and does so in a distinctive way and, with luck and good management, setting the company apart from its competition. Ideally, a mission statement should position a company in the same way that a brand is positioned—i.e. in the public's mind.

> The mission of an agricultural chemical company is not to sell fertiliser, but to help improve the performance and yields of the farmer's land.[8]

A third technique in the search for corporate philosophy is to 'hothouse' a solution. The participants are a communication consultant and representatives of corporate management. The former is external, objective and fearless. He has no personal or departmental axe to grind. He must also be single-minded. His is the coordinating voice, particularly important if he is dealing with management *en bloc*.

Let us suppose a group of four management executives (including of course the chief executive) meet with the consultant. They devote a whole day. The day is shaped like a funnel: the morning is broad, the afternoon narrow. They begin by individually delineating the purpose of the company, its long-term objectives, immediate goals and distinctive features. They discuss how it is seen and how this perception differs from the reality. Note that though this is a free-wheeling, free-ranging session it is definitely *not* a brainstorming. Brainstorming encourages a stream of consciousness: thoughts are built on, tangents proliferate. The purpose of our meeting is not to generate ideas plural, but to determine a definition, singular. Quality is important. The quantity is not. Thus the morning is preparatory to the afternoon. The consultant tells the team that they will definitely not solve the problem before lunch. This may or may not be true. But it has a relaxing effect on the team who feel encouraged to say what they like without fear of failure.

The result is a mess. But it is a *definitive* mess. *Everything* has been said. And nobody wants to add to it. Lunch is taken—preferably in another room—and so is some air. The team are encouraged to take another turn of the garden whilst the consultant returns to the room and begins to assemble the material. He lists all the key factors which have been made—ideally alphabetically, i.e. in an order which implies no sense of priority. These factors are of two sorts: those on which there is a great deal of consensus and those which are held, maybe by a minority of one, with a great degree of fervour.

Consensus, you see, may lead the group towards a safe solution: a maverick view may divide the group but may prove distinctive (and if it provokes them, it may provoke the company's publics).

The team returns to the room and narrow part of the day, anxious now to clear up the mess of the morning. They review the key points. Measurement at this stage is more important than judgement. (And it's always easier to measure than to judge.) The team are asked individually to allocate points to the factors. Which factors are more important and by how wide a margin?

Half the factors should then disappear from immediate consideration, being set aside for subsequent discussion of the total philosophy. For at this stage what is needed is *one sentence*, a definition of what the company is, what it stands for and where it's going. In fact the team members will polarise their scores—giving a few high scores and the rest low. In consequence, now barely a quarter of the factors remain. Then the hard work starts: judgement

We don't have a company philosophy but we're very philosophical about our dwindling profits takes over from research. A time limit is set. A sentence is finally hammered out. General agreement? Euphoric self-delusion? Fatigue-induced compromise? There's no way of saying. But at worst company management will have a good idea of what they think *matters* and how together they are. At best they will have made the crucial first step to writing the philosophy which in turn will guide not only their communications policy but all their corporate endeavours.

> The basic philosophy, spirit and drive of an organisation have far more to do with its relative achievement than do technology or economics resources, organisational structure, innovation and timing.[9]

15

Philosophy to message

The day after the day in the funnel, the participants look at what they have achieved. A few words on a piece of paper. All that effort for one sentence! (It's unique incarceration where the punishment precedes the sentence.) Was it worth it?

Johnson & Johnson in the US suffered one of the most potentially damaging attacks ever on a corporate reputation when in 1982 seven patients died after taking Tylenol. J&J's ability to tackle that problem so comprehensively, completely and quickly—to recover 85% of pre-scare sales in six months—was due in no small measure to the fact that the company had a philosophy to fall back on. It's a one-page document that guides J&J's everyday business and social responsibilities.[1]

> The credo outlines responsibilities to our consumers, our employees, the communities in which we live and work, and to our stockholders.

There was never a question in the corporate mind as to what J&J stood for and therefore what needed to be done. Accordingly, no valuable time was eaten up in deciding what attitude to adopt, what face to put on. A philosophy is rarely long. And a mission is always short—a one sentence statement.

Does all this suggest a simplistic approach to a complex subject? Simple, yes. Simplistic no. Robert MacNeil, eminent television journalist, respects the need to encapsulate:[2]

> In most of the stories television comes to cover there is always 'the right bit,' the most violent, the most bloody, the most pathetic, the most tragic, the most wonderful, the most awful moment. Getting the effective 'bit' is what TV news is all about.

Now, though a philosophy is not an extract but an encapsulation, the purpose is the same: to condense in such a way that the 'bit' sums up and represents the whole. To see how necessary this is—and to answer in another way the question we posed—consider what happens as we view the result of the television newsman's labours.

Try this experiment. Watch the news with family or friends and simultaneously record it, (preferably on a second receiver). Watch it however, as you normally watch it. Ten minutes after it finishes ask each member of the group what he or she remembers—subject matter and points made. Then compare the response with the events by playing back the recording. You will probably find that no single viewer, unprompted, can recall as many as half the stories, that barely a third of the facts reported in the remembered stories will be recalled, that those recollections will be imperfect and that the recollections of individual members will differ and in some cases flatly contradict each other.

The reasons are many but they can all be summed up as noise—the events in the room itself, the distracting picture on the screen, the presenter's manner, accent or clothes, a difficult vocabulary, the sheer volume of information, the language of an interviewee or spokesman, and more especially the lack of motivation of the viewer.

Nevertheless, the enormity of the communication task must not discourage us from attempting it. Rather it should encourage us not to add to the complexities by overloading the message. For the message has an important job to do. A statement of company philosophy may have to inspire staff, set personal goals, put all activities in context, unite separate and disparate components, remind the company of its social responsibility, etc., etc.

Yet it cannot afford to be too complex. Nor can it be so bland as to be meaningless. And when the message becomes a corporate *advertising* message (i.e. the paragraph of philosophy becomes, or is transformed into a headline, slogan or baseline for the consumption of the public), the process of concentration becomes even fiercer. The advertising message is the 'right bit'. And there *is* only one.

After the young Harold MacMillan had spoken in the House of Commons the elderly Lloyd George complimented him, but admonished him for trying to make as many as twenty points. For a member, particularly a new member, one point is maximum. A minister could possibly make two, a Prime Minister conceivably three.

But can one line possibly communicate or convey everything the company has written into its philosophy, itself an encapsulation of the thoughts and deeds of an association of people? To judge by the results in the posh newspapers and journals of influence the answer is a sad negative. How can 'WORKS WORLDWIDE' possibly convey what a company represents? Or how can a company hope to set itself apart when it proudly claims 'WE MEAN BUSINESS'? Every junior copywriter stumbles across that line—and its double meaning—and believes he invented it.

Double meanings of course are useful. Two messages for the price of one. Which is OK if both of these messages align with what you as a company wish to convey—i.e. both meanings are truly, philosophically, meaningful.

Edward de Bono warns against crystallisation. Crystals emerge only when everything else has been boiled away. 'A crystal is the antithesis of anything that is vague and amorphous.'[3] The trouble is that something important might have got lost in the boiling. We, the boilers, know what it is and know what the slogan or whatever is meant to represent. But the public know only the crystal, the slogan in its pure crystalline form, with no subsidiary meaning and expressing one basic, incontrovertible but hardly illuminating fact.

The point is this: by reducing the communication to a few words it is unlikely that the line will ever represent the philosophy. This is especially the case when the words are purely denotative. However, when imagination is applied to the facts and emotion accompanies reason, additional meanings—i.e. connotations—are communicated. The tip suggests more of the iceberg. There is, in de Bono's phrase, 'useful ambiguity'.

Ambiguity, of course, isn't always useful. When Sperry decided to communicate in their corporate advertising how important it was to listen, a significant proportion of their initial public believed they made hearing aids. Ambiguity must be researched. A small scale group discussion designed to discover if the desired public receives the desired impression is quick and inexpensive.

Nevertheless, even allowing for ambiguity and imagination, no single line can convey the whole of a company's philosophy. What it must do though is relate to it and, if at all possible, capture its essence. The important truth about slogans is that they have a life of their own, and for the majority of readers one which is totally detached from the life of the company and the philosophy which begat it.

There is considerable hostility to slogans both outside and inside the communications business.

Hate the company — love the slogan

The word originated in Scotland. 'Slogan' was a clan war-cry. It was then used to denote a catchphrase in both political and commercial publicity. Intellectual critics attack the practice of 'sloganising', reducing weighty matters to a few 'clever' or emotive words. *Chambers Dictionary* (1983) refers to a slogan as 'a substitute for reasoned discussion'.

Advertising people seem to have a love-hate relationship with the slogan. I don't believe today that anybody in the business conceives that advertising 'works' by the impregnation of messages into consumer heads, or that the incessant repetition of a slogan will result in anything but the recall of that slogan (and then not always that), or that recall has a direct relationship with sales.

Some of the advertising industry's most celebrated campaigns never used a slogan. J.Walter Thompson's distinguished twelve-year tenure of the Guinness account projected a consistent and clear image of the brand without a unifying slogan. And the universally admired Doyle Dane Bernbach campaign for Volkswagen has never used a baseline. Yet you always knew it was a VW ad and you could yourself sum up what the company and the car stood for without being spoon-fed.

On the other hand the same agency at the same time working on Avis produced a memorable and provocative slogan. 'We try harder.' In the field of car rental, as with most service industry companies, the company and the product are in effect one, so that corporate and brand advertising are hard to disentangle.

'We try harder' is a great corporate slogan because the reader *contributes*. Baselines, headlines or entire advertisements for that matter, which attempt to complete the communication transaction are advertising's equivalent of a pea-shooter, or one-way communication. 'We try harder' is open-ended. The potential customer completes the promise in his own terms, e.g. cost, cleanliness, time at the rental desk, and so on. Moreover, the corporate slogan is a standard for the staff to live up to. The consumer knows this. The company has put its neck on the block. And the staff wear badges to prove it.

Few corporate slogans, however, are equally on the button. Many attempt to sum up what the company stands for by a composite phrase. '*X* give you more to choose from.' 'All you want from today's . . . ' '*X* gives you more of what you buy a . . . for.' 'Total . . . that's our guarantee.' But putting your company name on a receptacle is not the same as conveying the company's *raison d'être* in a few words.

Difficult. Is it worth trying? One critic speaking at an international conference on corporate advertising thought not.[4]

> Slogans from corporate ads fall into three categories: the dream or corporate vision, which doesn't focus on anything concrete but tries to elicit warm feelings and confidence from the reader; the promise in which corporations at least make sure the reader knows who's talking; and the reality in which the

company mentions its products and services and makes sure the reader knows what the company does. But I think these slogans just take up space and detract from the company platform and corporate signature.

Perhaps. If that's all they attempt then they do detract from the 'company platform' or philosophy. And many slngans seem to be there—bottom right—because that's where a slogan goes. How many slogans are approved precisely because they sound like slogans and look like slogans and corporate management can be comfortable with them. 'We try harder' didn't sound or look like a slogan and it promised management a lot of trouble. I believe the example of Avis is sufficient evidence to prove that the part can express the sense of the whole and do it *distinctively*.

There are three causes of undistinctive corporate slogans. The first is fashion. Slogans, it seems, must be recognised as slogans. Just as all corporate identity must bear an autocratic family resemblance.

Secondly, the range of virtues a company can proclaim is somewhat restricted. When all companies want to be seen as good guys the vocabulary quickly becomes shop-soiled. I have a picture of hordes of company chairmen in London scrabbling around in Moss Bros for appropriate garments and assembling on the pavement in Covent Garden looking distinguished but undistinguishable.

Thirdly, corporate advertising which treats the company as distinct from its products, with the intention of making the company seem important (ego massage), is again restricted to a few key issues. Jacques Ellul would define them as myths. In *Propaganda, the foundation of men's attitudes,* he:

> . . . identifies the mythological structure of modern industrial culture. The myths are—of work, progress and happiness.[5]

Talking about who you are and what you stand for is easy. Making it sound interesting and original and different is difficult. Several fanfares have been written for solo trumpet. But if the trumpet you choose to blow is your own then the least you can do is write your own tune. Be specific rather than general and concrete rather than abstract. A distinctive style will help. But true distinctiveness is not an external application.

The search for a few words—the 'right bit'—is difficult and the failure rate is high. The end of the journey has hardly justified the travail or the expenses. A seeker of truth (in a cartoon in *High Life*) stands next to a guru on a mountain top and mutters unbelievingly: 'A bowl of cherries. That's it?'

'We mean business.' 'A company called TRW.' 'A tradition of progress.' That's it? Not always it ain't. Novo are a Danish multinational. They produce enzymes, insulin and diagnostic systems. From small beginnings and as a result both of inspired and painstaking research and of astute financial management, they are now world leaders in biotechnology and a star performer on foreign exchanges.

Another reason for their success is the emphasis their management puts upon all aspects of communication, the need for coordination and for keeping responsibility close to the desk of the chief executive, Mads Øvlisen. Øvlisen is ultimately responsible for the corporate philosophy. He calls it the company's *raison d'être*, the basic business idea. 'Why there is—and why there should continue to be a Novo.' He works on it with external consultants and his immediate colleagues—the board of corporate management.

The philosophy is regularly reviewed. But though adjustments are made to reflect developments and opportunities the basics remain and the company, despite its recent impressive growth, is recognisably the same company with the same values it was 25 years ago. The philosophy:[6]

> Novo intends to be an international leader in industrial, biochemical and health care products, processes and systems.
> Novo believes leadership can be achieved by continuing Novo's tradition of innovative advances in bioscience, biotechnology and medicine.
> Novo will be guided by the present and future needs of the global market place and the individual consumer. Novo is committed to the manufacture of products that provide benefits to society.

This appears in the annual report, in the monthly house journal and can be called up on the visual display unit in reception by any visitor to Novo's Bagsvaerd headquarters outside Copenhagen. A philosophy for Novo is not a one-page memo to be filed but a living presence.

Four years ago the company felt the need for a booklet to supplement its already considerable volume of company literature. There were several opportunities for the dissemination of information about the company of a general, background nature and several audiences who needed to know about Novo or whose better knowledge of Novo could help the company.

My company, The Creative Business, was consulted. We felt that, despite the diversity of needs, one book (rather than a booklet) would suffice, that the story of the company would interest and inform a seven-year-old schoolboy or a Nobel prizewinner; and that what was needed was a book not on 'what Novo makes' but 'what makes Novo'. It would be a book about the spirit of the company.

The Creative Business London were given access to all departments and personnel. As outsiders we were more likely to detect and interpret the spirit of the company. Also, company personnel invariably open up to external consultants. There is a deal of truth in the old definition: 'a consultant is someone who borrows your watch to tell you the time and then charges you.'

The investigation confirmed us in our belief that Novo was an innovative, research-based and wholly committed company. But how could that spirit be expressed—for example, on the book's cover? Then one morning we were in the office of the executive responsible for environmental matters. We were discussing a problem of pollution. He was confident they would solve it. He shrugged and said: 'It can be done.' Those four words don't replace the philosophy but they convey it. They say innovation, research, commitment. And they are, if indeed not a war-cry, then a motto for every member of the company. In fact the line frequently occurs in conversation at Novo offices.

Typical advertising slogans, particularly in the corporate field, no doubt deserve the censure of the intellectual critic and the advertising professional. They *are* a substitute for thought. They help to form stereotypes. By over-simplifying the endeavours of the company they devalue it. They are often vague and rarely specific. Instead of helping to establish a company's identity they diminish it.

But such messages are necessary if only because there is no way any of a company's external audiences (except those financially involved in its stock) will ever take the time to read its philosophy. The message—slogan, headline, baseline, book title or whatever—must act in its place. If not, as we know, a summation of the respondent's own choosing will replace it. It may be difficult to sum up a company but if anybody can and should do, it must be the company itself.

It may be difficult. It can be done.

16

Clarity begins at home

The obvious question (and therefore the one most often ignored or taken for granted) when companies communicate is 'who are we communicating to?' There are several possible audiences. Occasionally all are being addressed. None of them is entirely discrete. There are several ways of categorising them which we shall examine in the next chapter. The only division which concerns us at the moment is internal and external. This chapter is devoted to the former.

Internal company communication is notoriously bad. There are many reasons. The fault lies entirely with management. If the receiver gets it wrong the blame must lie with the transmitter. Noise is a factor but the sensitive communicator—in whose interest the communication is undertaken—has to find ways of detecting and counteracting noise.

Management may decide not to communicate for reasons of security or because it genuinely feels there is no reason for staff to know certain facts. But in my experience, and from discussions with both companies and consultants, the sins of management are chiefly of omission. There is a passive attitude towards communication. 'I know it therefore everybody knows it.' 'It'll filter down anyway.' 'We've got a very efficient grapevine.' 'What more can I do? I told Johnson. I assumed he told . . . ' And so on.

In communication we must never 'assume'. I once gave a speech to an advertising conference in Chicago. I interspersed the text with five short taped music pieces. My assistant put them together and allowed for pauses in between. We had a rehearsal in London. My assistant operated the recorder. Perfect. In Chicago I rehearsed again the day before the speech. I explained the tape arrangement to the sound engineer in the booth and gave him also a copy of my marked-up text. I gave my slides to the projectionist. We began the rehearsal. The first music piece started. It finished. I began talking. The booth window opened. The engineer yelled 'You want me to run this straight through?' 'No,' I said, 'stop after each piece.' 'You better come up.' I came up. The tape had been edited all right. Only the gaps in between consisted not of white or yellow leader to distinguish them from the sound tape but of *blank tape*! There was no way the engineer could tell when to start the next extract.

My assistant, on the other hand, knew the tape intimately: *her* rehearsal had been OK. Embarrassed, I apologised. The engineer spent half an hour fixing it. I told him I am known in the office for saying 'never assume.' And here I had assumed my assistant had inserted white leader. His colleague, the projectionist, said 'I had a boss like you. He used to say to me "never use that word again. You just spell it."' He proceeded to do so. 'Assume. It makes an ASS of U and ME.'

In communication we must never assume. And this is paramount in *internal* communications. The management may take a lot of convincing. Communication is assumed to be happening because communication is 'second nature.' How can the trivial business of talking or writing suddenly have taken on the status of a discipline like marketing, let alone a science like engineering? Besides, look at those memos, notices, newsletters. And there's a suggestion box . . . People assume they are communicating but don't really know and rarely bother to find out. And managements are people.

If British industry applied one-tenth of the professional talent and discipline to internal communications which it applies to, say, advertising its wares, then the state of industrial relations in this country would be vastly happier and productivity greatly improved.

Communication *isn't* something we're all good at. It requires understanding from us all, particularly those responsible for the contribution of others: Ray Mitchell is a consultant in employee communications for the CBI. He told me he prefers the term 'involvement' to communication.

> It's not just a note, something on the notice board . . . it's involvement in the company's activities.

He is critical. Companies don't simply omit to explain what is happening but *why*. One of management's biggest problems is to achieve change—and this demands that reasons are given. He talks to senior management. Very often they welcome him because they are *lonely*. He finds that *they* too are not involved by others. (Though this is directly their fault by not inviting information, by not creating the appropriate atmosphere.)

It is surprising what managements don't know. Not simply what's going on but what is not going on, i.e. things management believes are happening aren't happening.

Pea-shooter communication. One way. Lack of feedback. ACAS defines workplace communication as:

> The provision and passing of information and instructions which enable a company . . . to function efficiently and employees to be properly informed about developments.[1]

Employees need to know more than the basic instructions needed to carry out their work. They need to know, says ACAS:

. what is happening and why
. the way their jobs can contribute to company prosperity
. the future prospects of the company.[2]

Good communication means better performance, fewer misunderstandings, greater trust and job satisfaction. There is today much talk about employee participation. There can be no participation without good communication. By itself good communication will not eradicate doubt or bloody-mindedness or cynicism, but it will considerably ease the task if only because it clears the air and prepares the ground. Non-communication, remember, is negative communication.

My experience and researches show that companies who are good at internal communication are good at external communication. There are, I suggest, at least two reasons for this.

First, employees are spokespersons for the company. They are ambassadors, living advertisements. The fact of good human relations will be transmitted, as will the messages conveyed along the internal communication channel, to the outside world. 'It's a good company to work for.' It's an impression received from employees, past employees, their families and friends.

Nick Winkfield of Research Services Limited attempts to quantify the importance. A company has 5,000 employees. Each has twenty acquaintances. Each of those has twenty acquaintances. There will be a primary audience of 100,000 and a secondary audience of 2,000,000!

Bob Worcester produces some research figures to prove the point. In a Corporate Image Study in 1983 MORI asked how respondents regarded certain UK companies and how they had learned about them. They then compared the favourability scores of the total audience with those of various sub-sections. In each case the biggest lift in favourability occurred among those who knew someone who worked at the company—a 12% or 14% percentage lift compared with, at most, 2% for 'seen advertising'.

Effect of ways of knowing on favourability.
Very/Mainly favourable to. . .

	Co A %	Co B %	Co C %	Co D %
TOTAL	64	66	71	65
Know through. . .				
Seen advertising	66	68	73	65
Heard or read news	67	67	76	66
Know someone who works there	78	80	83	72

The second reason why a company good at internal communications is likely to succeed externally, is that the investment of skills and resources pays off. It will learn lessons from the exercise which can in turn help it when it communicates externally. One of these lessons is the title of this chapter— clarity begins at home. Another is a theme of this book—communication, both external and internal, is a person-to-person activity.

Of course in a company which gets both internal and external communications right, there is a strong relationship between the two. The employees of the company which is 'good to work for' will not be surprised by the corporate advertisement they see in the paper. It may have been posted on the notice board the week before. But if not then the news it contains will be known to them. The advertisement will be seen by neighbours and friends. The employee (we hope) will associate himself with the company and the message.

Sir Austin Bide, boss of Glaxo and a believer in participation, says employees require two things above all—a sense of security and an association with success. Good communication can help with both. It can internally transmit information about what the company is doing for the employee; and externally communicate the company's achievements which, apart from attracting new business, enable the employee to identify with success.

It is more difficult of course to identify with success if you haven't been told about it first or, more especially, if your own personal success is either circumscribed or unrecognised. People are concerned first with their own well-being and any executive involved with communication (internal or external) who forgets it is going to find life very troublesome.

One who hasn't forgotten is Ray G Howell of Hoechst UK, the British subsidiary of the German conglomerate. He quotes Graham Cole, a management consultant:[3]

> Often there's a startling, dangerous gap between the information companies give employees and the kind of information employees really want. The workers are interested above all in things which affect them personally: companies waste time, money and also goodwill by telling people anything but.

Howell instigated a communications workshop at Hoechst to discover the quality of their communication and where improvements could be made. It stressed the need for the involvement and support of top management—since the decisions concerned policies which affected people. The investigation revealed that:

> The dominant Hoechst UK management style was people oriented but managers found it easier to be effective as benevolent autocrats than as developers.[4]

The company was good at providing information. It was less good at two-way communication. They devised improvements. These included briefing groups to include news on trade-union negotiations and management committee activities 'plus organised feedback arrangements.' They incorporated communicating ability in the performance appraisal of managers and supervisors. They circulated management minutes more widely. They used their internal news bulletin more effectively by including explanation and discussion of controversial issues. They replaced, wherever possible, paper communications by face-to-face sessions. They used the term 'confidential' less often on internal reports and memos. Howell doesn't know if 'they've got it right,' but at least he is sure that his management is aware of change and can take the team through the difficulties that it brings.

Dunlop did a similar exercise. They discovered that only 62% of Dunlop Group employees usually/always believed group management information; 23% said they believed it half the time. According to MORI surveys this level of credibility is only *slightly* below average. Employees were asked about their sources of information. Almost half mentioned the grapevine.

	Get Information From	Prefer To Get Information From	Difference
	%	%	%
Senior management of the company	5	28	−23
Local management	16	45	−29
Immediate boss/supervisor/ foreman	39	49	−10
'Grapevine'/gossip	45	4	+41
'Dunlop' News	43	23	+20
New annual report to employees	13	14	− 1
Outside media (newspaper/tv/radio)	9	2	+ 7
Friends/relatives outside Dunlop	3	1	+ 2
Notice boards	32	27	+ 5
Loudspeaker system	1	2	− 1
Union meetings	22	19	+ 3
Letters/leaflets with pay packet	4	9	− 5
Letters/leaflets sent from company to home	2	3	− 1
Union newspaper/magazine	2	2	0
Divisional newspaper	5	6	− 1

Source: MORI 1980

The figures show that employees prefer to receive information from their immediate boss or from local or senior management of the company. As to the *content* of information, few felt they were given too much. They felt they were:

> ' . . . under-informed on future employment prospects, and the reasons behind major management decisions . . . new company investment . . . new equipment . . . and changes affecting their working conditions.[5]

The result of the exercise was a more open style of management. There was more emphasis on departmental consultation and face-to-face contact between line managers and shop floor and office employees. Kingston Pratt, who commissioned the research, was cautious about results. The success depended upon the 'enthusiasm and determination of individual managers.' 'Twas ever thus.

The key factor in any communications programme is monitoring. Unless management is sensitive to how its messages are received and how the relationships between transmitter and receiver are changing, then the success of the exercise is severely limited.

A comprehensive change in communications policy is worthless if management's model (actual or implied) is unchanged. If management still sees communication as a one-way process nothing will happen other than a surface show of activity which, by raising then dashing hopes, may in fact leave the situation worse than before. If management believes communication is a two-way process but the relationship remains static throughout, the situation is little better. As Howell of Hoechst says:

> 'It is necessary at all times to remember that the word 'organisation' is associated with the word 'organic'. Every organisation is a living thing which reacts and adjusts to its environment.[6]

Our model tries to accommodate this unceasing interchange. Communication is dynamic. It is a game of continuous volleys on a shifting course with differing perceptions about your opponent. But perhaps there is a limit to the number of matches you can play at once? Multiple tennis with 10,000 employees?!

Is good communication the reason few *small firms* have strikes? The Government's Think Tank found:

> . . . evidence to support the widely-held view . . . that very large plants . . . are more prone to labour disputes than smaller plants.

So reported Frances Cairncross of the *Guardian*:[7] The Think Tank:

> . . . listed as one of the principal causes of the car industry's lousy strike record 'poor communications between management and labour.' Management, it pointed out, often communicated with its workforce only through the trade unions and shop stewards.

Two-thirds of small firms have no trade union members on their payrolls.[8] Size makes it harder to run a company and harder to communicate.

Of course. When you consider that a large manufacturing company regularly addresses audiences of millions who aren't by definition interested in their product, surely it can't be that difficult to communicate professionally to an audience of some 10,000 who manifestly are not only interested but vitally *concerned*? What does a house journal cost? A pound a head? What's £10,000 compared to an ad budget of several millions?

British Leyland began improving its internal communications under Sir Michael Edwardes. The jewel in the crown was Jaguar. When a new chairman, John Egan, arrived at Jaguar in April 1980 he encountered a strange paradox: a burgeoning reputation for the new XJ6 Series III and a deluge of complaints from owners and dealers about failures and breakdowns. One of Egan's first moves was:

> . . . to set up a communications system to tell everyone in the company what the problem was, and how it was going to be tackled. The slogan of the campaign was 'In pursuit of perfection.'[9]

Jaguar's success was not due entirely to improved communications. But it could not have happened without it. Note too that he applied the skills and techniques of external communication to the problem. He encapsulated the company's new philosophy in the four-word slogan. It was a message to everybgdy: management, shop stewards, shop floor, dealers and, importantly, suppliers. It was a goal for the company—and for each individual. And the individual could *identify* with the company's success. The company's success would be his.

Contrast Egan's methods with the attitude of so much of British management. Reticent, self-effacing, modest, afraid of new-fangled— probably American—techniques of communication, it speaks, if at all, only when it has to and to as few people as necessary, and monitors not at all. It puts away its pea-shooter and assumes that because what it has said is important (i.e. because management has said it), others will listen and act thereon. But generally it does not communicate, even with a pea-shooter, assuming that a message from on high will naturally find its own way down, thus denying the science of communication any law save that of gravity. Then one day management discovers—almost certainly by accident—that a member of staff who ought to know, in fact knows hardly anything about how the company works.

Paradoxically, it would seem what those below management *do* know about is management style. Not what they say but how they behave. There are, it can confidently be asserted, more employees than there are management. Consequently, the focus is much stronger from below. The image may be faint but it will not be blurred or multiple. Whereas what each member of staff does is of limited concern to the chief executive, what the chief executive does (or does not do) is of vital concern to the employee. Not just what, but when, where, how and (aided by guesswork) why. Management is a constant preoccupation of staff. Staff may not be a constant preoccupation of management. The point is that staff preoccupation concentrates upon a smaller field of vision.

How accurate is the average assessment of a subordinate by the managing director? Is it as accurate as that of him by his subordinates? And since researches show that 'subordinates react most effectively to those matters they judge to be of most *personal* interest to the boss'[10] it is a fair bet that employee activity, given a situation of inadequate communication, will be concerned not so much with the achievement of the company goal as with the satisfaction of some (vaguely assumed) personal needs of the boss.

I have suffered this syndrome. A junior writer who has met me once and hears from a colleague of a personal idiosyncracy will incorporate it in an advertisement regardless of its relevance to the task that advertisement has to perform. My personal foibles are not so much information as noise. If I am not aware of the noise then my feedback is inadequate. Once I discover it I must remedy it.

It could be argued that too much information contributes noise. Certainly, major decisions which affect corporate policy may have to be communicated to a restricted few (e.g. managers) in the first instance. Certainly, confidential information which may benefit a competitor should be contained. And information which could be divisive and affect company morale needs to be carefully considered, prior to selective release. Too much information may overwhelm the receiver and, by clogging the communication channel, considerably reduce the transmitter's ability to priorise and control it. However, these caveats are exceptions. Open communication is effective and normally much easier to live with. Just as 'honesty is the best policy'. I have yet to know of MORI reporting that employees complained of receiving too much information.

Information has been described as 'anything that reduces uncertainty'. Achieve that and internal company relations are bound to improve. Internal communication must be afforded the same degree—if not amount—of professional discipline as external communication. It can (as we shall see) employ the same techniques. It must be led from the top and involve everybody. It must be 'consumer oriented'—i.e. be concerned with the personal wants, needs and desires of the workforce. It is useless if it invites no feedback or ignores the response it gets. It must be continuous. And above all it must be monitored.

What form it should take and how it can be measured are subjects for further chapters. Meanwhile, it is time to consider the other audiences whom we have provisionally lumped together as 'external.'

17

Hello out there

'The prime objective of Shell corporate advertising,' says the agency media planner,[1] 'is an all embracing one addressed to the community at large.' Other targets are smaller. ITT, whose image bore features of Allende, went into their 1974 corrective communication programme with the following priorities: 'opinion-leading segments of government, the civil service and the professions, business leaders, the media, and the company's own employees.'[2] Nigel Rowe, ITT's assistant director for public relations, says:

> It was felt that a broader definition of the 'target audience' would lead to confusion and conflict in programme planning and unacceptably high costs.'[3]

The target was further reduced by accepting the fact that those on the political right would be sympathetic and those on the left hostile, irrespective of what was communicated. Therefore ITT concentrated on those in the spectrum's middle.

When the Independent Television Contractors Association commissioned The Creative Business to write and produce a film documentary on how the television companies regulated the content of commercials, the audience was a little over 600. What's more each of them could be named. Irrespective of who else saw the finished film the target audience was the membership of the House of Commons and the objective was equally clear: to convince MPs that the self-regulatory system of advertisement vetting is effective, in the public interest, and more efficient—because less bureaucratic—than a state system.

Occasionally the target audience could fit comfortably into one room (e.g. the board of a company, a group of financial analysts or the Royal Family of Saudi Arabia). However big and however many, audiences are not discrete. A financial analyst, a chairman, an MP—they are all people. And communication is a person-to-person activity. As people they do not live in hermetically-sealed boxes, no matter how tidy that may seem for myopic media planners and marketing men. It might suit their books (or rather documents) to pretend that, say, an analyst will receive only those messages directly addressed to him. But it is neither true nor good marketing to do so.

A financial analyst reading a mailing from a multinational may also see a commercial for that company's brand on television or pass a display in a shop window. His image of the company is being formed by all these impressions, but whereas the first message is addressed to him *directly* the others are indirect: he may be an actual or potential consumer or he may be 'out of the market'. Nevertheless, all the impressions will be important and will contribute to the attitude and possible decision he has to make. For example, the analyst may read a company's internal house organ. He is definitely not the target audience. But the impression he receives will directly affect his view and therefore his expressed opinion of the company's internal communication policy which, in turn, could affect *his* public's attitude towards the company which, in its turn, could affect the share price.

Similarly, a buyer of industrial equipment may also buy that company's stock. He will thus be a receiver of two messages—as customer and part owner of the company! This is another reason for coordination of communications and consistency of image.

A politician, influential in a major decision affecting a corporate advertiser, may see a television commercial for which he is a prime target. However, seeing it simultaneously with some 16,000,000 others alters the nature of the communication and the importance of the message. It is both more important and more public.

Furthermore, the use of a public medium may prove a more successful way of communicating since there is less of a feeling of being got at. He may feel less of a target. He may choose to identify with the issue rather than react to it. He may behave, initially, like a member of the public. This could be an essential first step towards understanding and subsequent action. He is more likely to act on behalf of the public if he has become involved as one of its members.

The diverse audiences of corporate communications are separate but not discrete. Indeed their very overlapping serves the corporation's purpose, provided the communications are planned and coordinated. Robert E Kirby, the chairman of Westinghouse, told a *Fortune* seminar exactly who his audiences were, even gave figures.[4]

> In my case there is the financial community, maybe 50,000 people. Then there are the customers and potential customers—about 500,000 of them. And there is the universe of our employees—160,000 strong. And our stockholders—205,000 of *them*.
> There are the government officials—local, state, federal, foreign, legislators, administrators, regulators. All over us. All of the time. Thousands of them. And then of course there is the general public.
> I may look on it as my prime responsibility to build good products, deliver them on time, and make a profit for my corporation.
> But I have another responsibility—to help all these audiences understand what we are doing and why.

Another American, Anthony Galli, writing in the *Public Relations Journal* lists the following as 'target areas for corporate advertising objectives:'[5]

1 Government agencies and legislators.
2 Employees and prospective employees.
3 Plant committees.
4 Customers and prospective customers.
5 Suppliers.
6 Stockholders and would-be stockholders.
7 Acquisition-minded management.
8 Financial community.
9 Competitors.
10 Consumers.
11 International and multi-national investors.
12 General Public.

Whereas a third American, Thomas Garbett, cuts the cake this way:[6]

1. General Public

2. Financial

Stockholders
Brokers
Analysts
Portfolio managers
Fund managers
Banks

3. Opinion Leaders

Journalists
Authors
Educators

4. Employees and Prospective Employees

Federal
State
Local
Legislative
Regulatory

5. Customers

Consumers
Industrial and Commercial
Original-equipment manufacturers
Government

6. Trade

Distributors
Wholesalers
Dealers

Back home, Norman Hart provides the following list:[7]

(a) Customers and prospects.
(b) Employees and trade unions.
(c) Shareholders and investors.

(d) Suppliers.
(e) Local communities.
(f) Opinion formers.
(g) Government departments.
(h) Local authorities.
(i) Educational bodies
(j) Specialised groups.

The *Financial Times* in 1983 began a continuing research project into corporate advertising. With Research Services Limited they sought:[8]

> To measure the relationships between corporate advertising and corporate image and where such relationships exist to try to describe the factors that influence these relationships.

They enlisted the help of 50 major companies operating in the UK. They asked each to fill in a questionnaire. Question 6 concerned target groups. They provided a list and asked which were primary and which secondary. The list read:

. The entire adult population.
. The upper (AB) social grades.
. Activists/opinion leaders.*
. Government and government agencies, national or international.
. Business community.
. Financial community.
. Private investors/shareholders.
. Suppliers and customers.
. Employees, current and potential.
. Students.
. Local communities.
. The media.
. Others (write in).

*e.g. trade union leaders, political pressure groups, academics, etc.

From all this it might be concluded that there are as many lists of audiences as there are observers of the scene. If we take the two British examples we are puzzled first by the *FT*'s lumping together of customers and suppliers, then by Hart's omission of the media, and next by the use of the phrase 'opinion *leaders*'. Hart, notice, refers to 'opinion *formers*'.

The concept of opinion leaders, i.e. important people in society who set trends for others to copy and who ordinary folk look up to, has outlived its usefulness. As Tim Traverse-Healy said in his keynote address to the world PR Congress in Bombay:[9]

> The old concept of communicating through opinion leaders was mostly one of filtering information *down*. We may talk today of communication inwards

and outwards but no longer, I suggest, of communication up and down. We live in a society that is becoming progressively and rapidly less and less stratified and therefore we must now assess the weight of the argument rather than only the status of the person voicing it.

Many of the so-called 'opinion leaders' are no more than sensitive observers of the social scene who detect trends, maybe articulate them and give them momentum. 'Opinion formers' is a better description.

To arrive at a list of audiences, we could do worse than consider a hypothetical situation and those concerned with its outcome. A chemical company has grown. It is both successful and highly regarded. Now it needs to increase its manufacturing capacity. The plant is situated near a large lake. The plant could be enlarged with some risk of pollution exceeding company-accepted levels. These are well below the levels decreed by the government. This has been a key factor in the company's reputation. The new extended plant could, however, raise the pollution level to just below the government level. To keep to the previous level would mean vast capital expenditure—enough to make the venture profitless. The second option is not to expand. The third is to expand elsewhere with the strong probability of the company, a major employer, leaving the district altogether.

Who then will be affected by the company's decision and with whom therefore will the company need to communicate?

1. Internal

The staff will be augmented. They may have to move. They will be called upon to be spokespersons, particularly in the local community.

2. Local

The lake may be polluted. The company may leave. Either will affect the local community. The local authority may need to hold a public debate. Will the local youth be more, or less inclined to work there?

3. Influential Groups

Environmental groups will be concerned. So for that matter will the anglers, not to mention the Chamber of Commerce.

4. The 'Trade'

Suppliers of material and services may be affected by the decision to stay or go. They may also be identified with the company in any adverse publicity.

5. Government

They will need to be reassured that the company is still acting within the law. They will monitor the situation.

6. The Media

The national and local press, radio and television will regard this as news. There is strong headline material here. Dead fish. Lengthening dole queues. Irresponsible chemical giant. Pettifogging bureaucracy.

7. Financial

The banks who will help finance the capital expenditure. Will the analysts recommend 'buy' (expansion) or 'sell' (confrontation)? Will the shareholders ask questions at the AGM?

8. Customers

Will the damage to the company's reputation also hurt sales? Or will the increased capacity mean a better service? Or both?

9. General Public

How will it see the company from now on? How good a corporate citizen? Will this change in perception affect, directly or indirectly, consumption of the company's products?

These are just some of the questions. The audiences are not finite. However, I believe that any additional publics can be subsumed under the above categorisations. Let us review them, taking into consideration the previous categories we have noted.

1. Internal

All staff—management and employees. Union representatives. Plant committees.

2. Local

The community in which the company operates. Each factory or office will have its own community—neighbourhood residents, local authority, community organisation, educational bodies.

3. Influential Groups

Of course all audiences are influential. These are more influential. Indeed, being influential is their reason for being. These are activists, opinion formers, academics, educators, specialised groups.

4. The Trade

These are the members of the supply and distribution chain without which the company could not operate—distributors, wholesalers, dealers.

5. Government

This comprises government departments, (particularly in areas such as product safety, consumer protection, environment, etc.), agencies, national or international, political parties and individual Members of Parliament.

6. The Media

Newspapers, magazines, radio and television stations, news agencies—international, national and local. Trade and financial publications.

7. Financial

This is the most comprehensive audience. It comprises shareholders and investors; the narrow *financial* community and the broad *business* community (including competitors); the groups who are interested in (and could influence) the company's ability to obtain funds e.g. banks, investment houses, brokers, analysts, portfolio managers, fund managers, etc.

8. Customers

The consumers of the company's products, the prime target audience of its central advertising and marketing effort.

9. General Public

This is everybody. It includes potential and lapsed customers, unlikely customers and those out of the market, those who can influence a decision (no matter how remotely) and those who can't.

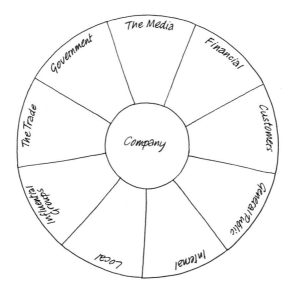

The company is at the hub of the wheel. Nine publics are at its outer edge. We have considered one of them—internal—in detail. It is time to look at the others.

18

The external audiences

This will be a rapid *tour d'horizon*.

Local

The local public is in daily contact with the company. Contact is so close it may be taken for granted and *undervalued* by the company.

The neighbourhood represents a microcosm of most of the *other* audiences. Within the locality live the general public; customers; suppliers; influential groups of all sorts; local government officials and local representatives of national parties; the financial and business community, possibly including the headquarters of major companies; maybe even competitors; and the local media, no doubt staffed with the odd stringer for a national daily paper.

Local people are a major source of investment capital. The local authority is a major receiver of the company's generated wealth. Local shoppers may make decisions about the company's products which are qualitatively different from those elsewhere, influenced (favourably or unfavourably) by what they know (directly or indirectly) about the *company*, as opposed to the products themselves.

Management needs to be concerned with community relations. Are social issues discussed internally (i.e. with the staff, who are part of the local audience) and with community representatives? Are visits arranged for local societies? Are they in turn addressed by company spokespersons? Are the company's facilities offered to local groups? Are local charities and events supported? Is the company a good corporate citizen? Is the office or factory an eyesore or a delight? Is the company solving problems or contributing to them? Is it a good place to work?

Many of these questions the company can answer itself. Some need researching. Some can be answered by direct contact with the local public via the media. The importance of the local audience must not be underestimated.

Influential Groups

I once described corporate advertising as 'advertising designed to influence the influential'. It still applies though I may have to revise my view of what constitutes influence. All audiences, of course, should influence sales. Otherwise why address them? Some audiences however are more influential and influence major decisions which could favourably or unfavourably affect the livelihood of the company. Many of these groups constitute obstacles to a company's progress, necessary (they would argue) constraints on free-wheeling enterprise. Others could become either foes or allies depending upon the outcome of the dialogue. But dialogue there must be. As Tim Traverse-Healy[1] puts it:

> It is now seen not to be practicable to operate without the consent of interest groups whose voices are increasingly articulate and whose actions over the years are becoming better co-ordinated.

But the dialogue has barely begun. The communication gulf between the wealth creators and the joint beneficiaries is still broad. And, as we have said, the onus is on the communicator.

Unfortunately the framework for the debate has been set by the critics of business. Intellectuals seem to reside *outside* the business community. They are certainly, as Max Ways says, estranged from the economic system, these 'armies of teachers, journalists, scientists, artists, fictioneers and entertainers'[2] through whose eyes the rest of the thinking public is made to see the world in which they live and work.

Whereas business as a whole needs to influence the so-called 'public debate' on the economic system—an amorphous concept admittedly—individual businesses must seek to influence any targets who may themselves influence decisions affecting their futures. These are not the shadowy figures known for a generation as 'opinion leaders'. For one thing they are likely to be followers. For another, as Bob Worcester points out, 'the ability to mould public opinion varies enormously depending upon the subject'.[3] No, the group a company wishes to influence are those whom the company knows have specific influence on a specific topic. Opinion leader communication is impossible without specifying who the leaders are and what opinion the company wants them to hold, change to, or modify.

Alcoa in the US defined their audience by means of a preliminary research survey which asked the respondents about their extracurricular activities.[4]

> Have you within the last year
>   a) Voted in an election?
>   b) Written something that was published?
>   c) Actively worked for a political party?
>   d) Written to an elected official?
>   e) Taken an active part in a local civic issue?
>   f) Addressed a public meeting?
>   g) Written a letter to an editor?

Yes to item (a) plus two or more of the other characteristics represented the qualifying mark.

The Trade

No public has grown in importance as much as the retail trade, particularly the supermarket chains. Manufacturers of fast-moving packaged goods are rarely in the driving seat. Key account buyers in a handful of national chains are the company's primary target. In the grocery business we have long passed the age of the exhortatory ad in *The Grocer* telling the retailer to stock up now and reap his rewards. Though still influenced by announcements of big television advertising budgets, the 'retailer' is now able to dictate terms to the manufacturer, to ask for a contribution to his own advertising which ironically supports his own products (made by another manufacturer but conveying the retailer's brand name) which are in direct competition. If the manufacturer is not the brand leader he may not even get on to the shelves. There may be room only for BLOB—brand leader and own brand.

In such a situation the manufacturer often has to find means of talking to the trade first—and tailoring his offering to the particular needs of each retail chain. The fashionable term for this is 'trade marketing'. There are dangers of course. The brand values which he has built up over the years may be dissipated if he does a special deal, if he allows the retailer's advertising message to swallow his own, if there is inadequate consumer advertising support for the brand, etc.

Growing retailer professionalism in marketing means that the manufacturer has to strengthen his selling message to the trade whilst at the same time ensuring that his other public messages are consistent with it and supporting it. Above all, it needs to maintain and project its reputation. As Theodore Levitt says:[5]

> The better a company's reputation, the better are its chances (1) of getting a favourable first hearing for a new product . . . and (2) of getting an early adoption of the product.

In non-grocery, non-consumer product fields the situation is less bureaucratic but the need for dialogue and communication of message is nevertheless strong. After all, very few manufacturers sell direct to the public. They rely on distributors, dealers and agents. These are the company's communicators to the customers but how often are they treated as more than mere channels, namely as audiences in their own right?

BASF Agricultural Chemicals make it a policy never to sell direct to farmers. The agricultural community see their ads in the farming press. They also see distributors' ads (subsidised by BASF). BASF, however, keep up a regular and systematic dialogue with all their distributors, not merely via area representatives but by means of seminars. They believe that educating the distributor in the latest techniques of marketing is just as important as presenting him with the facts and figures on the latest addition to the herbicide range.

A company must also consider its suppliers. It needs to make sure a supplier understands the company's systems, needs and market opportunities.

Government

This audience is rarely directly addressed in public though there seems no reason not to consider the professional techniques of commercial communication, even when the communication is behind closed doors.

Government departments, government agencies, local authorities require information. Could this information be better presented? Could it be regularly supplied, even ahead of time? Government officials, despite all rumours to the contrary, are human and appreciate well constructed, brisk, indexed presentation. They welcome background information on a company—not just what it makes but what it thinks, and what its policy is on the more sensitive issues (e.g. equal opportunity employment, pollution, youth training).

Generally, the official gleans this information from other sources. His file almost certainly contains articles, reports, depositions from interested parties. Does it contain an *unasked-for* statement by the company? Of course, it may contain the company's corporate advertisements. Governments are a key target for these. Occasionally ads are addressed directly to responsible officials and legislators concerned with specific controversies. No corporate advertiser believes an advertising campaign will directly influence a decision. Rather it hopes to make the government aware of the size and nature of the battleground.

The advantage of local government as an audience is precisely the fact that it is local and presumably accessible. A live presentation of the company's position on a key issue could be the most meaningful form of communication.

The Media

There's a paradox here. Media are a means, not an end. Journalists are communicated with in order for the message to be further disseminated. They are runners in a relay race with a distressing habit of dropping the baton or changing it for a stick of rhubarb. Nevertheless, they must also be regarded as a genuine audience, a receiver from whom feedback is required.

Communications normally occur only when times are bad or frantic. Is it any wonder that the journalist gets a one-eyed view of the company? How about lunch in the canteen and a slide show maybe, on a normal day? It won't make news but it will provide background.

Most media provide two channels of communication for a company— editorial and advertisement. If the media told the story in the way the company wants it told, on the days it wants it told, it probably wouldn't need advertising. But advertising is industry's own channel. It can—within the constraints of the law and decency—do what it likes. Nevertheless the newspaper lives by news and features of general interest. So it makes sense to consider not only if the press release satisfies those criteria but that the advertisement does also.

Financial

This is a vast audience, a spectrum from the individual with a dozen shares in Shell to the manager of the pension fund.

The financial community comprises the stockbroker, the banker the individual investor (ranging from the sophisticated to the very naive), the institutional investor, the pension plan, the mutual fund, the insurance company, the bank, the trust department and the security analyst.

Bob Worcester divides 'the City' into three discrete audiences. He believes their views are very different from each other:[6]

> There are the institutions (pension funds, the bank, investment analysts in major institutions), there are brokers who deal with your industry and there are city journalists.

A corporate advertisement is addressed to most if not all of these publics and though it may be targeted more precisely at the security analyst (maybe with the direct objective of raising the share price, there is little doubt that the general impression of a go-ahead company will affect attitudes of other audiences, such as the institutional investor, if only by making the latter a little more aware of the company. Familiarity breeds favourability. One commentator defines the role of financial communications thus:[7]

> To tell the financial community what management is going to do to increase the value of the enterprise.

In the area of corporate communications, image is made flesh. An impersonal perception of a company can be measured in a rise in the share price and an increase in the (paper) wealth of the company. According to the *Financial Times*:[8]

> The campaign by British Electric Traction to persuade businessmen in the City that it is no longer a sleepy, sprawling conglomerate rife for takeover is beginning to show results.

The results are measured precisely. Two paragraphs later we read:

> BET's shares are now hovering around 270p—double the level of two years ago and valuing the company at £548m.

There are other aims of communicating to the financial community. Advertisements for example can be designed to increase the trading in shares; draw attention to a corporate development; test the water for a forthcoming venture; invite demand for the annual report, etc. But if the advertising is to help the portfolio manager or the individual investor it must be newsworthy, informative and useful.

Too often communication comes too late to help not the audience, but the company itself. When take-over threatens, the silent company finds a voice. Rather shrill it must be said. Reg Valin of Valin Pollen refers to a dawn raid in the City. Afterwards 'the chairman of the company taken over was heard to say plaintively that he hadn't even had a chance to talk to his shareholders.'[9] A constant theme in corporate communications is the need to communicate in good times as well as bad . . .

The acquiring company also communicates of course. It puts its reputation on the line. It may even damage it since it is unlikely that the message or the manner will be in keeping with its usual style. Often the advertisements are bombastic or wheedling and the format is determined by the pressures on time and the typography of the accommodating newspaper.

A battle is no place for contemplation. A financial audience needs to know a great deal about the company beyond even that contained in, or recounted by, the annual report. The analyst, for example, will need to judge the company's management, its marketing and financial skills, its planning and control techniques, research and development capabilities, and so on.

Customers

There is no business without a customer. Every company is working for customers. The company communicates with a customer *via* its products, services and advertising. The customer is rarely communicated with by the company *on its own behalf*. For example, customers are rarely the chief target of corporate advertising. (Banks and other service industries are exceptions since it is difficult to separate 'corporate' from 'product'.) Nevertheless, corporate advertising does have an effect on sales, particularly in the industrial as opposed to the consumer field. Companies in both fields often use a corporate umbrella as a means to promote a collection of individual products or brands.

Corporate, as distinct from product, communication is rarely directed solely or primarily at wholesaler customers. They are, however, part of *other* audiences (e.g. local, financial and general public) and therefore have an ambiguous relationship with these messages. As a customer they have an interest in the company: it's a club which they have elected to join. The performance of the company in communicating to 'everybody else' is probably scrutinised more accurately by a customer than a non-customer. If nothing else, selective perception will increase the probability of the advertisement being read. (Just as we always look at an ad for a big-ticket item we have already purchased.) A company can't afford to ignore a customer wherever he or she may be or whomsoever it is specifically addressing.

General Public

The general public is an all-inclusive term. The danger is that it can mean everybody and therefore nobody. Whereas a popular brand may *need* to communicate to everybody, it is difficult to contemplate a company having to do so. Some companies, however, feel that need quite deeply. Some adopt a stance on behalf of business in general. Mobil has been a continuous, big budget, corporate advertiser believing that:

> Businesses must make themselves accessible if they are to demand access (to the media); they must contribute to public understanding if they are going to request public support.[10]

ITT's cutting off the right and left of the spectrum, Alcoa's careful honing of target groups are not for Mobil. The whole US public (and for that matter a vast amount of the UK's) is its audience. It sponsors public service broadcasting, it contributes to public debate—initiating it quite often. Whether it would choose such a broad target audience were gasoline not a mass consumer product it is difficult to say.

The CBI is in no doubt as to the importance of the general public to the corporate communications strategies of companies not 'in the consumer business'.

> A massive office building dominated by the corporate logo, their recruitment advertising, press reports of management of structural changes, are all in the public domain.[11]

The *Reader's Digest*, with an axe to grind, discovered a 'gap' in the market. The Great American Public.

> It needs to be told about the positive side which business plays in strengthening the national economy, cleaning up the environment, holding down prices, rebuilding the cities . . . all the good things which companies often do and about which the great American public doesn't know or is underinformed.[12]

Such as spending levels on corporate ads in the *Reader's Digest*.

A job needs doing. Business is discussed very little on television or radio. Whether there would ever be a genuine popular interest in business matters, problems, successes, or personalities is difficult to estimate. There is certainly little material available on which to base an informed guess.

All this, of course, begs the question whether an individual company should spend its money on behalf of business in general, let alone whether it should regard the general public as a worthwhile audience, particularly as it is by definition expensive to reach. Not per capita of course: in total spend.

But the general public is like a slice of cassata—lots of incidental goodies. Potential employees for example. Corporate advertising (let alone the less direct forms of communication such as sponsorship) can never replace recruitment advertising, but it can assist it by showing the type of company it is, indicating the opportunities which lie ahead (for the company and the recruit) and expressing the company philosophy.

Potential customers are part of the general public. Corporate advertisements might provide the first meeting between them and the company. So are the various interested groups. Corporate communications to a general audience might prove a more effective way of convincing them of a company's goodwill than a direct avowal or pages of reasoned argument. And a company's employees are also part of the general public. The most important of all a company's audiences—internal. The wheel has come full circle.

19

Public paths

Each of the nine audiences is receiving impressions, forming images of the company even if the company is not consciously communicating or co-ordinating its communications. The mosaic is forming. What isn't known is imagined. Northcote Parkinson gives warning:[1]

> Failure to communicate creates a vacuum which is gradually filled with misrepresentations, drivel and poison.

OK, OK, says the company. We know. We must communicate. We know what we want to say—to all nine publics. But how do we reach them?

Corporate communication is not as straightforward as product advertising or promotion. It demands more thought. The problem will determine the solution. We are miles away from blanket coverage and cost per thousand. Here the paths aren't as well trodden, some you may have to hack out yourself and others you might think lead somewhere else.

Choosing will mean weighing options according to the particular audience and the particular objective. The City's major sources of information so one survey revealed,[2] are stockbrokers (40%), annual reports (25%), press (22%), direct contact (11%) and advertising (9%). On the other hand, in a survey of US professional and managerial people[3] 34% said their most important source was advertising.

How to begin? The choice is perplexing in its size and diversity. Letters. Film. Editorial. Sponsorship. Speech. Corporate ads. Announcements. Direct Mail. Etc.

We need to categorise again. And we have as many media as we have audiences. There are nine means by which a company communicates with its publics. Or, to be more accurate, there are nine convenient groupings of all the various media. They are:

1 PRODUCT
2 CORRESPONDENCE
3 PUBLIC RELATIONS
4 PERSONAL PRESENTATION
5 IMPERSONAL PRESENTATION

6 LITERATURE
7 POINT OF SALE
8 PERMANENT MEDIA
9 ADVERTISING

As we review them, assess each for its potential to assist or hinder effective communication. Which is the noisiest?

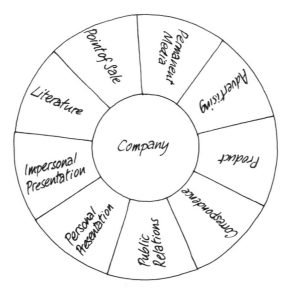

Product

In product as opposed to corporate communication, the most important message from the company to the consumer is the product itself: how the product *performs*. Similarly the most important message back is *purchase* of the product.

In corporate communication the product is still a potent force. Any amount of prestige advertising can be as nought if the product fails to deliver. However, in many companies the danger to a company's reputation may be lessened when the association between the company and the product is not apparent to the customer, e.g. in the case of a conglomerate, a recent acquisition or a company with a strong brand-led policy.

Companies can communicate verbally and graphically by means of the packaging, adding corporate reassurance to a brand.

Correspondence

The letter, telex, telephone or memo is a potent medium still for communicating with staff, trade, media, influential groups and even selected customers. Indeed, selectivity is the clue to personal correspondence. Cascading of information to employees, inundating editors, wearing out your welcome with customers or boring the pants off managerial colleagues is to be avoided and a waste of notepaper.

Used wisely, personally commissioned and personally addressed communication is very effective—as any recipient of a well-crafted direct mail shot will testify.

Public Relations

In a sense—and it depends how you define PR—this whole book is about public relations. If you accept Graham Kemp's description[4] that PR 'represents the interface between an organisation and its audiences and sometimes embraces the techniques used to create that "interface",' then anything goes. The industry's own definition is a shade more exact:

> The deliberate, planned and sustained effort to establish and maintain mutual understanding between an organisation and its publics.

Public relations is at a crossroads. Actually it's on the grass verge in the middle of the roundabout looking at all the exits and where it's been, a little unsure of itself, hoping it won't get breathalysed ('I haven't had a gin and tonic for a decade'), or mistaken for a press agent ('I'm in a profession now old boy').

PR in the, admittedly, limited sense we are using it in this chapter means 'press relations'—getting the company known to the media and measuring its success initially by linage but primarily by favourable attitude shift.

(I apologise to any PR practitioner giving up this volume at this point. I appreciate that public relations lays claim to the title of a 'multi-disciplined management function'. In fact many of the functions PR people undertake are covered elsewhere in this chapter. We suffer from an inadequate and chameleon terminology.)

PR can get a company much 'unpaid' publicity in national and local media provided the story is news and not guff. The company release which fails to appreciate the media or the individual journalist will end up spiked or, worse, treated as a news item of a different sort. Press releases which are thinly disguised advertisements are meat and drink to diary writers. But real news gets in, gets read, gets noticed—and does more for a company than any corporate advertisement. For the simple reason that editorial is impartial.

Editorial is an uncertain means of communicating a corporate message but when it works it generates not only consumer interest but the interest of other media. Furthermore the company can order reprints (or tapes in the case of radio and television), and 'merchandise' the editorial.

Personal Presentation

All other channels are a substitute for face-to-face. When an opportunity occurs for a company spokesperson to put the corporate case it should be taken with both hands, a firm voice and a carousel of slides.

The audience may be remote from a purchasing decision—e.g. schools, clubs, societies. But they are part of the general public and/or local community. Besides, you never know who may be in the audience. Furthermore the experience of putting the corporate case to a real live audience will help the spokesperson in his or her next communication, live or otherwise.

There are innumerable conferences, at least 10% of which are of some relevance to one of a company's audiences. Failing that, the company can run its own—e.g. on a critical business or industry issue—and generate media attention. There are internal sales conferences, conferences for the trade and press conferences (to be avoided unless the news can't be communicated any other way).

Face-to-face communication you would think is frequent within companies. Not so. Management chickens out. Few companies practise that key ingredient of successful US companies MBWA—'Management by walking about'. They prefer to send paper or put up notices. Excuses for *not* speaking are usually bogus. The cost is minimal compared with that of a page in a colour supplement. The disruption is more than compensated by the potential increase in productivity. The presentation can be televised on closed-circuit or taped and copies sent to the rest of the organisation.

In times of crisis face-to-face communication is the most appropriate channel. Prior to BL's Recovery Plan Ballot in 1979, Harold Musgrove, managing director of Austin Morris, and a team of executives:[5]

. . . put the product strategy across to some 18,000 employees—on day and
night shift—talking virtually continuously to groups of 1,000 people at a time.

But UK management is, with notable exceptions, shy of speaking to
employees. Managers are conscious of their position and so, fearing (what we
know as) psychological noise, when they do manage to mutter a phrase or
two to a passing employee they manage to increase it.

Face-to-face communication must not be regarded as a chore but as an
essential part of the job. Means have to be found to make it less formal in
those circumstances when formality would be counter-productive (noise
making). ACAS is, as ever, full of practical commonsense on the subject:[6]

> Face-to-face communication is direct and swift. It should enable discussion,
> questioning and feedback to take place but ought to be supplemented by
> written material where information is detailed or complex and where records
> are important. When spoken methods are used it is important that:
> * the chain of communication is as short as possible;
> * the frequency and timing of meetings are carefully considered;
> * managers are fully briefed on their subjects and able to put them across
>   clearly and consistently;
> * opportunities are provided for questions.

And if you require an even more systematic approach, contact the Industrial
Society and ask about Team Briefings.

Impersonal Presentation

In an impersonal presentation the human factor is subordinate to the
non-human or absent altogether. Videotapes, films, slide shows, film strips,
sound cassettes all come in this category. During the Tylenol crisis Johnson &
Johnson employees were continually updated on developments through
individual letters from the president of the company and through videotapes.

Exhibitions provide a company with a simple and inexpensive way of
communicating with the neighbourhood. They can take place in a public
building or the company's reception. Seminars can be combined with
exhibitions. Local and company personnel can attend.

A noticeboard is another form of impersonal presentation. But noticeboards
are generally a mess. If, as I believe, the model for all communication is
person-to-person then the company must find ways to humanise this
impersonal medium. Items have to be kept separate. Today's news has to be
seen to be immediate. Important items must not be swamped by second-hand
car sales.

Sponsorship basically is an impersonal presentation. The company's
identity is stuck with varying degrees of adhesion, to an event. The event
very rarely allows company people to participate (though the chairman's wife
may pat the odd horse). However, they provide opportunities for face-to-face

contact in the theatre, hall, bar, tent or private box. And you can always publicise the event. Though you would be hard put to emulate one US sponsor of a television programme.

'XEROX BRINGS BACK CIVILISATION.'

Literature

This is the most worn of our public paths. Some companies produce literature as if it was their end product.

A well designed and well produced annual report is now a *sine qua non* of any respectable company. The content of course is paramount: statistical data relevant to the company and the industry it's in, corporate objectives, earnings by specific products or divisions, results, other performance details, prospects, etc.

New York security analyst Fred Greenberg looks for 'incremental information' from a report. He cites Novo as a rare example of 'complete and balanced scientific analysis which allows the reader to make his own judgement'. Sometimes the design gravy hides the meat. Worse it disguises the fact that there's less meat than there should be. Some companies use annual reports to ward off comments by shareholders at AGMs. Though the design of annual reports differentiates one company from another, the terminology—as with other forms of corporate communication—tends to homogenize them. Chairmen have a limited vocabulary.

"I am confident..."	THORN EMI 1983
"I am confident..."	ALLIED LYONS 1981
"I am confident..."	ASSOCIATED DAIRIES 1982
"I am confident..."	IMPERIAL GROUP 1983
"I am confident..."	ERF 1980
"I am confident..."	BLUE CIRCLE INDUSTRIES 1982
"I am confident..."	WHITBREAD 1980
"I ...am confident..."	BOOTS 1981
"We are confident..."	BASS 1983
"We are confident..."	DEBENHAMS 1981
"We are confident..."	BARRATT DEVELOPMENTS 1981
"We are confident..."	GOULD INC. 1981
"We are confident..."	TIME PRODUCTS 1980
"I am, therefore, confident..."	SKETCHLEY 1981
"I am therefore more confident than I was..."	H.P. BULMER 1981
"I am nevertheless confident..."	SCOTTISH & NEWCASTLE BREWERIES 1980
"Long term, I am confident..."	ASSOCIATED BISCUITS 1980
"I view the future with confidence..."	ARGYLL FOODS 1983
"I have every confidence in the future..."	GRAND METROPOLITAN 1983
"We can look forward to the future with confidence..."	ROYAL INSURANCE 1981
"The future...to which we look...forward with confidence..."	GUINNESS 1980
"We look forward with confidence..."	GEC 1983
"We look forward with every confidence..."	SAINSBURY'S 1983
"Nevertheless we remain confident..."	CPC 1980

There are other forms of report. The corporate brochure or company book is not necessarily a regular item. It is less rigid, more impressionistic and satisfies a wider audience. A few companies issue a social report (or it is contained in the brochure) dealing with the company's role in society and detailing its community activities.

The report to employees has become essential to most companies. If a company has a good house journal then the annual results can constitute the major part of one issue. Otherwise a separate publication is distributed simultaneously with the annual report papers. Often the company includes the employee report in its mailing to investors.

GKN, Metal Box, Shell are a few of the companies issuing employee reports. Many more publish house journals. ICI and Unilever magazines are professionally produced but private publicatons which can hold their own with commercially produced magazines. Though meant for internal consumption, these publications are very useful to other audiences—influential groups, particularly MPs.

At a more popular level company newspapers provide both corporate and social news. Tone of voice is important here. Management must not be seen to be 'jollying the troops along'. The paper must include items of direct personal interest to employees and allow them to contribute. Managed properly, the employee newspaper, as research by the British Association of Industrial Editors affirms:[7]

> . . . is still the most widely used form of employee communication—and still the most popular.

In the research into *Dunlop News* referred to earlier, the item which scored highest on the 'most interesting' measure was 'News about Dunlop products' (71%) followed by 'News or information on how the company as a whole is going' (60%), Sports/Social Activities/Hobbies and Personal News Items (both 55%) and News/Items about Dunlop Divisions or Groups (50%). That seems to me to be a reasonable balance. The least interesting item was Women's Features (19%).

More formal literature is of course also produced for employee consumption, especially handbooks which contain information employees need to know. ACAS believe:[8]

> Written communication is most effective where:
> * the need for the information is important or permanent;
> * the topic requires detailed explanation;
> * accuracy and precision in wording are essential;
> * the audience is widespread or large.

John Garnett, presiding genius and evangelist of the Industrial Society, is adamant that a document for action—by no matter whom in the company— should never have more than 24 pages:

Otherwise it gets passed to the 'expert' and the man who should do something about it never reads it.[9]

Macmillan in the US once produced an annual report for children.[10] I don't know if they repeated the exercise. But companies such as Shell regularly

provide schools and educational authorities with booklets and wallcharts. Teachers accept such material with reservation but appreciate that some form of trade-off—a commercial stamp duty—is part of life today. It is a means by which public issues can be effectively presented for discussion in schools. According to the International Advertising Association:[11]

> The amount of material is greater at the primary and secondary level, than at university level, and more privately-provided material is available in the US and UK than in most other countries.

Promotion/Point of Sale

These are normal channels for a company's products, though rarely used to spread the corporate message. It is an area commonly known as 'below-the-line' to distinguish it from the media from which the advertising agency derives commission, the 'above-the-line' advertising. Competitions, displays, banded offers, free gifts, trial offers hardly seem the area for a corporate message. Which is probably a good reason to consider it.

Permanent Media

The French term 'média permanent' is an appropriate description of the collection of items on which a corporate identity appears—the signboards, vehicles, uniforms, notepaper, environmental design. Here it is patently the company and not its products which is communicating—or trying to. But for a manufacturer of crash helmets the environment is the street and the medium is the product itself.

Advertising

We devote three chapters to corporate advertising, the other communications channel designed for the exclusive use of a company. Occasionally, however, the company strays into consumer advertising, adding a corporate endorsement to a product message or offering a corporate publication as an inducement to readership.

This chapter has outlined the various media categories available. Though it has barely scratched the surface of each it will, I hope, serve to stimulate thought about the ways companies communicate.

20

The wheel

Let's recap and assemble the pieces. A company communicates to nine audiences:

INTERNAL
LOCAL
INFLUENTIAL GROUPS
THE TRADE
GOVERNMENT
THE MEDIA
FINANCIAL
CUSTOMERS
GENERAL PUBLIC

It uses any or all of nine channels:

PRODUCT
CORRESPONDENCE
PUBLIC RELATIONS
PERSONAL PRESENTATION
IMPERSONAL PRESENTATION
LITERATURE
POINT OF SALE
PERMANENT MEDIA
ADVERTISING

The wheel has the company at its hub and the audiences at its rim. In between are the means of communicating with those audiences, the channels. Nine publics. Nine channels.

Note the illustration on page 118 has deliberately not lined up any public with any channel. It would be customary for 'advertising' to align with 'customers'; 'public relations' with 'media'; and 'personal presentation' with 'the trade'.

I want to suggest that each of the nine channels be regarded as a candidate when a company considers communicating to each of the nine publics. In

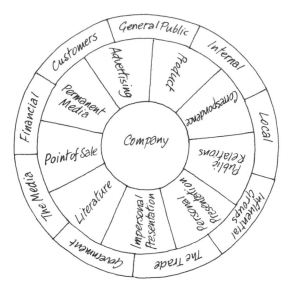

other words the inner circle (of channels) in our diagram *rotates*. (If I had wanted a fixed diagram I would not have chosen a wheel.) The wheel is not a model but a checklist—and a thought starter.

It reminds a corporate communicator that he or she has 9 x 9 options to consider. A total of 81 combinations of medium and audience. Now the majority of them may be impractical, even absurd, but the act of reviewing them will, in my experience, do two things: stimulate some fresh thoughts and encourage the thinker to regard corporate communications as a totality rather than a series of discrete messages to discrete audiences. The result may be a higher regard for the subject and its better coordination.

Michael Edwardes takes a comprehensive view of communications. There are usual and unusual channels. At BL:[1]

> On each occasion when an important issue was at stake the company view was communicated directly to employees as well as through normal union channels. This often meant sending letters to employees' homes (where they could calmly and deliberately consider the situation with their families), the issuing of factory briefing sheets and posters. When we felt a particular issue had wider significance we used newspaper advertisements.

A company needs to take a holistic view of communication because it is communicating all the time (even if it doesn't want to or doesn't realise it), to all of those nine publics. The communication which is taking place, even if unplanned or unconscious, is creating impressions and images are being formed. Is the company willing to do nothing about it? Perhaps it is. But far better for that to be a conscious decision.

The wheel's outer circle reminds the company of all the possible recipients of a message—i.e. those who may receive it even though not specifically addressed. The secondary audience may be regarded as a bonus. The staff will see the corporate advertisement and identify with the achievements it chronicles. Or a security analyst will read the employee annual report and receive an impression of industrial democracy at work. Or a local MP will read the house journal and have ammunition for a debate.

Conversely, the secondary audience may be an embarrassment. The directors' salary brackets enumerated in the annual report will be seen by the shop steward. The chairman's speech to his company's trade federation attacking, say, retail domination, will be picked up by the press-cutting service of the retail trade. An off-peak television commercial addressed to chemists informing them of the forthcoming television campaign will be seen by those very people whom the company seemingly is about to push the chemists' way.

Why is it that communications in business have been conducted in closed channels? How can management have fooled itself for so long that messages in one area are of no concern in another? Can management really believe in watertight communication compartments (advertising, public relations, packaging, design, etc.), when the consumer outside in his wisdom sees the company and everything marked with its name as one? Management has only to consider the company's grapevine to know that messages can't be hermetically sealed.

Specialisation, of course, is part of the reason. It is a peculiarly, though not exclusively, British disease. Specialisation happens early: children have to be streamed, choices have to be made, irreversible science/arts decisions agonised over. It's all 'either/or'. We call the all-rounder a jack of all trades. Yet 400 years ago we rejoiced in renaissance man who could fight, play a lute, sail the seas and write a sonnet. There's an old Spanish proverb (there generally is) which says 'the man who is nothing but, is not even'. Try telling that to your average administrator.

Convention, habit, laziness and the vested interests of the specialists encourage a company not to do anything to the pigeon holes of commerce. The company (maybe it's the chief executive—it's hard to say who) decides to develop a new product. Research and development are given a brief. The product development team may be told what's going on and look in from time to time. If R and D is successful of course they take over, maybe cling in a consultant new-product-development specialist. Consumer research is favourable. The marketing department is now in the act and a team appointed to mastermind the launch. The product development team have retired to their ivory tower, R and D to their lab. The NPD consultants are replaced by the advertising agency who prepare the launch advertising. Meanwhile a pack is being designed. With luck someone in the organisation is looking after all these activities. 'They're taking place in parallel,' he says. Only parallel lines have a habit of never meeting.

The wheel, is a means of breaking down pigeon-hole thinking. Ask who is responsible for all the activities it shows—all 81 options. Traditio.al answers won't do. They fit *part* of the pattern. The advertising agency addresses the customers, the general public, occasionally the trade and very rarely the financial community (specialist financial agencies do that of course). And the means it employs is advertising. That is what you would expect from something called an 'advertising agency', though it does indulge in literature, point-of-sale and promotion, and new product development. Generally, however, those activities are delegated to specialist outfits. Impersonal presentations are also a specialist area, inside and outside the company. Though some outside production outfits handle both impersonal and personal presentations. Permanent media and packaging are the province of design groups. Though the best design groups are generally aware of more of the other activities on the wheel than the other specialists. The average public relations company will be concerned with 'PR' in the sense we've used it here: 'editorial', and with personal and impersonal presentations and literature. If you ask them 'who's in charge?' the answer can only be the company, the hub of the circle. Which is how it should be. Though obviously one person should have control and he should never be far away from the chief executive (as we'll see in Chapter 24, when we discuss integration).

Let's call him CC (Communications coordinator). Where does he go for help? Each of the specialists we have mentioned will have its own row to hoe. It may be hard to take their recommendations at face value. Because no one service company can both advise and practise in each of the nine areas, CC is tempted to call in a consultant—a management consultant probably, marketing consultant perhaps, or a corporate communications consultant—whichever seems the most appropriate. The consultant, however, caf carry out few of the activities he may recommend. This can be considered an advantage since he will recommend those things which need doing rather than those things he can do.

The nearest existing organisation we have to the all-planning-all-doing outfit CC is seeking, is the more sophisticated public relations firm. It prefers the term 'corporate relations'. It is a far cry from the popular image of a PR man (though not as far as it might be), with its marketing reports, research analyses, communication audits and the like. It is unlikely to become involved in advertising itself—nor will the agency let it. Instead, it cooperates with agencies or forms an association with one to provide a 'complete communications package'. This suits the agency since it can offload all those bits and pieces it doesn't want to get too involved with, but which it can now be seen to be offering the more thoughtful advertiser who has an idea—heretical though it may be to utter it in the agency's boardroom—that advertising isn't perhaps the complete solution to his problem.

Of course it generally *is* the answer to the problem of mass communicating the benefits of fast-moving consumer goods, though even here the attention most agencies pay to complementary answers is token. These other services are called 'below-the-line', 'support', 'ancillary' and other pejorative names. They promise more work than reward. Advertising, you see is relatively less onerous and more expensive to buy. The agency, traditionally, has been on a fixed commission from the media. The more the client spends the greater the income, the more the media raise their prices—the greater the income. It's hard to see the '2p off coupon' through all the cigar smoke.

However, the situation changes when we come to corporate affairs. Mass communication is unlikely to be the main consideration—even a candidate. Corporate advertising is more selective and then not an automatic choice. In the world of corporate communication the problem determines the solution. The agency's real contribution is thinking time—and that is notoriously hard to cost. There follows the creation of communications and their implementation. But the media on the inner circle of our wheel, other than advertising, are not famed for rich pickings.

The big agency is therefore in a quandary. It appreciates the importance of the exercise to the client, it wants to be involved if only because the client's chief executive is. Annual reports and even identity schemes are very close to chairmen's hearts. Unfortunately they are not activities which the agency has done well or profitably. The solution is usually a compromise—the job is sub-contracted; a freelance team is brought in; juniors are given the assignment (much to their annoyance since they are trying to do ads to impress their peers in other companies, win awards etc., and regard this crap as demotion).

The truth is that no service company—agency consultant, PR company, design group—exists which is capable of taking on the job of helping CC in as comprehensive a manner as he would wish. His best bet is a good 'full-service' agency where that term is not candyfloss and includes PR, or a 'multi-disciplined' PR company probably with an agency connection. Should CC be concerned more with planning help and have a limited amount of practical execution and implementation, preferring subsequently to brief outside specialists, then a financial agency or a corporate communications consultant could fit the bill.

'Corporate communication' is a no man's land somewhere between advertising and public relations, with various assorted troops on either flank. The PR man's view of advertising is almost as jaundiced as the ad man's view of PR. Neither is very likely to recommend the other's channel to a client. The client suffers—compromises, chooses a single solution instead of a combination, handles the coordination himself.

The irony is that it all seems so simple to the people involved in the communication, the real people that is—the company and the audience. As we noticed, to the man in the street all messages are making impressions and client suffers—compromises, chooses a single solution instead of a combination, handles the coordination himself.

The irony is that it all seems so simple to the people involved in the communication, the real people that is—the company and the audience. As we noticed, to the man in the street all messages are making impressions and contributing to the image of the company—one company. The company, for its part, knows that it has various things to say to various publics and wants help getting them across with the optimum efficiency. It needs convincing that the agency understands its problems. It suspects that the agency has a different set of maps, that its view of the communications world is Ptolemaic compared with its own Copernican view which puts the 'company' rather than 'advertising' at its hub.

Which brings us back to the wheel. We need to add two inner rings at the centre. Their use depends upon the nature of the company and where it is communicating.

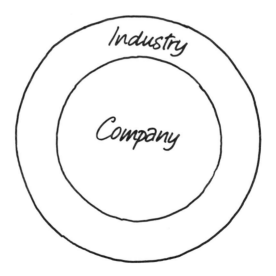

The first inner ring is 'industry'. A company's image can be affected by the image of the industry of which it is part. Shell is an oil company. It is part of the total 'oil companies' image. And 'oil companies' are part of Shell's image. Industries come together for joint action or are lumped together by outside critics. A conglomerate in many industries may attempt to embrace anonymity by dissociating its group name (e.g. a holding company or group of initials) from any of the industries in which it is involved. In which case the subsidiary company is seen as part of the industry, though probably also as part of the group! The conglomerate may end up associated with *several* industries.

The industry therefore constitutes a filter through which the company's image is perceived. The company may decide to counteract the filter, though over-reaction may draw attention to it.

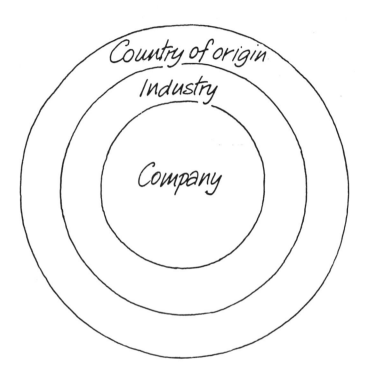

The other inner ring is country of origin. Whereas British is barely perceptible as part of, say, Cadbury's image in the UK it is significant in the US. Here Citroën is a French car first and a car second. Few companies who trade abroad appear neutral though some make serious attempts (and often heavy weather) of appearing local.

The wheel then is a corporate communications checklist, a reminder of the audiences, the means of reaching them and two components which could affect the resulting image. It also provides a company's corporate communication director with a wide range of choices, wider than he will need but containing possible practical options he otherwise may not have contemplated. It is then a practical tool. All the more useful because the divisions are equal in size and the inner wheel will spin without bias (see page 124).

Corporate communications is a comprehensive activity. The disciplines it comprises are wider than those of specialist service companies. 'Advertising' deals with part of it. 'Public Relations' with considerably more. A new term—and a new type of service is required. At The Creative Business we call it 'Communication Management'.

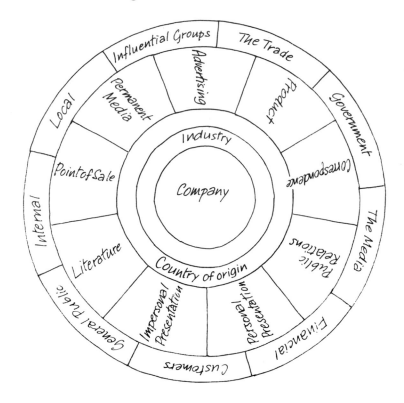

21

Image or images?

A company is complex. An image is simple. A company speaks to many audiences. How can that single simple image represent the company or be appropriate to—if even received by—all of those audiences? Corporate image, to repeat, is:

> The net result of the interaction of all the experiences, impressions, beliefs, feelings and knowledge that people have about a company.[1]

A multitude of pieces form the mosaic—the company's product or products; packaging; its corporate and product advertising; direct and/or indirect experience; corporate identity (logo, letterhead, livery, etc.); and all the impressions created by its communications. But is the mosaic's picture the same for two different publics?

> It's one thing to tell a corporate treasurer reading *Fortune* that Manufacturers Hanover is financing a nuclear power plant in Spain. But it's something else to tell that to the average television viewer who has been asked to keep his thermostat down because of an energy shortage in New York.[2]

Whereas a solid growth record and excellent prospects may attract the security analyst, the customer is more interested in a quality product, and the potential employee in job satisfaction. Nick Winkfield relates the dilemmas of a multinational company:[3]

> How can you present yourself to investors as profitable, and to purchasers as offering good value for money? . . . Can you advertise your exports (i.e. technological transfer) to newly industrialising countries, without alienating your domestic trade unions?

Surely it's difficult to project the identical image to all of our nine publics? And even if it could be done, is it advisable since the needs are so different? What other options are there? Basically two—centrifugal and centripetal. The first—totally separate images—would be anarchic. Similarity would be accidental at best. The second—where each separate image contains an element of a central or 'core' image—does at least ensure that each communication is helping, and is being helped by each other.

Is the latter feasible—or merely abstract geometry? I happen to believe it's feasible. It needs a strong personality at the centre—in both senses of that term; a clearly delineated and perfectly articulated philosophy and a strong and powerful executive in charge. Given that, peripheral identity aberrations won't damage the central image.

The company has to decide what it wants its core image to be and has to accept the probability that all its publics will not be equally sympathetic to it. Unless of course it chooses to project a bland image which all audiences are equally apathetic to.

To achieve any degree of success a company has to negotiate three minefields. The first of these is its own *products*. It is difficult to separate the corporate image from that of the company's brands. Unless it has adopted a brand-first strategy in which case, of course, it won't want to do much corporate communication at a company level. But if, say, it's Beecham, how is that image affected by the image of Beecham Powders, even—for some of us—Beecham Pills? If it's Rowntree Mackintosh, is the image of Fruit Gums a more dominant factor than that of Yorkie which has ten times as much advertising spend but one-tenth the company branding?

And how feasible or advisable is it for a company to maintain a consistent image over a proliferation of different brand names? If individual brands, despite carrying the company endorsement on packs, have been promoted on their own behalf, what hope has the company of communicating a 'proprietorial' image? There are two areas of dual branding exemplified by Nabisco and Sterling Health. The former tag each product or advertisement with a Nabisco triangle top right. The latter put a 'family' of variously branded health products together in one advertisement and claim ownership of the lot. Nabisco's way is simpler, takes longer and is more effective. The Sterling Health way seems to ask the viewer or reader to take in too much information in one go.

Nabisco's method reveals planning *ab initio*. Sterling Health's solution is an afterthought. A total communications policy means that each of the company's products and each of the product's communications fits into a single philosophical framework. Knowledge of the corporate image is enhanced by each press ad, pack design, end shot. And the corporate image in turn helps the sales of the company's new products. Before a new Nabisco brand with its own brand name has had time to establish its own *brand* identity, the company identity on the pack on the shelf is radiating reassuring impressions to the shopper.

Of a sample of housewives faced with a new biscuit called, say, 'Ranch' and told it was made by a 'well-known food company', perhaps 50% would say they were likely to buy it. Add the Nabisco triangle to the pack and that figure might go up by some 10%. The Nabisco route is one way through the minefield of corporate vs. brand names. But not many companies are in

Nabisco's position and the option, though available for a new company, isn't there for an established one.

The second field is mined with differing activities. Whereas our previous category saw a dichotomy between company and brand, here there is a dichotomy between one part of the company and another. They may be addressing different audiences. They may not. As a Watney spokesman bemoaned:[4]

> People like our pubs, but, however unfairly, they do not think much of our beers.

Yet pubs and beers are close. What are your chances if you're a conglomerate whose growth has been inorganic? 'The man with the gong. A man of many skills.' British Electric Traction: 'The talent that makes companies flourish.' Or to quote an ex-colleague, Dr Virginia Miles: 'XYZ brassieres, another fine product of the American Meat Packing Corporation.'

How relevant is a company's existing reputation for each of its activities? Is BASF a chemical company when it markets sound tapes? Are the publics for pesticides and cassettes so totally discrete that there is no problem of confusion? Has Dolby taken care of the noise? Do consumers see product compatibility the same way manufacturers do? Research is essential to help a company find out. The company may be forcing incompatible pieces into a contrived whole. Conversely a company's reluctance to call a new venture or acquisition by its own name may worry the consumer less than it worries the company. Research may be necessary to check compatibility—or *reveal* it. It may result in halting a proposed acquisition or merger since the addition would blur or mar the corporate image. It may result in setting up a separate division which contains its own identity and projects a separate image to all but the company's employees and shareholders.

The third of our minefields is, in a sense, far more personal. It's something we each recognise about ourselves. *Persona*. Who are we today? A conglomerate, of course, has schizoid problems. Some communications people are convinced that you can't do a corporate ad for a conglomerate.

> You really need a company that's perceived as being in one kind of business to do a really strong totally integrated job.[5]

But problems of dual personality aren't confined to conglomerates. Each of us is complex. We play different roles according to the context.

William James divided the elements of the 'me' into three categories: the material me, the social me, the spiritual me. Can the company's three '*mes*' possibly project sufficient of a common image to be recognised as the same company? Is the social self compatible with the material? But James isn't content with one social self.

> Man has as many different social selves as there are distinct groups of persons about whose opinion he cares.[6]

Does a company run the risk of alienating one group when it chooses to don a specific self for another group? For, as we have seen, secondary audiences exist. Wall Streeters, says Friedlich, want to know:

> . . . about the ingredients in your product and profit more than they want to know how you feel about Motherhood.[7]

The financial audience needs to be reassured that the company's management knows what it is doing. Sponsorship of the Macclesfield Under–15 trampoline team might constitute noise. Only a whisper perhaps. But suppose no other sound is heard? It then assumes deafening proportions. A company which dons its social self at every opportunity may be suspected by a 'social' public of having a material self it wishes to hide, and by a 'material' public of having no material self worth talking about.

Yet I am convinced that the company which is true to itself (i.e. to the philosophy it represents and has articulated) will find it comparatively simple to be consistent, and thus to project a 'core' image. The response the company provokes is 'that's typical!' — which may be supportive or the reverse. But either way it's proof of consistency. What we do in our material, social and spiritual roles may be vastly different in nature but as an expression of our personality they are, as the saying goes, 'in character'.

When RSCG conduct their character analysis (see page 64) and construct a *marque personne*, each trait is of a piece. Unilever is an Anglo-Dutch multitude of disparate companies, yet there is a recognisable Unilever style. Attend, as I do, Unilever seminars and meet different nationalities from different companies and the theme survives the variation. 'Unileverness,' says Olins, 'is best summed up in the word "moderation", the quality of being reasonable.' Each Unilever company 'will behave predictably, in a way the rest of Unilever will understand.'[8] If you know the company from personal experience or observation, that word 'moderation' fits.

We form our perceptions quickly since we must make sense of our environment. If a company is consistent then the early impressions are obviously more likely to be correct and the subsequent communications we encounter work synergistically. On the other hand if the company's view of communications is not holistic, if the messages—in content and style—are inconsistent, then we are in danger of forming a first impression that is only partly 'true'. We may try to rationalise the dissonance between it and our next impression. The task becomes progressively harder the more conflicting impressions we receive.

You can prove this yourself—in retrospect. Here are the names of two UK companies. Pause for a moment and consider—what is your image of each?

Cadbury. Reckitt and Colman.

The first, I suggest, is much clearer than the second. Yet you have heard of both. They are both large and successful UK manufacturers. One, however, has a centripetal identity policy; the other's is centrifugal. Each succeeding impression of Cadbury probably confirms the previously assembled sub-totality of image. Each succeeding impression of Reckitt and Colman is more difficult to reconcile with the sub-totality. Reckitts Blue. Colmans Mustard. Dettol. Gales honey. Robinson's Barley Water. Colman's Casserole Mix. Steradent.

Now, none of this may matter. Reckitt and Colman rarely promote their corporate personality outside financial and corporate statements. My purpose in this little exercise was simply to prove a point: the cumulative effect of successive transmissions of similar identities projects a coherent image, whereas the cumulative effect of successive transmissions of dissimilar identities projects an incoherent image.

Yet incoherent images may result also from a company which uniformly brands its products. Ford in the US recently ran three separate corporate campaigns—simultaneously. Ford Motor Company, in the most corporate of the campaigns, used their first station wagon as a peg for a forward looking statement: 'There's a Ford in America's future'. The North American Automotive Operation wing of the company showed an assembly line with inspectors, and the line 'At Ford quality is Job No 1.' NAAO also featured Jackie Stewart talking from the shoulder above the baseline: 'Ford has it. *NOW*.' According to *Ad Age*'s Detroit correspondent, Jay McCormick:[9]

> Ford ad executives claim each of the campaigns appeal to a different target audience and that when those audiences overlap, the campaigns complement rather than clash with each other.

Each ad was the work of a different agency. The question surely is would one Ford agency, given all those assignments, have come up with three baselines? (Your prejudice is as good as mine.)

The triple campaign is justified with terms such as 'symbiosis' or a rather superficial media segmentation. 'Ford has it. *NOW*' is aimed at 'young, sophisticated car buyers'. 'Quality is Job No 1' is thought to appeal to 'just about everybody'. 'Ford Future' is directed at 'decision-makers, predominantly in Washington and New York'.

That is a very neat rationalisation prepared by the self-deluded for the consumption of the gullible. It has as much contact with the real world as 'visual manifestation' manuals have with life as it is lived. Corporate identities (which we pursue in Chapter 25) are often tangential to the company's *raison d'être*. The new neat logo and contemporary typeface, uniformly applied, serve a purpose in coordinating the look of the company and possibly raising the morale of the staff. But unless it is seen and experienced as an expression of corporate will and endeavour it is no more than a fresh coat of paint on a rickety building. It is not part of a new message. It is noise affecting the old one. Or, as Rodney Fitch puts it:

> The alternative to a new board of directors is not some new stationery and a logo.[10]

A corporate identity change can be seen as a soft option. It may be difficult to reach a decision—which face do we put on?—but that requires far less effort than self-analysis. What sort of company are we? What is our philosophy? How do we articulate it? And, ultimately, how can that be expressed in every form of communication?

The company which takes a corporate identity programme seriously is less likely to project conflicting images. For this type of company image is the *result* of a comprehensive intellectual exercise. The company which takes the soft option, on the other hand, is concerned only with cosmetic adjustment. As Daniel Boorstin[11] says:

> A corporation which decides to rebuild its image has decided less on a change of heart than on a change of face.

And the face it chooses is unlikely to resemble the face the public already knows or, worse still, match the character of the company either now or in the future. But even companies which take the operation seriously are victims of the future. Will their current identity (and subsequent image) be relevant when they make the next acquisition or move from consumer goods into capital goods? Every company must change. Each financial year chairmen reflect on this.

> Your company has passed the time when its position was wholly dependent on the sale of beers, wines, spirits and soft drinks, very important though these remain, and will continue to remain. The purchase of J. Lyons and Company in 1978 has proved to be . . . an outstandingly good investment . . . The Lyons brand names retain their strong appeal and respect among the public, and in all these circumstances—and not without considerable thought—your directors have decided to recommend to shareholders that the name of the company should be changed to Allied-Lyons . . . In our new title we are attempting to brand the old and the new—a highly appropriate exercise in view of present activities.[12]

Image or images? As Allied Breweries move from beer and pubs to groceries and so forth, the name is probably inadequate. The name Lyons is appended, not, it should be said, because this is a joint venture. Lyons has been bought. Allied own them and 'Allied' is the dominant personality in the joint name. The identity and perceived image have been slightly modified by the inclusion of the name Lyons in the name of the operating company. However at *brand* level, as the chairman already recognises, the name Lyons is a valuable property ('strong appeal and respect').

Not only must a company make sure that each of its communications transmits a message compatible with the corporate personality, and thus leaves impressions with the receiver which reinforce its perception of the core image, it needs also to consider how the company's identity and the brand's identity *relate*. The two identities have different jobs to do. There is no golden rule, no fixed line of demarcation. It varies from company to company and, within a company, changes over time. It may suit a company to use the corporate name as an endorsement or even a brand name. It may (as in the case of Allied Lyons) be more prudent to allow the brand a life of its own and communicate proprietorship only to shareholders and the financial community. It may choose to stamp everything it does and everything it sells with the same name (e.g. Philips), in which case every product ad is to some extent a corporate ad and vice versa. Nevertheless, though it may be extremely difficult to disentangle them, the two identities—corporate and brand—exist and their roles and relationships must be defined. The company which brands everything with its name gains in recognition and synergy what it loses in flexibility. It may project a consistent image but the price is eternal vigilance because the risks are large. Consequently a venture into a new area might have to be cancelled because the image is not compatible with the public's current perception. Or research is not undertaken, the venture goes ahead and the corporate image becomes blurred. Constant indiscriminate use of the company name can seriously weaken the strengths of the company's identity.

Not many years ago in Austria you could buy doughnuts marketed by Shell. Would *you* buy a Shell doughnut? (What would it taste like?) Should Shell *be* in the doughnut business? How could it happen? Quite easily. There are shops on service stations. Many of the motorist's necessities are bought in from suppliers and branded Shell. One motorist necessity is food. Today Shell to all intents and purposes is out of the doughnut business. It rarely becomes involved in subsidiary activities which don't fit its corporate personality. And then it uses a different brand name—e.g. Temana for pet care and air fresheners.

In this chapter we've looked at some of the problems of projecting a consistent image and tried to negotiate three minefields—different products (and the different needs of company and brand), different activities and different aspects of the company persona. There is another problem. Mines are also laid at sea.

22

Image or images?
(deuxième partie)

We were discussing an international campaign for a food product. The man with my job in the French agency said: 'I'm looking for a potato peel.' What he was actually looking for was 'appetite appeal'.

That took me a few seconds. Other problems of communication take longer, such as the classic unanswerable question about the ability of advertising campaigns to cross frontiers. In May 1963, at the International Advertising Association Conference in Stockholm, a gentleman from Reckitt & Colman was explaining its international advertising philosophy.

> We have an international brand called Harpic, a lavatory cleanser. In Germany we talk about efficiency. In France we use lavatorial jokes. In England we say it cleans round the bend. And as you know, in England, everybody is clean round the bend.

The Brits in the audience laughed loyally. What of the rest? There were headphones for simultaneous translation. My colleague, an Anglo-German, listened in. 'And as you know in England everybody is standing on the corner,' is what the translator said. So, in a way, the speaker was making his point. I'm ambivalent on this issue of international campaigns. My head says yes. My heart says no. And I haven't yet heard from my liver. The proponents declare that people are people—which is pretty incontrovertible. And quote Coca Cola.

I remember sitting in McCann, New York, one of 30 men of middle management from Interpublic's burgeoning empire, watching a presentation on the Coca Cola international campaign. The fast-talking presenter screened pictures of ten pretty girls, each a Coke model from a different country. We had to guess which was from which. None of us did very well. This pleased the presenter, but the prospect of lowest common denominator womanhood saddened a few Europeans.

Later in the seminar the same presenter showed us the Coca Cola Battle Plan, or how they brought the good news from Atlanta to Venezuela. We wrote notes. At the next table my French colleague, a wry aristocrat with excellent English and a gold pencil, attempted to keep up. After ten minutes he gave in, tore the yellow sheet from the pad, screwed it up, took out his

Dupont lighter and set fire to his inadequate notes. At that moment a fire engine screamed down Lexington Avenue. Régis turned to me, shrugged and said 'American efficiency'.

In those days—the early 1960s—uniform international advertising seemed not only possible, but simple to execute. Speed was annihilating distance. The jet age was beginning to neutralise national characteristics, iron out idiosyncracies. It was the high point of Coca-colonisation. Earnest but enthusiastic men sat at international headquarters with impressive global titles. Coordinating. Which meant making sure that the logo and consumer promise were identical throughout the world so that the Yugoslav peasant on his next visit to Colombia would feel at home.

These corporate executives manipulated the world like puppet masters, much of the time blithely unaware that the strings had been cut. Occasionally the international executive would pack his battle plan and a couple of drip-dry shirts and go see. He would settle little local problems and wing away. International fire fighter they called him back at base. But he knew he also had to be something of an arsonist if he was ever to justify a return trip.

Have we learned anything in the past twenty years? We're less naive, less arrogant and more pragmatic. We're less inclined to impose a uniform solution, whether we're talking about a single international brand or the bigger question of international advertising as a whole.

There are very few international brands which start from an international base. Peter Stuyvesant ('the international passport to smoking pleasure') was one. But deliberately setting out to become international by assuming an international origin is wrong-headed. Even the internationalist is born *somewhere*.

Brands are born somewhere. Companies are born somewhere. Unless the company makes a conscious effort to erase its birthmark, that fact will serve as a constituent of its identity and that of its brands (an inner ring on our wheel).

There are examples of rootless international brands. You and I may know that Philips is Dutch and Nestlé Swiss, but neither of us learned that from its consumer advertising. In fact it is each company's policy, at least in the UK, to adopt its host country's nationality. Philips sounds English. Nestlé becomes

Nestles, an English word, and a cosy one at that. So rather than have no roots they now have English roots.

Esso have for a half a century successfully promoted their UK presence with the result that 62% of the British public interviewed in 1979 thought the company British and only 25% thought it American owned. Shell, on the other hand, an Anglo-Dutch company, was perceived as being British by only 60%:

> . . . and 24% thought it to be American (a conception shared by over 90% of Americans).[1]

The similarity of these figures might suggest that Shell, because it is (half) British, felt it didn't need to try so hard as Esso, or that the other filter through which images are projected is having an effect, i.e. 'oil companies are all the same'. But Esso *operates* in this country. Its sign is everywhere and it contributes to the country's wealth from the North Sea. Talbot may be French owned but the name is English and the car is made here. A Fiat car is *not* made in the UK. 'Our biggest problem is that we are made in Italy' says Guliano Lonardi, Fiat (UK)'s managing director. 'All research always confirms that the country of origin is instrumental in creating the image stereotypes of a particular brand.'

The country of origin is part of the total image of a car. Volvo's image is shaped in part by the image of Swedish engineering: the safety of the car is consistent with our perception of a Swedish obsession with the state's concern for the welfare of the individual. Citroën's Frenchness is inevitably part of Citroën's identity—everywhere except, of course, in France where it is taken for granted. Abroad, the fact of its being French may not feature in the advertising but it *is* known and therefore forms part of the mosaic.

If a company wants to transmit a message uniformly in many countries, it must take into consideration that abroad that message will almost certainly be received together with information about its country of origin. Whether that added information is part of the message or is noise is a decision for the company.

Unless a company chooses to assimilate, its country of origin is part of its corporate reputation and part of its brand's identity. Consumers rush to judgement. They abhor vacuums. They need to pigeon-hole products and companies. Brands must belong. Companies must be 'fitted' in. And very often advertisers make use of country characteristics to support the brand, even to form its main message. The personality of the country becomes the promise. Air France is France in the air. Whatever France is famous for, is Air France.

> If you hear other airlines talk about their charm, their comfort, their friendliness, their good food, and their *savoir vivre*, one could assume there are only French airlines. Bon voyage! Your Air France. The Airline of the French People.

Lufthansa *is* German efficiency. IBM *is*, despite its UK campaign, the best of US business know-how. Perrier is 'eau là là'.

People buy international reputations. They buy international brands. They do *not* buy as stateless citizens of the world. International jet setters are constantly appealed to in, for example, airline magazines by international advertisers such as banks and hotels. But while the consumer seeks an international facility, he likes to believe that what he is getting from the Bombay branch of Barclays is a recognisably British Barclays service, from the Valetta Hilton a recognisably US Hilton service.

Star performers who succeed internationally do so, I maintain, not because they embrace internationalism but because they have a specific characteristic recognisably associated with their origins. In show business there *are* some international performers who seem to be stateless: they appear in night clubs, circuses, cabarets and are destined to wander the world like the Flying Dutchman. But unlike the Flying Dutchman their names aren't known and nor are their places of birth. But a *star* succeeds internationally because of, not despite, his or her national, even local, characteristics. Chevalier, Monroe, Wayne, Montand, Streisand belong to the world precisely because they are quintessentially and recognisably ethnic. Alec Guinness plays a hundred roles but remains English.

Surely Guinness is black and Irish?

International brands likewise are creations of their homelands. McDonalds, Coke, Levi's . . . are as American as apple pie (more than can be said for McDonald's apple pie). The received image abroad is inevitably US influenced and cannot be identical to that perceived by an American. Beefeater Gin is a London gin and is known wherever it's sold as the 'gin of England'. In the UK Gordon's might be so perceived and the locals might regard the emblem of the beefeater with less awe or interest than the foreign drinker, for whom it is a symbol of British tradition and a mark of quality.

But even without national costume, a brand or company originates from a specific location. A star is born somewhere. When you buy a Coke or a Big Mac you are also buying a piece of the country—part of the American way of life. Marlboro is international because it is American. Perrier because it's French. Johnnie Walker because it's—Scotch.

The company which operates internationally has to decide early on how much of its national characteristics it wants to transmit and if it needs to counteract those characteristics which it regards as noise. It must also decide how much latitude it can afford each operating company in projecting the identical image, how much local consideration should be allowed to modify that central image. An international communications strategy is simple to devise but difficult to keep. Denis Bradshaw of Whitbread, comments:[2]

> The main challenge is holding together the corporate image while maximising the local potential.

Different markets are at different stages of development. Brands likewise.

> If suddenly we were to enforce the company image it would upset the business at the local level. It is a fine balancing act, which must in the end retain sight of the international objectives.[3]

But which international objectives? Those of the brand or those of the company? The former affect the company if the company name is associated with it in the brand advertising. International, as domestic brand strategy can choose to impose company identification. A brand is a wholly artifical creation which—provided the company can hide its parentage—may be able to avoid transmitting national signals. *May*. But it's virtually impossible for the company unless it operates entirely through local franchises. And then it has somehow to ensure that the values of the brand are being maintained. So it produces a bible (the pattern book) to ensure just that. And having produced it for one country it uses it in others. The consistency-over-time which is sought from the individual country becomes consistency-across-borders from the various operating companies. Before you know it a set of rules has replaced the guidelines and the brand is not merely being projected in a similar way throughout the world in order to leave customers with a reasonably consistent image, but the *identical advertising material* is being used.

International campaigns are tidy; save advertisers time and production costs; massage head office egos; ensure, at least, that advertising which worked in one place will be used in another place instead of untried local advertising (particularly in less sophisticated countries). And today the impact of satellite and cable is annihilating distance and difference even more effectively, generating a desire—at least from those who seek to benefit such as international agencies and international media—for more and more international brands promoted on identical platforms and wearing identical clothes.

What effect this will have on the image of the companies who manufacture those international brands is difficult to say. There would seem to be a danger of homogeneity—mega-corporations brushed with the same tar. All of them in the mega-corporation industry. It may be more difficult to determine a distinctive positioning and project a clear image—and therefore all the more important. As a senior official at the EEC Commission said in 1973:[4]

> Most people know so little about ITT in Europe except that you are so big and powerful, that it is hardly surprising you are mistrusted. If the facts were known perhaps people would feel differently about you.

Non-communication is negative communication. We may see a future of identical brands communicating internationally identical messages in identical forms; and, simultaneously, identical companies consciously communicating hardly at all and projecting indistinguishable images.

Then again we may not. International brands demand conformity. This is easier with services such as airlines or banks, and with big budget brands which portray a national 'star quality' (e.g. Marlboro, Coke, Schweppes). However, the pace of conformity will slow, may even be reversed, despite the blandishments of the pundits and professional communicators and the problems of coordination which different markets and campaigns may bring. Coordination *is* possible despite complexity. Absolute uniformity is not the only way to guarantee a consistent image though it may serve the company as evidence of a consistent *identity*. If a company's mission is 'to make a busy housewife a better cook without taking up too much of her time', then the dialogue between the company and the housewife in country *A* may vary considerably from that in country *B* due to cultural differences (e.g. attitudes to cooking, to working wives, types of meal). Europe is regarded by some as a single market. Yet a recent analysis by US agency Needham Harper & Steers:

> ' . . . showed that not one of the 50 most heavily advertised brands in Britain is marketed throughout Europe with the same name packaging and advertising, because local tastes (and regulations) differ'.[5]

Will cable change all that? I doubt it. Nova will still be a lousy name for a car in Spain where it means 'no go'. British will still mean good quality breakfast items (bacon, tea and marmalade) but not a good deal else culinary to the French. The famous Comfort demonstration of the fluffed up sweater taking up more room in the drawer will still be a loser in Hong Kong where there's a premium on space. Green labels on tea packets will still mean unripe tea to one African tribe and freshness to another.[6]

One dominant societal trend in Europe is individualism. Diversity and complexity will rule for a little while yet. Advertising works best when the creative person can empathise with the consumer. He is more likely to touch human emotions if he can feel as his audience feels and demonstrate that feeling. Advertising has to be human and that means it has to be particular. It is difficult if not impossible to be particular without being national or—better still—local. Whilst advertisers pay more respect to customers than to products, then diversity rather than conformity will be the rule.

A company when it communicates on its own behalf or that of its brands, must allow for diversity. To implement a package solution may fool a company into believing that its image is identical universally whereas local adjustment—or even a major change—to the message content may be necessary. Not, it should be added, to change the image but to preserve it. Unilever trains its executives, both international and national, to appreciate international objectives whilst at the same time using their intimate knowledge of the local marketing and commercial culture to ensure that those objectives are not inhibiting the achievement of national goals. To Procter and Gamble this may smack of compromise. Colgate might say: 'If it works here it'll work there'. For them and others like them satellite broadcasting is the crowning of all their beliefs. At a satellite broadcasting seminar a (moderate) Unilever spokesman said:[7]

> We must provide the right product for the Belgian housewife, even if her French and Dutch cousins want a variation. Our starting point is the target consumer and not a search for a possible common denominator which will enable us to use pan European media.

We talk blithely of an age of change (as if preceding ages weren't), but nobody survives change without being flexible. The question for corporate 'image makers' is how far flexibility can go without changing the central image beyond recognition.

It depends of course on what business the company is in and the strength of that central image. Said Mark Twain of Thomas Cook:[8]

> He has made travel easy and a pleasure. He will sell you a ticket to any place on the globe, or all the places and give you all the time you need and much more besides . . . Cook is your banker everywhere and his establishment your shelter when you get caught in the rain.

In a group discussion in the UK, a lower middle class lady said she would love to go on a Thomas Cook holiday but she was afraid she would be the only one there without a crocodile handbag.

In its UK base Thomas Cook operates in a heavily regulated environment and competes by means of quiet added values. However, in the deregulated travel world of the US Thomas Cook is seen as a sharp buyer, passing on savings to the consumer in the shape of competitively priced tickets. Thomas Cook is flexible but it is quite recognisably the same gentleman. The lady would recognise the US office—and so would Mark Twain.

None of these pieces is the entire mosaic. An image is not a crystal. It is a synthesis—the net result of a mass of impressions. Shell regularly survey impressions around the world. Despite variations according to the country, class of market or consumer segments, basic common Shell image denominators do exist (e.g. 'technically advanced', 'quality products', 'large', 'old-established').

It is conceivable that one company can speak to several publics on several different subjects and retain a core image even though those publics' needs are different. The new recruit needs to realise that the company will still be in business in thirty years time. The security analyst needs to know that the company will perform well in the immediate future. The customer needs to experience the product today. The MP in the host country needs to sense that the company is a good citizen.

> Compromises will generally be necessary but the best possible compromises can only be made if we start with a thorough understanding of the needs of each market and each target group.[9]

Image X will not be totally relevant for all four publics. And an image entirely suitable for one will probably be wrong for another. But there should be common elements. If we regard the core image as X then the four images are *X1, X2, X3* and *X4*.

The company of course shouldn't think first of its image but of its personality (or philosophy) and how that is expressed. Is it of a piece? Are the company's many activities consistent with it—and with each other? Is the physical identity in line? And the behavioural identity? Is the style of the communication appropriate? Making sure all are answered in the affirmative is not terribly difficult. Variations in message content, in communication purpose, in audience can then be accommodated and the core image will remain intact.

Images overlapping a central image . . . the security analyst recognising the brand as a product of the company he knows from the annual report . . . the customer with a complaint receiving the sort of attention from the sort of people the television commercial has led her to expect . . . the customer in Singapore recognising the ad in *Time* and the bank in Orchard Road as manifestations of the same personality.

23

Media relations

Editorial and advertising occupy the media, the one by right the other under sufferance. The advertiser pays for the privilege to rub shoulders with world leaders, events of genuine importance and celebrity doings. He must stay in his allotted space—a tenant of a stately home condemned to house arrest in the lodge. He is allowed out from time to time when the proprietor or one of his servants considers he has done something that merits public attention. Occasionally he escapes, disguised as 'advertorial', though usually he has to pay for his freedom: he has help on the inside from one of the servants whose features are also disguised. But most of the time he peers out at the surrounding activity somewhat resentful that the rent he is paying for the accommodation is helping to maintain the house and the grounds.

If editorial and advertising are two sides of the same coin then, says the journalist, both sides can't land face up simultaneously. The media, all in all, are successful at keeping them in their place. The cases of advertisers influencing editorial are rare. As are the cases of the media 'arranging' editorial to attract advertising. The twilight zone of the 'special feature' is today seen for what it is—a sponsored section of the newspaper. And its overuse (double glazing, pipe smoking, time sharing) debases an already devalued currency.

The integrity of the media is still cherished in the UK and the US. The rule is the stronger for the occasional exception. One cynical American writer sees editorial as a deep sea diver. 'You don't pick a fight with the man at the other end of the air hose.'[1] Thomas Garbett admits that:

> The problem sometimes exists at the upper levels, particularly in small operations when an economic pinch is being felt. But virtually all publishers recognise that they are on a downward spiral when their editorial content goes downhill with their readers and that selling out the integrity of their editors is probably the fastest way down.[2]

A company can pay to appear in the media—in an advertisement—or can do something newsworthy and, if necessary, bring that event to the media's attention. If the company is to maintain a consistency between advertising and editorial with the aim of projecting a cohesive image—which is one of the themes of this book—the task of keeping the editorial in line may totally frustrate the company with unfortunate results.

Whereas a company can within reason do what it likes in its own channel (advertisement), it is a guest in the editorial. Hoping to get his story across in his way with his emphases and in his language, our novice company spokesman will discover that his view of news and human nature is very different from that of his media contact and/or the editor.

The company may be tempted to avoid all future contact—even when it has news to convey. It may revert to complaining in a letter to the editor (meant for publication), or taking an advertisement with the specific purpose of 'putting the record straight'. Taking an ad is fine. 'Putting the record straight' will merely draw attention to the fact that the paper has, right or wrong, an opposed view on the issue. The ad serves to publicise the argument rather than the issue.

Most companies are conscious that unless a company gets coverage in the press or on radio or television (or at least its trade press), then it may be seen not to exist or to be in trouble. 'How are you doing? I haven't seen you in the papers lately.' The implication is that the company has something to hide. No news is bad news. Ironically, the reverse is the case with the journalist. If the company has something to hide that *is* news. Good news is no news. Which is exactly the reason the company needs to use advertisements. As Ann Burdus says:[3]

> The media currently appear to be a divisive force in society. This is not their fault: it is their nature. They deal with news and they deal with differences. They deal with problems and they deal with disagreements.

The qualities companies normally parade in their corporate advertisements—innovation, social responsibility, size, leadership, superior management, etc.—don't sell papers. What sells papers is when somebody proclaiming all those virtues is found in a love nest in Cricklewood.

> The evil that men do lives on the front pages of greedy newspapers, but the good is oft interred apathetically inside.[4]

News is incongruity. It was incongruous for man to fly. Now it is incongruous for an airliner to land in the sea. It is incongruous for a mother to have sextuplets, for sex to be paid for in Streatham—and with Luncheon Vouchers! And if your job is to maintain congruity of advertising and editorial, you may well prefer to ignore the latter altogether. The media's view of what constitutes news is different from your own. 'News,' said Lord Northcliffe, 'is what someone somewhere does not want to see printed; all else is publicity.'[5] Furthermore, the media's list of subjects and people it regards as news*worthy* may well differ from the company's. Business is not a subject *per se* for the popular press. Media's job requires them to be selective. They have no mandate to educate the public on business matters (or any matters come to that). They report events. Their selectivity reveals a bias. The Royal Commission on the Press found that only 14% of people quoted or mentioned in press stories were managers or employers' associations' officials. In contrast 41% were union officials. Is it any wonder that companies are tempted to opt out of relating with the media? They could agree perhaps with the late Nicholas Tomalin's assertion:[6]

> The only qualities essential for real success in journalism are ratlike cunning, a plausible manner and a little literary ability.

Squire Barraclough, who knows media relations from both sides of the divide is convinced that some companies set up PR departments in order *not* to have any relations with the media. But, for the umpteenth time, non-communication is negative communication. So the company is apparently caught in the trap: speak and be ignored or misreported; remain silent and be suspected of covering up.

Journalists are particularly sensitive to readers' interests. Items in a company press release are unlikely to interest more than a small minority of their general interest readers.

But business must speak up—corporately and individually. It has a duty to communicate. Silence breeds those very attitudes which ignorance and bad reporting generate. A company needs to communicate continuously if only to provide background preparatory to real news and to familiarise the media with the matters which concern it. Companies must not assume that linage is all. Continuous dialogue with the media may be 'working' even if no news stories appear. Attitudes towards the company and towards business may be changing, reaction to a future event may be more favourable because better understood. Comments Tim Traverse-Healy:[7]

> We should be much more concerned that a commentator understands the background of an issue than that he or she should make use of the form of words that we send them.

If a company is forced to use the advertising columns to put its case, so be it. But shouldn't it send advance proofs of those advertisements to the many journalists who may have refused to regard the item as news or the company as newsworthy? David Kelley, writing in the *Harvard Business Review*[8] compares economic and intellectual freedom:

> Journalists defend the freedom of the press in part by arguing that competition among ideas helps ensure that truth prevails over error—just as business argues that competition in the marketplace tends to ensure that good products and honest practices predominate. The arguments are exactly parallel.

But companies are notoriously reluctant to take advantage of their freedom with the result that they confirm the media's prejudices. And the media are notoriously selective, perversely idiosyncratic in their choice of angle, and so confirm the company's prejudices.

How then is CC, the communications director of our imaginary company, to relate to the media? The gamekeeper must turn poacher. If an advertising writer can communicate best by empathising with the target audience, then the communications director can communicate more effectively by putting himself in the journalist's chair. Indeed, some techniques of advertising can be of use here. The advertising writer begins by inventing a 'target response'. What does he want the reader or viewer to think or feel or believe as a result of this message? Clearly the response should be congruent with the company philosophy, should help reinforce the perception of the corporate image. This exercise concentrates the mind. It helps to make the interview and/or press conference and/or press release *single-minded.* Advertising people know that rarely is all of their copy read. They organise their material to ensure that the main ingredients come across quickly and succinctly but not totally. The journalist, like the consumer, will want to read more.

Though the company may need to provide more material than can be included in the story, background should be kept in its place. The story should be arranged the way a journalist arranges it. The most important points in the first paragraph, the second most important in the second and so on. Journalists' copy gets edited and the later paragraphs may go but not at the expense of the story. Similarly the press release may not be completely utilised (or indeed read), but the key issues will be assimilated.

The journalist will want help but not want to have his job done for him. CC may think like a journalist but he must not write like or for him. He may envisage the ideal headline but he dare not write it. Better to make the ingredients of the headline accessible and prominent. Tact, subtlety, restraint and a desire for the journalist to express himself within the parameters set for him are all necessary. The success of the exercise will be measured not by the media's parroting of CC's phrase but by the media's understanding and communication of the company's message.

The company must consider which 'angle' it would like to see and which it would hate, and endeavour to write the story to avoid the latter. It must act the devil's advocate, see what happens when any of the sentences are taken out of context and make sure, as far as possible, that such deliberate or accidental editing will not turn the story on its head.

CC knows that *people* make news. Human interest is the media's staple fare. Stories should be told in personal terms. The construction of a new hospital means fewer delays for patients, more jobs for builders, better facilities for hard-working nurses, etc. By understanding the journalist and the nature of the job CC is more likely to secure a story. By being single-minded—i.e. tying in all the events to one central theme and relating that theme to the corporate philosophy—he is more likely to ensure a congruity between advertising and editorial.

It is obviously a delicate operation. CC should delegate it only to those who understand the rules. The channel may be narrow but it will always remain open. Journalists' questions should be answered as frankly as possible. If a journalist asks for further information to a press release the spokesperson should try to answer fully and immediately. If necessary he will promise to ring back soon—and do so. Above all, he should try to avoid 'no comment': it can sound like a denial. And he won't say too much. The more he says the more danger of being quoted out of context. He puts what he wants to say in writing and keeps a copy. He doesn't put in writing what he doesn't want quoted.

The press release has to convey news and be a practical tool for the journalist. A thinly disguised and pre-digested commercial will be ignored and its embargo totally respected (news will not be released before the prescribed time or indeed at any time thereafter).

British journalists respect the tradition of speaking off the record, to provide 'background' without attribution. This trust is rarely abused. But it takes time—for relationships to develop and for trust to be built up. In broadcast media relationships are rarely long enough. The pace of the medium and the nature of the dialogue are quite different. The latter often happens live—with minimal warning or preparation. It is very difficult for a spokesperson to remember the argument let alone the corporate philosophy. The need for single-mindedness is even more imperative in the broadcast media. Everything should relate to a central point and the point should be reiterated. Politicians are often criticised for not answering the interviewer's question. They are not necessarily being devious. Often the question is a superficial attempt to sum up, to put the subject matter into black and white terms. Hence the politician, when forced to agree with a statement, resorts to: 'You said that. I didn't.'

CC knows where he is in the advertising channel. He is in charge. The message leaves him in one form and appears in the media more or less intact. He has probably researched it beforehand to ensure it's being heard the way he wants it heard. No such reassurance, however, in the world of editorial. The communicator has no power over the form or style or length or correctness or even the appearance of the message.

But if CC is a genuine communicator, then all his training and knowledge of communication theory will stand him in good stead. The business of media relations is not the despatch of cold releases but the constant dialogue of company spokesperson and journalist.

Who says what to whom along which channel and with what effect.[9]

The good communicator knows the importance of using the correct code, of avoiding noise, of feedback, of identifying and empathising with the respondent. Whether truly face-to-face with a journalist or sending a release or giving an interview on television, the communicator needs to observe the six cardinal rules of Dale Carnegie.[10]

1 Become genuinely interested in other people.
2 Smile.
3 Remember that a man's name is to him the sweetest and most important sound in any language.
4 Be a good listener. Encourage others to talk about themselves.
5 Talk in terms of the other man's interests.
6 Make the other person feel important—and do it sincerely.

Carnegie formalised these not as communication rules but as 'six ways to make people like you'. Nevertheless, being liked makes communication easier. (And Carnegie himself was not bad at communicating through the media.) Nor did Carnegie have impersonal press releases in mind or advertisements or correspondence. But the rules are equally valid. Person-to-person is the model, the touchstone, the criterion for all communication.

Harry O'Neill, executive vice-president of Opinion Research Corporation, interviewed a sample of US financial business editors. They offered the following suggestions for business to improve its relations with the media.[11]

Be more candid in your dealings with the media
Make appropriate, authoritative spokesmen available
Be less antagonistic or defensive in regard to the media
Recognise the corporation's responsibilities to the public and the public's right to know
Be more accessible, more responsive to inquiries
Provide more complete, detailed information
Be willing to give the bad news as well as the good news
Begin to share information early, as it develops; avoid delay
Make better use of public-relations professionals and staff those departments with better qualified and trained personnel
Provide more personal contacts with the news media

24

Integration

Ask the management of the average UK company two questions:
1 'What is your corporate philosophy?'
2 'Who is responsible for coordinating your communications?'

What sort of response do you think you'll get? From personal observation Bob Worcester believes that the job of coordinating *all* communication within any of the top 50 UK companies is too daunting. Thus, corporate and product communication are kept apart. However, he estimates that 38 of the top 50 have one person (or two) in charge of coordinating corporate communications and that *all* of them have a corporate philosophy.

Communication in a company is uncoordinated when vested interests hold on to part of the communication programme. Corporate advertising is regarded as the most important means of communicating about the *company* (as opposed to its products or services). The most visible certainly, the most important possibly, but the only form by no means. It is inextricably related to all other forms of corporate communication (product advertising, design, packaging, corporate identity, etc.) and unless that relationship is recognised, much of the corporate advertising endeavour is wasted. Many companies seem to feel that corporate advertising by itself will project the company's image ignoring the rest of the elements which constitute the synthesis, either because they are seen as unimportant or because the luminosity of the ad campaign will divert attention from them. But a corporate image is the net result of a mass of impressions created not simply by words and graphics but by *deeds*. Corporate advertising can work at full power only if it truly reflects those deeds: and the words and graphics are an expression of the corporate philosophy. Otherwise a corporate ad is all tip and no iceberg.

The projecting of a company's image is not the exclusive responsibility of the PR or advertising people. As we have seen, everyone who comes into contact, directly or indirectly, with any of a company's publics is contributing pieces to the mosaic. Whether or not the pieces form a comprehensible total picture depends upon the degree to which the company communications are coordinated.

Is there a corporate philosophy? Has it been articulated? Is there a succinct definition of company purpose—a 'mission'? Has that message been communicated to each member of the company who communicates with the public? Have the company's suppliers and communications advisers been told? More specifically have the company's salesforce been adequately briefed about the relationship between the company's products and the company's 'mission'?

Is somebody, if not coordinating, at least *aware* of all the interfaces between the company and its publics and the impression each of these is creating? Are the chairman's speech writer, the pack designer, the product advertising creative group, the editor of the company newspaper, the sales promotions manager, the recruitment director, the press officer and the junior who looks after the notice board on the first floor conceivably in tune? Who is the conductor? And who is orchestrating?

It is a problem that has concerned commentators on both sides of the Atlantic. Yet the solution is clear. And though the implementation may cause difficulties, they are insignificant compared with the importance of the subject.

> In this most crucial of all areas of communication no one is minding the store fulltime. There is no one division responsible for representing the corporation to its key audiences.

So writes designer Walter Margulies.[1] The advertising manager, the PR director, the consultant—none of the usual communications people can make the vital decision on which corporate communications are based. Only the chief executive, aided by his board of management, can determine the philosophy. Wally Olins, writing more specifically on the subject of corporate *identity*, detects the same problem area. Who's in charge?

> It cuts across traditionally separate activities, it implies a different and in some senses a contradictory sense of standards from that normally applied in organisations, it implies taking a wider range of factors into acount . . . modern management systems have not allowed for this discipline within the organisation's structure. There is no corporate identity manager or design manager to liaise, for example, with a product and brand manager to see that the products the company produces accurately reflect the style of the company; to liaise with a personnel executive about the way in which the style of the organisation emerges in recruitment literature, etc.[2]

The essential functions of the chief executive (according to Chester Barnard, an ex-president of New Jersey Bell and early management writer) are:[3]

> First, to provide the system of communications; second, to promote the securing of essential efforts; and third, to formulate and define purpose.

The chairman of the board of Eaton Corporation said:[4]

> A chief executive can no more delegate the responsibility for communication than he can for earnings per share.

The control of corporate communications must be the responsibility of the chief executive. Margulies is hopeful. He believes that contemporary chief executives are more aware of the need for, and techniques of communications, of:

> . . . a growing recognition that marketing the corporation through a systemised yet flexible corporate communications plan is as much a function of business (and management) as producing and selling the product or service.[5]

Whether or not the chief executive is the original founder of the company (in which case the company's image is largely his own), he should have the sharpest idea of what the company is about and what it should be communicating—*at all levels*. Unfortunately, his influence becomes muted by the time committees, planners and interpreters have got in on the act. The lines of communication are normally very long. Unless a Michael Edwardes is in charge. He is clear about the role of communications and the need to coordinate:[6]

> The first step was to bring to bear on internal communications, the skills which the company possessed through its external communications and public affairs people. The responsibilities for communicating both inside and outside the company were brought together. This had the immediate effect of shortening the internal communication chain, and to elevate its status and importance in the company structure.

Another way to shorten lines of communication is to have a fire at the factory. Crisis management (see Chapter 33) demands instant access. Similarly, when a company becomes involved in controversy advertising (e.g. putting its view on a vital contemporary issue) the decision is nearly always that of the boss. We have discussed the need to communicate in good times as well as bad. Internal lines of communications should be as short when companies are being proactive as they are when they are being reactive.

Designers of corporate identities demand a close working relationship with their clients—and at the highest level. Olins wants the relationship to be personal and enduring. The designer lives with the client, observes him at work, discusses the company's beliefs, distils its spirit. Terence Conran was asked to design a new interior for an advertising agency where I was creative director. Our first meeting had nothing to do with square feet, windows or number of personnel. Instead he wanted to know my philosophy of running a creative department.

The leader of the company must be the leading communicator—and vice versa. Journalists, when they contact a company on an important story, seek out the *decision-maker*. Unfortunately few UK companies prepare the soil in which decision-makers can flourish. One executive in a big multinational told me *à propos* an advertising research programme: 'We're awfully good at making certain. We're not so good at making decisions.' Committees replace the individualistic articulate leader. Committees by definition aren't individualistic and a glance at a committee report reveals how articulate they are.

Some chief executives seem too busy making decisions to communicate them.

He doesn't even tell me whether he wants tea or coffee...

Which of course is nonsense—what are decisions for? Communications need to be integrated into the structure and the operating procedures of the company. Indeed, Margulies believes that:[7]

> In certain instances, the corporate communications effort may even transcend in immediate importance the company's other ongoing marketing activities.

If the chief executive cannot be personally involved in corporate communications he must nevertheless retain overall responsibility. To whom does he delegate? Almost certainly a position will have to be created—adjacent, metaphorically, to the chief executive—even though the appointment may be made from within. The previous training and current activity will not be as important as his or her attitude—and proven ability to communicate.

The chief executive of Sperry in US, Paul Lyet, has a vice president for communications who reports directly to him:[8]

> If it's his job to communicate he can't be effective unless he's tuned in . . . For example, when we have a financial statement, I see to it that he gets a copy of whatever I see . . . He's in my office at least as much as any other executive . . . I believe in the saturation theory. He knows my thoughts about acquisitions, about plant closings. He knows what the board is thinking about . . . just think how much more effective he is because he knows those things . . . this makes me more effective in this communication job that *I* have to do.

Kirby, the chairman of Westinghouse, at another *Fortune* Seminar in 1977 delineated a character study of the person in charge of communications. It deserves quoting in full.[9]

> I need more than just someone who can make a great media buy or create a zingy commercial or write a great speech or plant a favourable story in the hometown newspaper.

I need someone who is acutely aware of the crosscurrents of public opinion—financial publics, customer publics, stockholder publics, employee publics, government publics and general publics—and what problems or opportunities they may present to me.

I need someone with a clear understanding not just of the techniques of communicating, but of the overriding issues that I have to live with every day—nuclear acceptance, capital formation, job creation, tax structures, technological advances, doing business as a m.n.c. and on and on.

I need the kind of communications counsel that takes into account not only the short-range objectives but the longer-range strategies that will make or break my company in the future.

I need the wide-vision thinkers who understand the corporation, the nation, society—and how they can all work together.

In 1972 a survey of the hundred leading US corporate advertisers conducted by the *Public Relations Journal* revealed that the concept for corporate advertising programmes originated with top management 15.7% of the time; in 1977, 22.9% of the time.

Others will need to be involved before the communications are effected. For example, in the case of corporate identity, those with a more 'scientific' or financial frame of mind (who may regard the exercise as mere window dressing), will need to take part early in discussions on corporate philosophy so that the identity can be seen as a natural outcome, obeying some inner logic. In the case of corporate advertising, the views of the product advertising people must be sought in order to harmonise the effort.

Though an associate can coordinate policy throughout the company's communicating sectors (advertising, sales promotion, packaging, financial relations, press relations, product planning, design and internal affairs), the boss must be responsible for setting that policy, masterminding the overall corporate communications strategy and overseeing the coordination of all the disciplines involved. (And many US corporate bosses actually get involved in writing corporate ads, e.g. United Technologies, Mobil, TRW, Sperry.)

The mere act of coordination may reveal dichotomies between corporate and product advertising. Company management could have assumed that corporate endorsement of individual brands was stronger than it is. Alternatively, the corporate endorsement may be very strong but the brand values being communicated may be inimical to the corporate values adumbrated in the company philosophy.

The closer the coordination the greater the synergy. Whereas an isolated and intermittent corporate campaign—inspired perhaps by a desire to solve a particular 'image' problem—can present an inconsistent picture of the company. Corporate advertising *per se* is not a tactical weapon. Companies may have to react tactically (e.g. to answer criticism or respond to a crisis), but even then they should be able to draw upon their previous corporate communication as a fund of goodwill. Tactical ads—what Margulies calls[10] 'sporadic, from-the-hip advertising'—do not contribute much to that good-will. A few charts, a quotation from the chairman's statement as the headline and a paragraph of accountant's copy over the corporate logo, all assembled by a committee, does not constitute the basis of a corporate communications programme. For that is, after all, what each corporate ad should represent. What is the point of coordinating all the communications activity if the corporate ad is always tactical and never strategic?

Corporate advertising needs to be both strategic and continuous. In the US, where corporate advertising represents a far greater proportion of the total ad-spend, companies frequently change their campaigns. One commentator[11] has remarked:

> If companies changed their corporate strategies as often as they changed their corporate advertising, they'd be knee-deep in confusion.

The corporate ad being a reflection of the corporate philosophy will be answering *the basic questions* about the company—its nature, identity, capability, goals. These are all strategic questions. Only in the manner in which it is *used*—e.g. how it complements the product advertising or financial communication—can it be called tactical.

David Ogilvy has decreed that 'every advertisement is an investment in the image of the brand'.[12] Likewise, every item of communication is an investment in the image of the company—provided the communications activities are integrated.

Integration is of two (related) sorts. The activities are harmonised and/or the central theme is reinforced. For example, IBM (whose theme integration is self-evident), use their press advertisements also to invite prospects to attend a seminar and a demonstration. ICI are very clear about their identity. Their management knows what it is doing. Their corporate ad themes last several years ('Pathfinders', 'Ideas in Action'), and truly reflect what they are about in various areas of endeavour. Their corporate advertising is not tactical. It is not being used to correct a misconception. They have a clear corporate identity. It endorses a vast range of products. Their chief executive is a communicator. ICI will move from its 'monolithic Millbank headquarters' because

> . . . it gives out the wrong messages. We are supposed to be a lean and hungry company. This (referring to the walnut panelling in his office) creates the impression of a company which is mighty, powerful and unchanging: in other words a British institution. Any company that thinks it is a British institution is on the way out.[13]

Dunlop ran its corporate advertising campaign in tandem with its product advertising and claimed that each helped the other in terms of impact and awareness. Mobil's corporate identity programme, Olins maintains, is a conscious part of its philosophy:[14]

> Mobil wants to tell us that it is a useful, effective organisation, providing wealth and generally making the world a better place to be in.

Mobil subsidizes printed guides to the Victoria and Albert museum. Xerox in the US sponsors education programmes on television but it addresses other communities in ways which generate less publicity but which echo their concern:

> . . . training programmes for inner-city minorities, financial aid to higher-education and cultural pursuits and the participation of corporate executives in community affairs and public activities.[15]

Financial, like corporate advertisements, can be coordinated with other communications activities to draw attention to corporate or product developments or to generate enquiries for information on the company. Corporate ads and product ads are read by the same people presumably playing different roles. The potential investor reading the *Financial Times* might be an industrial purchasing officer. Are the two ads compatible? Is there a 'core' image? And when he becomes an investor does the annual report reinforce this image or could the presentation of the facts and figures have originated from any of a number of companies? Does the mailing include examples of the product advertising or the employee report?

When the annual report is sent to journalists is it merchandised? Does the release highlight salient points? Does the design of the report itself communicate? When AGB, Europe's largest research company, diversified into publishing, computer software and conferences, we were asked to design their annual report. We asked the chief executive, Bernard Audley, what target response he was seeking. By way of answer he told us that the dominance of their research business overshadowed their three other activities. Accordingly, on the cover of the report we used a four-square motif which we followed through on the inside pages, using the key graphics as identification marks.

The report won the *Observer* Chivas Regal award for the month of publication. The whisky was welcome. Even more welcome was the paper's review of AGB's achievements which began by saying that *all four divisions* of AGB had had a very good year.

If it's important that investors should be acquainted with the company's communications, how much more important is it that the staff should have advance warning of what is about to happen. But how often are employees shown their company's television commercials ahead of their neighbours?

Novo is a perfect example of the rule that a company which communicates well internally does so externally. *Novo Post*, its house journal, is professionally produced using staff personnel. It appears regularly each month and gives each of Novo's 4,000 domestic and international employees a (nearly simultaneous) update on major developments—research, production, financial and structural. Staff association meetings are covered. Personal stories are few but important. The company's philosophy statement was first published in *Novo Post*.

Novo's annual report, product packaging, booklets to the trade, press kits (releases and background information), advertisements and internal induction books clearly originate from the same company. This is not a matter simply of an imposed house style but of a working philosophy articulated, communicated and universally understood. The building is equally of a piece. It was recently extended. The chief executive, Mads Øvlisen, spent many hours with a leading Danish architect:

> The physical surroundings are so important to the image we create. Novo is in health care and biotechnology. We can't be seen as elaborate and conspicuous. Nevertheless people work here and too clinical a look would be inhuman and unfriendly.

He describes the design as 'clean, straight lines and surprises'. He was anxious to break up the rigidity of some of the design, insisting on a discreet pattern on a carpet here, on softening a corner of a ceiling there, on heating the first-floor bridge which joins the two buildings and carpeting it so that people would be encouraged to stop and talk to each other.

The building has an auditorium. How should it look? Most of their key staff have an academic background. But Novo is a business and the last thing Øvlisen wanted to remind them of was a lecture room. Novo is a Danish company. 'The auditorium mustn't look like New York City.' There would be no decoration. The colours would be Novo's colours. Apart from that, 'the room would be its own decoration'.

The security analyst presented to in Wall Street by Novo's financial director Kåre Dullum with an accompanying audio visual show would find the information and the slides in perfect accord. And a visit to the head office would reinforce that image. This unity does not arise by chance or from the obsessive vision of one man. Øvlisen has not been chief executive long. Novo's reputation for coordinated communications and corporate identity pre-dates him by three decades. The clue is in the organisation chart which at Novo is regarded more as a management tool than as a blessed icon. Communication is Øvlisen's overall responsibility and also the concern of corporate management, the board of five who run the company. Internal communications are a constant item on their agenda. Novo illustrates Roger Falk's dictum:[16]

> Minimum interference but maximum communication might be said to summarise what a central management should work for.

At a *Fortune* seminar, Hugh Redhead spoke on the sins of corporate advertising. His fifth sin dealt with:[17]

> . . . the failure to amplify the corporate advertising with all of the other
> necessary corporate activities to build a results-producing programme.

He devised a checklist in the form of questions. For example, shareholder
meetings. Are they well planned? Are the questions anticipated? Ditto for
meetings with the investment community. Are they frequent? Do the
speakers rehearse? Are the visuals good? Do your top people participate?

How about your annual reports and quarterly earnings statements? Are
they inviting to read? Are the disclosures and explanations absolutely
believable? Is the public relations effort tightly geared to corporate objectives?
Are the public relations one-sided, or is there a free two-way flow of
information and questions? Are the employees geared in? Ditto for distributors, dealers, and franchises. They all work for you: they should be aboard.
Are the boards of directors used as a working communication tool?[18] Novo
would score alpha on all of that.

What this chapter has been about—indeed what this book is about—is what
Kotler has chosen to call 'organisation marketing'. He defines it as:[19]

> Those activities undertaken to create, maintain or alter attitudes and/or
> behaviour of target audiences towards particular organisations.

As Kotler points out, 'organisation marketing' has traditionally been the
province of the public relations department:[20]

> It can be argued that public relations is essentially marketing management
> shifted from the product/service to an organisation. Many of the same skills
> are needed: knowledge of audience needs, desires and psychology: skill at
> communication; capability to design and execute programmes aimed at
> influence.

My own term for this overall function is communication management, since I
believe the person in charge of coordination needs to be able to implement
product communication into the overall plan. Otherwise, I endorse Kotler's
definition.

The only overall communications I'm aware of are the company logos on the workforce's protective clothing

Kotler noted at the time a move towards greater coordination. He referred to an appointment at General Electric of a vice president of marketing and public affairs:[21]

> . . . who will be responsible for all corporate activities in advertising, public affairs and public relations. He will also handle corporate marketing, including research and personnel development.

Sperry, whose vice president for communications we learned about earlier, make communications part of every manager's job and write it into the job description. One American journalist noted that:[22]

> The growing trend is not only to see the corporate advertising as part of the total marketing strategy but also, to some degree, to infuse all the company's communications with the theme of the corporate message. This is leading the corporate PR executive, more and more becoming known as the director of communications, public affairs or similar wide-ranging titles, into greater responsibility in the total marketing picture.

Whether marketing is taken over by corporate affairs, or corporate affairs subsumes marketing, or advertising and PR merge in fact matters less than that communications are regarded holistically by someone close to the chief executive and that the chief executive has supreme responsibility.

American companies take corporate communications seriously. That last observation on the changing role of the communication director in the US was written a decade ago. Meanwhile, Bob Worcester[23] surveys 100 large UK companies and discovers that a third of the people questioned don't know who their spokesperson is.

25

Corporate identity — reason or razzmatazz?

At our cocktail party, Anthony's personality was conveyed by the physical and behavioural cues which he consciously and unconsciously transmitted. Brian received impressions, and these formed his image of Anthony. When we speak of changing the image of a company we are talking about the *effect* of our actions. All we can actually cause is a change of identity. We can hope that this will have the desired effect. Anthony's tie and business card were physical cues. His manner of speech and conversational gambits were behavioural ones.

In industry, 'corporate identity' is strictly physical—it comprises visual cues—but it serves also as a guide to corporate behaviour. The identity programme can be used within the company to stimulate and/or coordinate corporate behaviour. Externally, corporate behaviour can be assessed against the promise of the corporate identity.

Is this claiming too much for a few squiggles and a piece of type? Most of the time—in an ill considered house style or uncoordinated programme—yes. It depends on two factors: the quality of squiggles and, to a far greater extent, the quality of the thinking which has produced them.

Corporate identity then (as opposed to identity in the fuller sense) is the sum of the visual cues by which the public recognises the company and differentiates it from others. And when there's more than one public? The same thing applies. *Aéroport de Paris* has four publics. The technical operation deals with civil airport authorities in different countries. The *Opération de L'Escalier* provides a service to airlines and airports and represents airlines who don't have their own staff. The passenger operation concerns itself with information and passenger handling and PF deals with passengers' freight.

Four diverse publics. Is there a need for a unifying identity? Ask the staff. To the questions 'who do you work for?' and 'where do you work?' there is but one anser 'Aéroport de Paris'. Which often elicits the reply, 'You're lucky' (the questioner assuming therefore that they work for Air France). Le Creative Business is currently designing a corporate identity programme which will identify—and *differentiate*. As my colleague François Schwebel says:

> There will be an Aéroport de Paris way of selling perfumes and carrying out engineering projects.

As with personality and image, identity is a fact. Each company has a corporate identity even though it may never have employed a design company or even heard of the term. A customer will see the company's name portrayed on its products, correspondence and vehicles in a style (or styles) of lettering or typeface in certain proportions in certain colours. Every physical manifestation of the company which the public experiences is a visual cue, part of the corporate identity. Let us hope that each is aiding recognition and discrimination. For Lufthansa, according to their worldwide advertising director, Ernst Tschoepke:[1]

> The corporate identity is the visualisation of the company's characteristics by means of the systematic presentation of all the company's equipment, services and buildings. In other words, the way we look to the public eye, our self-image and the expression of the company's style.

Lufthansa's style (though we would use the word 'personality') is clearly communicated by its corporate identity and by its behaviour. What we experience second-hand via Lufthansa's literature and advertising, we experience also first-hand in the seat of the Airbus. There is consistency between the visual identity of the ad and that of the aircraft interior. There is the more important consistency between that house style and the efficiency of the airline which we equate with the clean lines, lack of fuss and direct communication of the cues we encounter. The first consistency we can measure and check rationally. The second is emotional, subjective and unscientific.

The design world is uncharted territory peopled with genuine seekers of truth, honest craftsmen with no pretence, and fast buck merchants. The guiding precepts are subjective and the vocabulary is largely impressionistic. When a junior in a small-town studio and an international communication company (after a massive study and design programme) arrive at an identical logo, is it any wonder that management, particularly accountants, regard corporate identity schemes with a mite of scepticism?

A logo is not a magic token or philosopher's stone. And it certainly won't cure all the ills of a badly run company. Nor can it change the company's image overnight. But companies are tempted to think so—and this contributes to the cost. Because if the benefits of a house style are so wondrous then no self-respecting company can pay peanuts for the treatment.

The designers for their part live in this *demi-monde* of image and reality. How can they charge a five-figure fee for something that can be communicated on the proverbial back of an envelope—and which looks like two minutes' work?

Companies don't like paying for ideas. One reason for the longevity of the commission system in advertising is the fact that it is far easier to pay for something which can be measured—e.g. time and space—than a creative idea which can't. Similarly, design consultancies never begin work by *designing* anything. And they never begin their presentation by *showing* anything. But they're very good with words (despite the chameleon terminology) and everything is documented. The examination precedes the diagnosis. The diagnosis precedes the operation. The operation is followed by post-operative consultation and in the case of the client's financial director, a period of convalescence.

It's not all like that, of course. The reputable designer exaggerates neither the work required nor the resultant benefits. But he does, rightly, insist on professional standards. He will not provide a tray of goodies from which the client can select. He will demand a preliminary investigation. He will insist on knowing what the company is about. He will inevitably act as a management consultant (and ruffle feathers thereby), though his concern is not cash-flow but communications-flow. He regards himself as a problem solver. The company therefore has a problem. Otherwise, why call him in? Why change what it's doing? Any professional problem-solver needs to have the problem thoroughly defined. Perhaps the client's delineation of the problem area is flawed. Often in my experience the client's statement of the problem is itself *part* of the problem. One trade association called in The Creative Business and said it needed a leaflet. We soon suspected that the leaflet was their knee-jerk reaction to any problem. Sure enough we discovered that they had more leaflets (on many subjects) than they could possibly distribute. What they needed was a complete overhaul and coordination of their total communications.

The good designer—like the good communications coordinator—will ask 'the question behind the question'. He may as a result answer not the problem as stated but the real problem. And that he will have to state himself. He will give the client not what he thought he wanted but what he needs. And make him want *that*. And the solution will be relevant to the problem, organic. Real cream from that particular bottle of milk. Not artificial cream.

The professional designer will not presume that his solution is the only correct solution. It could well happen that a design answer could appear quite independently of the preliminary labour, that the route taken was shorter and begun at a different starting point. That is an occupational hazard in the business. He can reassure himself however with the knowledge that the problem determined his solution, that the thinking was thorough, that the design obeys an inner logic. Not some abstract design logic but the inner logic of the company.

If it fails to obey that then the whole exercise is a waste of money: the design will work *against* the company. A clean, clear-cut, contemporary corporate identity applied to a shambolic slum of say an office equipment company will be seen as a con. The dichotomy between identity and reality will make the reality seem worse—by comparison and by having attention drawn to it. The company will be seen to have its priorities disastrously wrong. If the company intends to become what its corporate identity suggests it already is (and the aspirational and inspirational potential of corporate identity are not to be denied), then the gap musn't become a chasm. As in all things, timing is of the essence.

When SAS introduced its new corporate identity some two years after the airline had restructured staff and redefined its purpose, the chief executive, Jan Carlzon, explained the delay by saying he wished to 'minimise any impression that he was working only on cosmetic change'. He had already been accused often enough of indulging in empty razzmatazz.[2]

Razzmatazz is easy and not necessarily expensive. If all a company wants is a façade it doesn't have to pay for the laying of foundations let alone the digging up of drains. I am always suspicious of anyone who recommends or asks for an 'image-change'. It says he is not at all concerned with the reality. Unfortunately a slick identity change *can* create an image change and at a superficial level the trick may seem to work. Long enough maybe to carry through some short-term tactical coup in the market-place, real or financial. But long term, the dissonance between appearance and reality will harm the company. And a subsequent 'image-change', even professionally carried out, will have to overcome a 'cry wolf' reception from its publics.

An identity change must say more about a company than the fact that its identity has changed. It must say that something has happened—for the better. Change within the company must trigger change in its corporate identity. It has reorganised, gone into new areas, taken over other companies, expanded geographically etc. Any of these developments can cause a company to consider how it projects itself to its publics, old and new.

The degree of change to the identity must be commensurate with the degree of change within the company. A totally new look may give a totally wrong impression for company *A* which has merely added a division. Whereas a slight modification to an existing logo may inadequately represent the radical change of heart which has taken place at Company *B*.

Furthermore, a company must consider the investment which an existing identity represents. Is the new identity recognisably a descendant of the old? If it is—and the accountant pricks up his ears—does the company really need to spend all that money on changing 200 different pieces of stationery, seventeen office entrances, a fleet of lorries, and advertising the change in the media and trade press? If it's not a recognisable scion of the old company is it in danger of confusing—even losing—loyal customers? The change has to be carefully thought through. It may need more communication (and more frequent communication) than had originally been estimated. It may need a two-stage (expensive!) transition. All this costs more money. No wonder many companies delay decisions or find excuses to postpone the project entirely.

Very often their decision is easy to justify. And in other than cost terms. 'Recognition and reputation are difficult to build.' 'Design is a fashion industry.' 'Today's contemporary design will be old-fashioned in a couple of years.' (Very true this. The designer seeks a contemporary but classic solution.) 'A lot of successful companies haven't changed *their* logo. Look at Coca Cola.'

Indeed. Coca Cola's original script is alive and well. Adjustments have been made to its surroundings. A swirling stripe was added a decade ago. (That was probably the most expensive stripe in the history of corporate communication.) But fundamentally Coke's livery is 90 years old. We have an example closer to home which is over twice as old.

'We're sorry Mr Peters we can see no reason whatsoever for changing the design.'
'But ma'am it *is* over two hundred years old.'
'And throughout that period it has served us very well.'
'But the world is changing ma'am.'
'It has always been so. Which is another reason why our . . . what is your term?'
'Corporate identity ma'am.'
'Corporate identity should remain steadfast.'
'But ma'am a contemporary design for a contemporary world would communicate adaptability.'
There I have the better of you Mr Peters. What could be better proof of adaptability than surviving a merger? In fact two. Scotland. Then Wales. You must admit that the design works well. It incorporates our three separate divisions. It is instantly recognisable and distinguishes us entirely from our competitors. What more could you ask of a flag . . . er corporate identity?

Change is, of course, often necessary—in cases of mistaken identity. This can be caused by confusion of message, of product area or design, or of name. Confusion, that is, with another company or simply confusion created by a dichotomy of the corporate identity and the activities performed by the company. Walter Margulies relates the story of United Aircraft which had extended:

... its airspace-based technological know-how to a wide variety of other fields, including electronics power search and transmission, industrial processes, electronics, communications, marine propulsion, appliance automotive systems, laser technology and automotive diagnostics and control.[3]

Dissatisfied that it was known chiefly as an aircraft manufacturer 'when it was not confused with United Airlines'[4] it changed its name to United Technologies.

Corporate symbols have a longer life than corporate logos. Names denote as well as connote. Symbols by and large only connote. US Rubber, British Ropes, British Oxygen, Radio Corporation of America—all changed because they moved beyond rubber, ropes, oxygen and radio. The temptation when moving from a restrictive name is to become completely free, seek the anonymity of initials (e.g. BOC, RCA) rather than choose a name which relates to the company's activities without restricting it too much in the future (e.g. Uniroyal, United Technologies).

A corporate identity is not something a company decides whether or not to have. It's got one whether it likes it—or plans it—or not. What it needs to do is to fashion it according to what it believes it stands for. And, as we'll examine in the next chapter, fashioning it may actually help it appreciate *what* it stands for.

What then is the purpose of a planned corporate identity? Coordination and consistency in the design and the implementation may be seen to bespeak the same virtues in the organisation itself. It may not actually be the case. There may be a dissonance between identity and reality which the employees will notice before anyone else. Uniformity in design may be seen from their viewpoint as an artifical neatness unrelated to the actual shambles they work in. But the decision to undertake a corporate identity programme is evidence, generally, of a desire not simply to look efficient, but to become so. The work involved first in framing the brief then in coordinating the departments involved and finally in implementing the design does in fact serve as an exercise in corporate cooperation. At worst, a company which successfully survives a corporate identity programme is seen to be efficient and well-regulated merely for having done it. At best, the exercise has revealed the company to itself and realignment, maybe of the company's structure, certainly of the company's thinking, goes hand in hand. In the case of United Aircraft, as Margulies points out:[4]

> A study of the company's communication needs led not only to a new name, United Technologies, but to a classification and strengthening of the corporation's sense of its own future, as well as a plan for compatible acquisitions.

A corporate identity programme helps guarantee that what the company represents (makes, sells, stands for) is identified with the company and with no other. Recognition and discrimination. The corporate identity helps position the company—i.e. occupy a place in the consumer's mind *for* something and *apart from* the competition.

A corporate identity programme thus helps a company in:

1 Identification.
2 Differentiation.

Lufthansa recognise both aspects.[5]

> The corporate identity is essentially the packaging of our services, and certainly provides an effective way of giving us a clear differentiation from our competitors . . . In addition we gain an expansion of our advertising effort by association with the corporate identity. The more consistent and uniform the visual presentation of Lufthansa the more we increase the effect of our advertising efforts.

It also increases the effect of other company efforts. The salesman's company is now better known. A launch pad of reputation has been created for new products. Packaging works harder.

The symbol becomes shorthand for the personality of the company. If the personality (or reputation) represents values, then the symbol itself comes to represent values. It thus has a *worth*. The company can easily prove if this is the case—and exactly how much. It could, for instance, show respondents in a research group two packets of, say, soup identical in every way except that packet *A* has no symbol and packet *B* has the company's symbol. Which would consumers prefer to buy and how much extra would they be prepared to pay for packet *B*? The symbol is part of the branding. Branding is a device by which a company reassures a consumer that past satisfaction will be repeated.

But does a symbol have any value *on its own*—i.e. unassociated with a company and its reputation? Would a logo consisting of an abstract design and an unknown name have any intrinsic value? Strictly speaking, shapes on a piece of paper have no value of their own. They acquire value by what they *represent*. All shapes and words convey meaning of some sort. Our sample logo may not represent a company but the lines could—by previous association—suggest all manner of things (cleanliness, modernity, speed, technological efficiency). As could the word. Indeed fictitious companies have scored well in research experiments, have been perceived as more innovative and resourceful than actual companies. Two abstract shapes can be compared for consumer perception along several dimensions (e.g. tradition, financial stability, inventiveness), and one can outscore the other by a factor of four. Yet the shapes seem aesthetically indistinguishable and, in themselves, meaningless. But meaning they undoubtedly have. The shapes are associated with similar shapes which themselves are associated with qualities. For example, a pattern of straight lines could remind the respondent of a similar pattern of straight lines seen in cartoons to indicate speed ('speedlines'). The logo would then be judged on the relevance of speed to the accepted image of the company. Similarly, a pattern of curved lines might suggest the logo of another company and the characteristics of that company would be considered against the image of the first company.

Words and names are impossible to disconnect from meaning. Even random jumbles of letters convey some meaning. Typefaces convey meaning. The 'correct' typeface helps communication. The unsuitable face constitutes noise. In 1973, at a party at *Punch*, I was shown a dummy of a new magazine which United Newspapers were about to publish. It was being produced for British European Airways (as it then was). They had a very good name: *High Life*. Two executives asked me what I thought of the logo. It was lettered in a fine italic script. 'Er . . . well . . . if 1947 comes back you're made.'

When people ask your opinion they generally seek your approbation. I tried to be helpful. The logo could not afford to be self-conscious. It had to stand up to all sorts of cover subjects, month in month out. It had to proclaim the name of the publication. It should be modern without being trendy, classic without being old-fashioned. I had another drink. Next day I discussed it with a young art director. I suggested a simple *Grotesque* face. He worked on a few variants. We agreed one. He did a layout. The following day was a Saturday. I knew where I would find the executive. Twenty minutes before kick-off I accosted him outside Arsenal football ground. Putting my hand inside my raincoat, I said: 'Want to buy exciting logo?'

The *High Life* logo is the same today. Covers change. The name of the airline has changed. The logo remains the same. And nobody pays very much attention to it. Which is as it should be. It looks right. It's appropriate. By which I mean it's appropriate to the job in hand. The name *High Life* was consonant with the jet-set image of the businessman on expenses whom the airline was attracting and who would then pull in advertisers. The design was appropriate to the job of a cover.

Corporate identity logos, on the other hand, have several jobs to do. They appear on every visual interface between the company and its publics. The company name is either designed in a special way or is associated with a symbol. Perhaps a slogan is added. Partly because of the diversity of uses, partly because of the fear of the unknown, companies tend to play safe and choose a visual platitude. Again, because of the diversity of applications and the size and diversity of their activities, companies tend to play safe and choose an accompanying *verbal* platitude. Corporate identities become indistinguishable.

Corporate identity programmes thereby succeed in achieving the very opposite of their intended purpose of identification and differentiation. Research bears this out. One company, R H Bruskin and Associates,[6] for example, prints company logos individually on playing cards and asks respondents to sort them into two piles. Familiar and unfamiliar. This is a game anyone can play. Though most companies would be saddened by the outcome. Some company people are saddened too by the effect a corporate identity can have within the organisation. The uniformity and rigidity of the corporate identity can become a constraint. Instead of being an expression of a corporate personality it becomes an expression of management power, a centralising force, a set of rules, the design equivalent of a company uniform. Personal idiosyncracy is trodden underfoot.

Lufthansa insist that photography is used as its means of graphic illustration.

> Cartoons or so-called artistic graphics are never used, as they are too dependent on personal taste. The characteristic of photographic illustration is more honest, more realistic and more like a document than any drawing could be.[7]

Such single-mindedness aids efficiency. Efficiency is inevitably part of the corporate personality. It's what you want above all from an airline. All well and good. But has 'personal taste' been permanently grounded? And why, are illustrations used in the safety instructions? Or would photographs be too honest and too realistic?

Corporate identity has to be handled with care. In the wrong hands or wrong frame of mind it can become a weapon, instead of a useful tool—not just for management but for the entire company. It is in effect a crib, a prompt, a visual reminder of the creed by which the company lives. It is not simply something stamped onto the outer packaging of the product or to the base of the advertisement. It is a perpetual reminder of standards and of a way of doing things. Thus, the physical identity becomes the blueprint for *behavioural* identity, a guide to company performance in its business and social intercourse with its many publics: how a salesman presents, how incoming phone calls are received, the tone of voice of the house journal, the approval system, etc. All these actions are interpreted according to the principles embodied in the corporate identity. The corporate identity thus serves to identify and differentiate the company both externally and internally; to unite the company in a common purpose; and to keep that purpose constantly before each employee.

In 1973, BRS Parcels were not clearly identified and certainly not differentiated. They were confused with BRS. Indeed, when an executive from the National Freight Corporation visited our office to discuss the problem, *we* thought that BRS and BRS Parcels were the same company. So did patrons. BRS might concentrate on heavy goods and BRS Parcels on items which could be carried by one man. But the distinction had not been communicated to the public and was certainly overwhelmed by the overlapping of the names. Some 40% of incoming phone enquiries for BRS Parcels went to BRS.

Obviously the name would have to change. It was equally obvious that the new name would have to be merchandised to customers and used as the basis for the relaunch of the company. But before that there needed to be extensive dialogue with the staff. Did the external confusion betoken a similar confusion within? It did—to a greater degree than we had anticipated. Nearly everybody we spoke to—executives, drivers, depot staff—agreed that the name should be changed. Most of them knew what to! To the name of the original company—i.e. before nationalisation. In the south this meant Carter Paterson. In the north Bouts Tillotson. And so on around the country. The corporate identity was to achieve unity. The staff sought devolution. We invented the name ROADLINE and devised a simple symbol—a lower case *r* in the form of a motorway sign.

We threw out the 'B', ditched the 'S', kept the 'R' and dropped the damned Parcels

This was approved by the National Freight Corporation and the management of BRS Parcels. Now came the hard work. We met company officials who individually appreciated the name and worked with us devising a critical path analysis of all the activities needed to implement the design programme. There were hundreds of pieces of paper, there were signs at depots, on vans, on uniforms, in customers' windows. The cost was considerable. Yet less than two years before, two hundred staff had been made redundant. How could NFC justify spending all that money painting vans?

The critical path of our analysis—there is always one which is more important than the others and which affects all their timings—was a presentation to the shop stewards. We wrote it—and helped management to deliver it. It explained *the whole story*. The loss of income due to confusion. The lack of unity within the organisation. The need for a fresh start. The advantages of the new name and design. The marketing and advertising opportunities of a new launch. The timetable in detail. And above all how they would be affected and how they could help.

Behind the razzmatazz—the reason. We got their agreement. The imple-

mentation proceeded on schedule. Morale improved. The disparate organisation gradually became one—and profitable.

NFC now stands for National Freight Consortium. The employees bought
themselves out. Roadline is one of its assets. Whether they would have
wanted to own BRS Parcels is another matter.

26

The uses of corporate communications

A little girl was lost in a wood. She met a dwarf who asked her why she was crying.

'I am lost and hungry,' she said.

The dwarf told her not to worry and pointed to a stone on the ground.

'That is a magic stone,' he said. 'It makes stone soup. Just follow my instructions.'

The little girl couldn't believe this but she did as the dwarf bade her. She went to the running brook and filled a small saucepan (which the dwarf happened to have on him). When she returned he had lit a fire.

'Thank you my dear. Now if you dig over there you will find some carrots. Over there, some leeks. And over there, some turnips.'

She went and dug and sure enough she found the vegetables which the dwarf told her to wash in the running brook. The dwarf cut them up and put them in the pan together with the magic stone.

Soon afterwards the pan was bubbling merrily. The dwarf gave the little girl a glove and told her to put it on.

'Now my dear take the stone from the water. Throw it away. What you have left is stone soup.'

Corporate communications programmes are often the stone in the soup. The exercise is more important than the reason for the exercise, more important than the result. Whether it's a fully-fledged corporate identity scheme, or a one-off corporate advertisement in a charity programme, or a public statement, it provides a stimulus for the company—to design a corporate strategy (or re-examine it), to decide who it is, what it does, what it believes and how the people who work there can help achieve these goals.

Unless a company has a philosophy it can't have a message. Unless a company has a personality it understands and appreciates it can't coordinate its identity. The truths are self-evident. However, I'm not so sure about the corollary. Unless the company knows what it wants to communicate it shouldn't communicate. Communications and philosophy are interlinked.

The substance of a corporation's communication policy is created in the

process of evolving and developing corporate positions on issues, not for
public communication but for the operation of the business.[1]

I believe this apparently common-sense approach confuses means and ends.
Of course the ultimate purpose of corporate policy is to enable the company
to operate efficiently. However the *articulation* of that policy is meant for
public consumption. Further—and more importantly—the *act* of articulating
that policy will help to determine what it is.

'Most human beings,' said Aldous Huxley, 'have an infinite capacity for
taking things for granted.'[2] Companies assume they have a corporate
philosophy and that everyone understands it—either because they were told
on joining the company, or because they ingested it during their working life.
Yet experiments we've conducted with senior executives of major companies
reveal considerable differences of opinion among people whose job is not
simply to implement or represent that philosophy but also to determine it.

A corporate communication programme shows a company to itself. The
consultant has to be a confidant. Company disharmony about corporate
purpose is soon evident. The operation which began as a simple design
scheme escalates gradually into a full-scale management consultancy examination. And that raises the question: are designers the best people to be
discussing with us what we as a company ought to be doing? That depends
on the designers and the nature of the design consultancy. The term
'consultant' covers a spectrum from the recently fired executive with a year's
experience in a small company at one end to Peter Drucker at the other.

At the important end is a company like Lippincott and Margulies, who
embrace marketing and 'regular' management consultancy within their
services. It is an understandable progression. If corporate design is something
more than veneer, then the problems it answers and the philosophy it
embodies are legitimate territory for the person asking the questions.
Similarly with the corporate advertisement. That too will raise questions
concerning the company's purpose. It does not take long before the
questioning reaches marketing and product advertising. Is there an answer to
satisfy all the questions? Who has it? One executive or several? Has the
answer been conveyed to the designer, to the corporate communications
company and to the advertising agency? To repeat: the act of articulating the
policy helps to determine what it is.

The corporate identity, a symbol, a slogan, a corporate message, a
corporate advertisement—each is a discipline. Each acts as a catalyst. Each
serves to concentrate the corporate mind on what the corporation is about.
The space available is concentrated too. Having to describe the company in a
few words or a graphic design forces you to limit yourself to the essentials
and to make the resulting words/design as potent as possible. The slogan
should be more than a statement of leadership in the respective industry.

Perhaps it encapsulates that whilst communicating something else about the company?

Wolf power tools are sold to the general public. Their slogan is 'The tools of the trade'. This says both that they are basic and used by professionals. The statement is matter of fact, take it or leave it, uncompromising. It clearly positions the company, identifies it, differentiates it. All in five words.

Constraints of size and/or time act as *creative* stimuli. I often use the poster as a stimulus. Irrespective of the media schedule, what would we say about this brand or company on a sixteen-sheet poster? Five or six words on what has been called 'the pictorial equivalent of a shout'.[3] If it works as a poster it should work anywhere. The concentrated creative idea is like a Japanese paper flower—tiny, but it grows.

Even more constrained than the poster is the franking mark on a stamp machine. The Post Office allow you a four word message to accompany the company name. When our office manager was told this he came straight to me. 'They want to know immediately.' Constraints of space—*and time*. 'Applying imagination to facts.'

The tables were turned. Normally I play that trick on client management. We adapt a format we use in our product development where we show a projected new product in the form of a 'concept board', a reasonably well-finished drawing of, say, a packet of dessert mix and the made-up product accompanied by a verbal description. We will take four of these to a group discussion and ask respondents to comment on the products individually and to compare them.

With a company we begin by assembling separate collages of scrap art (pictures from newspapers and magazines), each representing a different company personality. For example, does it see itself as a technocrat, a patriot, a social scientist, a winner? We draw various 'Chinese portraits'—i.e. if the company were a car, which one, etc. From these initial sketches we produce four drawings of the company together with captions. Occasionally we write a paragraph of copy. The discipline of an A4 sheet, a picture and few words enables us to capture—with the client—the ethos of the company. We adjust, refine, redraw. 'That's it! That's us! That's what we want to say.'

The discipline of the corporate communication is a catalyst. Various forms of words precede the philosophy so that the exact form of words can be agreed upon—and that in turn becomes the basis of the philosophy. As the philosopher said: 'How do I know what I think till I hear myself speak?' Of course hearing himself speak may tell him that his thinking is *wrong*. The exercise may have revealed deficiencies in the philosophy or its implementation or, as is most probable, its coordination.

A communications consultant, PR adviser or designer who digs deeply enough and shows a company to itself may not be thanked for his pains. He may not, as messengers of old, be killed for bringing bad news. But his findings may be shelved and the communication may go ahead without the corresponding internal adjustment. The identity in other words will not fit the unchanged personality.

Some managements faced with a decision of this nature, take refuge in calling it 'just an image problem'. Something for the image-maker (the PR department or the ad agency) to correct. The fact that the problem is one of company performance, and possibly at the most important level, is glossed over. The internal PR department will realise it has gone too far. The communications consultant may shrug and find its exercise stalled at the end of stage one. The ad agency will turn out some nice looking and comforting ads. But the real problem remains untouched. The time bomb ticks undisturbed.

One advantage of treating all company communications as integrated 'as a wheel' is that everything radiates from the centre and everything seeks the centre. Some of the routes are quicker and the consequences of inaction more apparent. Preparing a trade ad or an article in the local paper may not show the company to itself quite so graphically as preparing an annual report or a corporate advertisement. But inconsistencies of performance and identity are demonstrated there as much as in any other communication.

The wheel reminds the company of the interrelation of all media and all audiences and therefore all forms of communication. Decisions at the periphery—e.g. which products in a range to promote and which to leave unassisted, or which event to sponsor (or whether to sponsor at all), or who should address the trade association conference and on what subject are all interrelating decisions. If they are made independently without reference to the centre—and it is surely imperative for each decision to be referred to senior management—then unless the company has laid down some positive and clear guidelines, it is unlikely that those decisions are consistent with each other or truly reflect the corporate philosophy. If, on the other hand, a philosophy has been articulated and communicated then each action will be second nature to the executive concerned. He will know if 'that's us' or not. It is not necessary to undergo a massive corporate identity programme to achieve this state of understanding. But it helps; the identity, as we saw, serves as a permanent prompt for action. Moreover, if thoroughly carried out (and not just a visual tidying up) the exercise has raised issues that previously, through design or mismanagement, have not been aired.

When a company speaks through its products it isn't seen to be putting itself on the line—and presumably doesn't see itself that way either. When a company speaks on its own behalf it is more directly declaring corporate responsibility.

This can have positive benefits. It can create confidence among company employees. It can improve morale. Merely the act of advertising can tell the workforce and the salesmen that the company is awake. Corporate advertising can pull together the divisions separated by function and/or distance. In a large company the corporate ad can inform the employee about corporate policy and direction. Again, the discipline of the advertisément works to the company's advantage. Concise statement, attractive layout, clever copy and above all reader involvement are precisely those characteristics normally absent from the usual management/staff communication. Furthermore, whereas an internal message would have been at best cursorily read, a public announcement in the popular press undoubtedly attracts attention and gives it added importance. (Not that the corporate ad shouldn't already have been communicated to the staff; it can anger subsidiary companies to hear of management decisions from general public announcements. Far better to send advance copies of the ad, maybe even of the publication if it is a periodical, to reinforce the communication and to send enough copies to ensure that the advertisement gets displayed on notice boards.)

A corporate ad shows the company declaring its belief in itself and its role in society. It puts up, in the words of Arthur Page of AT & T:[4] 'hostages to performance'—for the company as a whole and for each individual employee. But it also makes the company vulnerable if only because it has put its head over the parapet and identified itself, achieved what is known as high profile.

A company should not engage in corporate communication unless it fully understands the implications of high profile. The company is known for, and by, what it does and can expect continuous dialogue with its publics. People know whom to respond to. (But at least they'll probably spell the name correctly. Would Procter and Gamble be referred to in the quality and financial press as *Proctor* and Gamble quite so frequently if they had chosen high profile instead of their brand policy?)

A corporate communications exercise sharpens a company's focus. It concentrates the corporate mind and draws all constituent minds together. It sharpens the public's focus of the company. So that both internally and externally the company becomes 'more like it is'.

A corporate identity programme can also be used to correct faults, the diagnosis of which could have taken place long before the employment of design consultants. The new livery won't do that by itself but—as we have seen—the working out of the design programme and, more particularly, its implementation cannot happen unless the company improves its strategic thinking, organisation structure and internal communications. A professional corporate identity programme is thus both the result of change and the catalyst of change. The new symbol (or whatever) is not a superficial graphic but evidence of achievement—the flag on the mountain top. And if the identity is that important wherever the company puts its mark is imbued with the same qualities. The coffee cup bearing the new logo will be properly washed and thrown away when chipped.

Margulies said that the United Aircraft's change of name and design clarified and strengthened the corporation's sense of its own future. Pilkington's new scheme demonstrates that the company is:[5]

> . . . moving away from a 'smoke stack' manufacturing image and asserting its new technological strengths. The new use of the Pilkington name in every company logo is already adding . . . muscle to smaller units.

Corporate communications and marketing are more clearly related than their respective proponents within an organisation normally admit. They may interpret it differently but the same corporate advertising campaign can both help project a new and favourable image and sell hard. The two aims are not incompatible, as we shall see in subsequent chapters. Corporate identity too, as designer Michael Peters[6] insists, is also selling. Indeed, every company action must bear the customer in mind. If a corporate identity programme is carried out to make the company more efficient then the efficiency will presumably manifest itself in sales, profitability and the satisfaction of customers' needs. More directly, of course, if the new identity serves to make the company and its products more easily recognised and discriminated then the purchase mechanism is lubricated. Corporate identity has a further marketing function: corporate reputation becomes a launch pad for new products.

By associating ventures with the company name a corporate identity scheme reinforces the marketing effort. It imposes a strict discipline to ensure that the values are inextricably identified with one company.

A corporate identity scheme is above everything else *single minded*. At its most basic it minimises the risk of confusion. At its most effective it creates a synergy (2 + 2 = 5) whereby each of the company's diverse communication activities is helping the rest. The corporate identity reinforces the image of the company. The image of the company in turn strengthens the selling 'argument' of the individual company product. A corporate identity represents added value. (Value which can be measured, as we saw in Chapter 25.)

Imprinted across a range of products it represents a corporate endorsement, even if each of those products has its own brand name. The Cadbury name reinforces Marvel and Smash. Kelloggs on the other hand uses no other brand names. Heinz is uniformly Heinz with the exception of Ploughman's Pickle. Kraft means, among other things, processed cheese. When it introduced cheese in its original state it introduced the sub-brand 'Crackerbarrel'.

By and large, however, all these companies (and many others such as Nabisco, Johnson & Johnson, Ford) use their corporate name as a form of umbrella branding. Several products are united under one manufacturer's name. Occasionally a company will produce umbrella branding advertising, promoting some or all of that range in a single advertisement or campaign. Unlike corporate advertising which pushes the company, umbrella branding advertising pushes the company's products. Unlike corporate advertising, the ultimate consumer is the prime target. Whereas corporate advertising endeavours to treat the company itself as a brand, umbrella branding advertising endeavours to communicate a *corporate endorsement of the brand(s)*. Umbrella branding, whether or not communicated also by means of advertising, increases the familiarity of the brand. Each ad supports all the other products in the range—including those which are not advertised.

But there *are* disadvantages. If the image of the product and that of the corporate 'brand' aren't consonant the consumer could get very confused. Did the company name of Cadbury help Snack Soup? (Procter and Gamble could go into crisps without anyone thinking they will taste of soap.) A problem with one product can't be hermetically sealed if the corporate name is used. (On the other hand if the crisps fail and are withdrawn from the market Procter and Gamble's reputation is not seen to suffer. Indeed, the vast majority of their consumers don't know the name of the company let alone their reputation.)

To conclude, corporate communications is both a management tool and a marketing tool. The most useful form is the corporate identity programme but even a single corporate advertisement can act as a stimulus to the company to examine its corporate philosophy, communications policy and *modus operandi*. Indeed the communication itself may be of less importance than the exercise it generates (the stone in stone soup).

The exercise can comprise a thorough review of the company's perform-ance measured, if possible, against its publics' perceptions. A corporate identity programme is not simply the result, but also the *cause* of change. The identity represents added value. It enhances each product and supports the product range. If the scheme is properly undertaken and executed the resulting device is not a superficial graphic but visible evidence of achieve-ment. As such it can act as further stimulus—to further achievements.

27

Corporate advertising — some basic questions

Corporate advertising—what is it? Who does it? To whom? And why? These are some of the questions this chapter will try to answer, whilst no doubt raising a few more. Bob Worcester (who should know), defines it as:[1]

> ... paid-for corporate communication designed to establish, develop, enhance and/or change the corporate image of an organisation.

Notice that products are not mentioned. Philip Kleinman, writing in *The Guardian*, comments:[2]

> Oil companies no longer tell you how wonderful their petrol is. Instead they brag about how wonderful they, the companies, are.

And according to David Ogilvy:[3]

> Corporate advertising is talking about the corporation to promote its identity.

Products however aren't specifically excluded from corporate advertising. The *Financial Times*/Research Services Limited survey of corporate advertising provides this distinction between product and corporate advertising:[4]

(a) If the campaign aims at immediate short-term increases in the sales of *one particular* brand or product or service it is 'product' advertising.

(b) If it aims to increase sales of the whole range of a diversified company's products, brands or services it is 'corporate'.

(c) If it aims for longer term increases in sales of particular brands or services but by general or indirect means, such as a campaign featuring a range of its products or services, it is 'corporate'.

(d) If its objectives are not primarily to do with sales or marketing, it is 'corporate'.

(e) If none of the brands, products or services marketed by the company are featured in the campaign it is 'corporate'.

Definition (d) echoes Walter Margulies's comment 'if it doesn't sell a product it must be corporate'.[5] The *FT*, remember, are asking companies to categorise their past and current advertisements, so (d) and (e) are somewhat catch-all classifications. Nevertheless, the distinctions here are useful.

Corporate advertisements *can* include products, but as a means to an end.

Joseph Graves of Trans Union believes corporate advertising is:[6]

> devoted primarily to selling the corporate personality. Its first objective goes beyond the direct sale of a single product or service.

Corporate advertising has several objectives: to educate or inform any or all of its nine publics about the company's policies, operations, capabilities, objectives, beliefs and standards. Within this it can speak about its management and manufacturing skills, its financial acumen, its technological know-how, its research capability, social welfare, community activities, product improvement, innovation, resources for training and development. The aim is to impress the public(s), to create a favourable attitude which in turn will, directly or indirectly, positively affect a purchase decision. It can be as simple as the purchase of the company's products, or as complex as government or shareholder approval to the company's purchase of a competitor or the investor's purchase of shares. The line may be long but purchase—of some sort—is at the end of it. Advocacy advertising, charity advertising, decorating the media with beautiful pictures and a logo must lead, however circuitously, to purchase. For many years corporate advertisers and their agencies believed the scenic route was best. Then questions were raised: were the public sufficiently grateful to the provider of the view? And once they stopped did they forget where they were supposed to be going? More of which anon.

Corporate image advertising has been described by an American lawyer as a 'hybrid creature designed to use the means of paid advertising to accomplish the goal of PR.'[7] The disputed territory of corporate communication has never been better delineated. As I've said, corporate advertising is a substitute for perfect public relations.

Advertising though is industry's own channel. The company can (within the constraints of legality and good taste) say what it wants with the desired emphases. And in the order it wants. This is particularly important though often not appreciated. Company management often assumes a degree of public knowledge of the company commensurate with its own. When the unknown *XYZ* corporation proclaims its belief in the free enterprise system or good health, our reaction may be tempered somewhat by our ignorance of the company. Bob Worcester, as we noted in Chapter 1, recommends the would-be corporate communicator to think of three generations of corporate advertising:[8]

> 'Here's who we are', 'here's what we can do for you' and lastly 'here's what we think'. An attempt to convey the third without the basis of the first two is likely to be met with suspicion and even hostility rather than interest and credence.

This posits a somewhat orthodox—but no doubt accurate—view of how corporate advertising is meant to work: awareness of the company, leading to knowledge of its products, services and achievements, leading to favourable attitudes which harden into positive predisposition which leads in turn towards decisions which ultimately affect purchase (as described).

The advertiser must consider how far he is along the line with each of his key publics. He may know from direct experience—his own or his colleagues. Research will confirm his beliefs. But if he seeks to generate awareness he should be careful. He needs to establish a benchmark before he starts, and then measure movement. However, he should not be too dismayed if the reaction is slight. Corporate advertising by its very nature and purpose takes time. Nor should he be dismayed if the advertising recall is slight. His real need is for the awareness *of the company* to improve. Indeed, it would suit his book for the awareness of the company to improve but for that of the advertising to remain static. It may mean that the public treats the information as news rather than publicity, in fact isn't conscious of the advertising *qua* advertising at all. 'I don't drink Guinness because of the adverts,' said the man before the war, 'I drink it because it does me good.'

Presumably corporate advertising does someone good. The chief executive probably initiates it (certainly has to approve it) and therefore it has a job to do. If it doesn't, he may not do it again. Before we discuss why he does it perhaps we'd better know *who* he is—and *whom* he is doing it to.

He is in business in a large way. The larger the company the more likely it is to be a corporate advertiser. In the UK, of the top 100 companies 40 are corporate advertisers—but only 16 of the top 50.[9] In the US, 227 of the top 500—but 49 of the top 50.[10]

Companies whose mainstay is institutional products or service functions (financial, transportation and utilities), are more likely to do corporate advertising. Whereas 66% of industrial and 61% of service companies had done it in a five year period, the figure fell to 35% for consumer goods companies.[11]

But who gets the most out of it? A survey of *Fortune*'s top 500 management in 1976 (sponsored by the *National Geographic Magazine*) revealed that in the opinion of 79% of the respondents:[12]

> Companies most likely to benefit from corporate advertising are manufacturers of high-priced consumer goods; 72% industrial products; 61% packaged goods.

Certain product fields contain heavy corporate advertisers. Anthony Wreford[13] estimates that:

> The oil, chemicals and hi-tech industries account for 80% of the corporate advertising in the UK.

Companies are often forced into it because of the activities of their competitors. The hardest job, says Wreford, is to sell the idea of corporate advertising in an industry which doesn't do it.

According to Wreford's consultancy, McAvoy Wreford, there are six types of corporate advertising a company should consider. Apart from the *long term* 'theme' campaign, there are the specific *issue* advertisements which a company might need to raise in the media; advertisements which serve as *market preparation* (e.g. prior to a listing on the exchange or a take-over); infrequent but regular *financial* announcements; a variety of *tactical* messages; and statements on behalf of the *industry* of which the company is a part. As to *whom* it is done to, Wreford recommends the following: [14]

	Long Term	Issue	Market Preparation	Financial	Tactical	Industry
The Public	★	★			★	
Customers	★		★	★	★	
Government	★	★			★	★
Employees	★		★		★	★
Financial	★			★	★	

This list omits four of our nine publics (Local, Trade, Media and Influential Groups) whom we can regard as *indirect* recipients.

Here is a US audience breakdown of corporate advertising. [15]

Employees	23%	Public at large	76%
Financial Community	46%	Stockholders	29%
Opinion Leaders	37%	Trade (distributors, wholesalers	
Government Officials	20%	agents, etc.)	32%

Nearer home and more up-to-date are these preliminary figures from the *Financial Times* RSL survey. [16] The figures represent the primary target group for corporate advertising. In brackets are secondary target group figures.

	%	%
The entire adult population	16	(13)
The upper (AB) social grades	9	(38)
Activists/opinion leaders	6	(34)
(e.g. trade union leaders, political pressure groups, academics etc.)		
Government and government agencies, national or international	19	(41)
Business community	31	(63)
Financial community	19	(63)
Private investors/shareholders	—	(31)
Suppliers and customers	9	(56)
Employees, current and potential	—	(44)
Students	—	(6)
Local communities	—	(16)
The media	3	(16)
Others	—	(6)

With such a diverse range of publics (and of reasons) for corporate advertising, no wonder the end product has a drained look. In communication the ideal model is *person-to-person*. The corporate advertiser must think of itself and its publics as people in a dialogue.

   Once you think of the respondent as a specific person it becomes easier to be specific in your message. And if any form of communication could benefit from specificity it's corporate advertising. So—who *is* this person? It isn't anybody. It's somebody whose attitude the company needs to change. J. B. Orthwein, speaking at a *Fortune* seminar, listed a few specific candidates.[17]

> Somebody who recommends against buying our stock.
> Somebody who doesn't apply for a job with us even though he's just the guy we need.
> Somebody who rejects our request for a loan.
> Somebody who says he's out when our salesman calls but says he's in if our competitor calls.
> Somebody who says of one of our product's failures 'just what I'd expect from that outfit'.
> Somebody who writes a negative comment in his column for no apparent reason.
> Or who says something negative about us at a cocktail party when somebody mentions our company.
> Or a guy who works for us but hangs his head a little when somebody says 'where do you work?'

This admirable list of specific targets ('who') leads us naturally into the subject of 'why'. Indeed, Orthwein's list suggests several reasons. Very broadly speaking there are seven main reasons, the most important of which is to influence the purchase. This reason rarely exists on its own. On the other hand it rarely does not co-exist with the others: raise morale, improve recruitment, increase the share price, make themselves understood, correct a misconception, announce a major change (e.g. a new corporate identity). Corporate advertising rarely has only one objective. But then it rarely has only one audience. They choose advertising as a means of doing any or all of these because it has proved cost-effective; because the cost of a sales call is prohibitive; because research has shown in the UK that 35% of the target audience use ads to help them make up their minds about companies; because several audiences can be addressed at once; because the media adds value—credence, importance, by association; because it can be done fairly quickly and deadlines force decisions: because it helps the company focus on what it's doing; because the media choice coincides with the target audiences; because extra copies can be made quickly for merchandising purposes; because it massages the ego of the chairman, etc. etc.

   And of course the media are *news* media. An ad helps ensure that an issue is debated in a wider arena and more fully. This point was cogently made by Ann Burdus:[18]

Apart from communicating knowledge, corporate advertising can communicate through the stance it takes. It can encourage positive thinking, and it can communicate social concern. In our society today there is a need for corporate advertising with several objectives—to educate the public, to communicate the interests of the company, and to engender a positive attitude about industry and production.

The mass media enable this dialogue to take place—and to be *overheard*. The interested 'other' public subtly influences the debate. The advertiser knows that, say, his ultimate consumer is likely to read the ad aimed at the financial community; or his staff will see how he is 'selling' the company; or the specific target influence (e.g. an MP) is aware that others are aware of his being approached and questioned—moreover, they know what the question is.

The ordinary consumer who is normally not the direct target of corporate advertising is nevertheless not entirely apathetic towards it. It's *his* car they're talking about. It's *her* washing machine that company makes. The more the consumer knows about the company behind the product (especially the high-ticket items, consumer durables and the like), the better is he able to make a reasoned judgement. Background knowledge of a company may not be the chief determinant of a purchase but it could tip the balance. For example, a new product in a new field for the company may be chosen in preference to an existing competitive product precisely because the consumer has a favourable image of the company as a heavy investor in research and development.

Employees, similarly, may not be the prime target of the corporate ad. Nevertheless it is virtually certain that news of every public communication from the company will reach the employee. Selective perception is a powerful force. (If your name is Robinson I bet you spotted it on this page before you read this sentence.) Furthermore, friends and acquaintances will inevitably show him, or tell him of, the advertisement.

Corporate advertising, directly or indirectly, can improve morale; inform employees of the state, structure, performance and prospects of the company; focus the diverse activities in which they engage upon one clear objective or message; delineate career paths and set standards. It can also attract new employees, again directly or indirectly. Certainly, as Dunlop found, previous knowledge of the company via its corporate advertising assisted them in attracting applicants and presumably made the interviewing task easier.

In the financial area corporate advertising has been employed to inform investors about a company; to support brokers; to explain what the company does; to illustrate that it *knows* what it is doing; to debate an issue; to explain its marketing policy; to enhance the corporate reputation for, say, innovative or financial acumen; to elicit some form of action (e.g. write in for a report); to introduce a new name and/or office; to give a financial record. The last can be a simple all-type and/or a double-page colour spread or even a bound-in extract from the annual report.

Occasionally a company may wish to go over the heads of security analysts and talk to individual investors, or it may wish to explain to customers the reason behind a sudden price rise, or address the general public and answer a publicised complaint. Of course the security analyst will see these ads, eventually. The effect usually will be favourable. Analysts respect good communications: they are communicators themselves.

Corporate advertising suffers from ill-defined objectives. Specific tasks should be set, if possible quantified and measured against a benchmark. The purpose of the ad is to motivate a specific recipient towards a certain behaviour, e.g. a recommendation from the analyst; a favourable vote in the local council; a more understanding union; a readier acceptance for the new product range by the retail trade; an appreciation by the trade press of the qualities of a particular machine; an awareness from the general public of the new name and corporate identity or the fact that the company is very active in the North Sea; an appreciation by business, financial and political columnists of the scope of the company's business and its track record, etc., etc.

Each of these objectives can be addressed in a corporate ad and the attainment can be measured. Instead of a vague imprecation to the creative team ('Hey folks, make us loved') the management spells it out.

> Research shows that the student population thinks we only make farm machinery. Only 15% of university and polytechnic students know we're in avionics. We need to increase that to 45% within a year.

Now you're talking. Of course you may also be talking yourself out of doing an advertising campaign. The responsible recipient of that instruction could suggest alternative media (e.g. mailing academia's careers officers, student competition or sponsorship of an aeronautical event). But student media are reasonably inexpensive . . .

Garbett[19] says that being specific will 'allow you to determine whether the project is worth consideration'. Agreed—with one rider: it helps you to determine if there are alternative means of attaining the end. Knowing what the end is and how far away—a rare treat for many creative advertising people—is both a discipline and a yardstick.

Garbett[20] quotes a *Business Week* list of no fewer than 99 jobs that corporate advertising can do. These include subjects such as achievement, acquisitions, anniversaries, brand identification, change, crisis, customer's customers, delivery, distribution, diversification, energy, environment, financial, funding, government, growth, innovation, international, investors, labour, media, name change, packaging, philosophy, problem-solving, product line, product service, quality, recruitment, research, size, social responsibility, testing, trademark, union officials, vertical integration.

The list of specific objectives in these areas is virtually endless but each end is assuredly measurable.

Garbett himself gathers the jobs into ten areas:[21]

   1 Build awareness of a corporation's identity.
   2 Improve understanding of a company's area of business.
   3 Overcome poor attitudes toward a company.
   4 Explain corporate philosophy and policies.
   5 Illustrate achievement.
   6 Enhance a company's image as an investment.
   7 Advocate social change useful to a corporation.
   8 Secure support of useful legislation.
   9 Provide a unified view of a corporation to its employees.
   10 Aid in recruitment.

American commentators love lists. The longer the better. In 1950 at the height of the Korean War, *Printers Ink* magazine ran an article listing the '30 essential jobs for advertising when the product is oversold'.[22] Included were:

> . . . to maintain customer goodwill and acceptance of brands, to enhance the reputation of the company for making quality products, explain the shortages and to speed the news of innovation or efforts to ease the shortages.

Much of the advertising in the popular press during the Second World War was essentially corporate in nature.

One of the last casualties in war is corporate advertising

The final catalogue in this chapter is perhaps the most relevant and certainly the most useful, since it is the most recent and is quantified. The companies participating in the *Financial Times*/RSL Survey were asked to define the primary and secondary objectives of their corporate advertising (one primary and as many secondary as applied). Here are the combined responses of the first 32 companies:

	PRIMARY	SECONDARY
To improve awareness of the nature of your business.	34%	50%
To provide unified marketing support for the company's present and future products, services and capabilities.	25%	34%
To inform your target groups about issues of importance to the public and to the company, its industry or business in general.	6%	31%
To communicate the company's concern and record of achievement on social or environmental issues.	—	19%
To demonstrate the company's contribution to the British economy.	9%	38%
To improve the company's standing in the financial community.	13%	34%
To motivate private shareholders.	3%	13%
To improve your reputation as an employer.	—	22%
To improve your reputation as a company to do business with.	19%	41%
To overcome some bad publicity or correct bad image.	—	13%
To withstand or to launch a takeover/merger.	—	6%
Other primary (write in).	3%	3%

So much for what corporate advertising is—who does it, to whom and why. Before we discuss the important question of how, we need to look more closely at the relationship of (and differences between) corporate and product advertising.

28

Corporate and product — have they been introduced?

Do pigeon holes matter? Did they ever do much for the pigeons? Were the pigeons even consulted?

'Corporate' and 'product' advertising are basically different and the FT/RSL distinctions (see Chapter 27) are useful. But too great a concentration on their differences could deflect us from considering their not-so-uncommon common purposes.

Every product ad which incorporates the company name (particularly those where the company name is also the brand name, e.g. Heinz, J&J), is in effect a corporate ad. ICI, one of the UK's leading corporate advertisers since the 1940s recently halted its campaign, possibly because of management sensitivity. They had made cuts in the workforce. Redundancies and corporate campaigns don't go together. However, an ICI spokesman affirms:

> Employees . . . do understand the need for product advertising in the drive to increase sales and keep plants open.

And the heavy product promotion gives it a television presence. The product commercials allow ICI to 'maintain a degree of corporate identity'.

Many companies try to mix the two. Anthony Wreford says that the dividing line between corporate and product advertising has become much vaguer[1]. Products are being used to build up a corporate image and corporate advertising has become a method of product support, intended to give salesmen an easier job when contacting customers.

The dividing line is particularly vague with service companies such as banks. An ad which promotes one particular aspect of its service (i.e. a product ad) is also reinforcing the image of the bank as a caring/innovative/listening/action bank (i.e. a corporate ad). If it isn't then its communications are uncoordinated.

Purely corporate messages from UK banks are fast disappearing—except perhaps in charity programmes. It is not sufficient for a bank to show its head office and caption it. 'Customers,' says Matthew Lutos, advertising manager of Barclays Bank, 'will no longer accept bland corporate messages from any institution'.[2] A warning note, this, to any institution which pigeon-holes and fails to coordinate its communications.

'Corporate advertising,' he continues, 'makes all banks appear the same.' (A theme we pursue). 'People must be given the opportunity to examine products and to compare them with the competition.'[3] Banks, accordingly, are more aggressive and sell specific individual services rather than a general service, a product rather than an image. Nevertheless, the image must be maintained. And there are occasions when the sale of specific products is not the prime concern of the company, when the desired response has more to do with government legislation or consumerist pressure.

How to interest the reader? If the content of product ads is not available (i.e. the product), are the techniques? If Doctor Johnson[4] was right about the soul of an advertisement, what is the company *promising* the reader? If the fundamentals of product advertising are consumer benefit and consumer orientation, how can a corporation thrown back on talking about *itself* avoid becoming (sin of all sins) manufacturer-oriented? The answer is that, firstly, by and large, it doesn't and, secondly, when it speaks of benefit it is often forced to do so in the abstract, a barren yet (paradoxically) overcrowded area—as we shall see. The exceptional corporate advertisers manage to inform and interest and *involve*.

Professor Yankelovich, whose two surveys of corporate advertising have won favour with many corporate advertisers, has proved to his own and his sponsors, *Time* magazine's, satisfaction that:

> High-corporate advertisers had a significant advantage versus product advertisers with the same or even higher expenditure.[5]

> Corporate advertisers achieved higher familiarity with the same or substantially lower product advertising budgets.[6]

Bob Worcester[7] has some reservations about the Yankelovich conclusions and the definition of corporate advertising on which they are based. But he agrees with the main finding, that familiarity breeds favourability. (Which isn't surprising as he claims he originated the thesis in 1973!) If people, for whatever reason,

> . . . regard a company favourably in one respect, they will be predisposed to think well of it in some other respect even though they have little or no specific evidence for doing so.[8]

The proponents of corporate advertising assert that its effect on product sales is greater the more expensive the product, the less frequently it is purchased, the more considered the purchase and the less product advertising there is. (The last point I would have thought was self-evident.)

However, it might be asked (and frequently is) what would happen if the increased corporate advertising budget were allocated to product advertising, say of an umbrella branding nature? It could help project the corporate image and assist sales. Alas, I know of no controlled experiment which answers this conundrum.

So we must accept that corporate and product advertising are different but related, separate yet often intimate and mutually supportive. The guidelines for each differ but not exclusively. They overlap. As do the audiences. The differences are not of kind but of degree. However, if the corporate world differs from the product world, the corporate world of product *A* is very similar to the corporate world of product *B*. Corporate advertising has a homogenising effect. It seems to iron out differences between companies, let alone products and brands. Indeed, as we shall see in Chapter 29, it can even vaporise differences between industries.

All of which forces me to formulate—on the basis of evidence from both sides of the Atlantic—Bernstein's Law. It states:

> *Product advertising* takes minor differences and maximises them;

whereas

> *Corporate advertising* takes major differences and minimises them.

Product advertising adds value to competing products to aid identification and differentiation. The difference between two similar formulations of washing powder or perfume owes more to the ingenuity of the advertising agency than to the manufacturer. The way it is seen, the imagery which is applied, the consumer identification it elicits, the strength of the advocacy— all succeed in enlarging the miniscule gap between the product and its competitor and make that product a 'brand'.

Conversely, corporate advertising which takes as its raw material a company of diverse human beings and diverse activities in diverse locations and even diverse products and markets, more often than not succeeds in summing it up in a phrase of numbing ordinariness and parading a virtue to which all businesses lay claim. Advertising creative director Reg Starkey[9] says that:

> If the value of the advertising line is inversely proportional to the number of times it is used . . . lines like 'we mean business' and 'we care' must be worthless now.

'When everybody cares,' says Margulies, 'who cares?'[10] What then are the forces for homogenisation? There are at least five.

1.   Crisis of Identity

Companies grow, merge, acquire, change direction. This inevitably affects what they say about themselves and how they describe their corporate activity. They don a safe, neutral, off-the-peg identity to accommodate all the different identities they have subsumed or will subsume. It they're not sure of their identities how can they expect the consumer to be?

2.   Defensive Posture

Companies are not as confident about themselves as they once were. The age of arrogance has passed. Large corporations, multinationals, big business are all objects of criticism. Some of this is well founded. Multinationals in particular have been know to play the money-markets; to export sophisticated western products to unsophisticated Third World consumers; to bribe Middle Eastern agents; to trade with South Africa while pretending not to; to keep separate sets of books; to court dictatorships; to deny responsibility for pollution, lead poisoning, acid rain, distress, deformity and death. Is it any wonder that the framework for the debate between companies and their critics (whether government or consumerists or citizens' bodies) has been set by the critics? Accordingly, the corporate response is defensive.

3.   Issue Advocacy

This is really the reverse side of the previous coin. The companies put the positive view on behalf of themselves but more especially their industry—and even, on occasion, industry as a whole.

4.   Navel Neurosis

Corporate advertising is self-centred. It is not easy for a corporate communicator to speak objectively of a product. It is difficult to be detached about oneself. It goes through the motions, buys in outside consultants and commissions research but blinks at the findings and blenches at the proposals. The image is unlike the self image. Unflattering. Even unrecognisable. The company overreacts. It is thought of as impersonal. So it shows people.

In the mid–1960s GM ran a campaign which said 'General Motors is people.' Today, everybody is people. It is thought of as multinational. So it either focuses on one particular location or stresses local endeavour. It is thought of as worthy, so it stresses other more sexy virtues. And how about size? Economists like Galbraith are on the side of small companies because they are competitive and genuinely private. On the other hand:

> Large corporations possess something like political power in their ability to 'administer' prices, mould public opinion and influence the government.[11]

That was the *Harvard Business Review.* Here's another quotation:

> All global companies are now so complex, their administration so sophisticated, that no national government has civil servants or politicians experienced enough to comprehend them as a whole.

Accordingly, these big companies ask you to look at them through a reducing lens.

The main outcome of all this self-adjusting, self-effacing, so-called image correction is that companies are becoming more and more alike in their corporate pleadings and are in danger of losing that very thing which identity programmes are meant to achieve—IDENTITY!

5.   Abstractions of Personality

Corporate ads look like other corporate ads because they deal for the most part in abstractions, in qualities of character, in generalisations rather than specifics. Because it is endeavouring to communicate a *personality*, the corporate advertisement has fewer tangible elements to play with. Moreover, the characteristics of personality *A* are very similar to the characteristics of personality *B, C, D* and so on. Or, shall we say, the characteristics that the advertiser wishes to *promote* are very similar. And therefore the ads of *A, B, C* and *D* become less and less distinctive. The advertiser could of course achieve identity by promoting one of the less agreeable traits of behaviour such as 'meanness to old ladies' but is unlikely, by so doing, to advance his cause. Unfortunately, promoting public-spiritedness is not likely to do his cause much good either since his competitors are also promoting it. Besides, as we know, virtues can't be branded. (Though admittedly Guinness managed quite well for forty odd years with 'goodness'.) Distinctively portraying what a company represents is a tougher trick to perform than distinctively portraying what it *does*.

What inhibits the company in determining its philosophy, let alone concentrating that into a message, is the nagging thought that the concepts are themselves undistinctive, bland or pretentious nonsense. Conversely, the same team asked to promote one of its *brands* would quickly seize on an argument and confidently give it a 'positioning'. Likewise, in corporate communication, a company needs to position itself in its own mind and subsequently—and more importantly—in the target consumer's mind. It must appropriate a piece of territory, significant in itself and separate from that of its competitors.

But, says the corporate advertiser, product advertising is different. It's relatively easy to be single-minded when you're promoting a brand. Corporate advertising has a portfolio of objectives and a list of publics to fill an address book. To demonstrate this, Graham Barnes at Colman RSCG has prepared an archetypal brief for the archetypal corporate advertiser to the archetypal agency:

'To convey—to existing and potential employees, customers, suppliers, shareholders, opinion formers and government alike—that Widget Engineering are a huge, important concern with financial resources so large as to numb the mind but with all the nimbleness and friendly humanity of a cottage industry; are so successful that even Tony Benn would regard it as a retrograde step to nationalise them; are technologically innovative but make supremely reliable, commercially useful products; are leaders in their field but never complacent on product quality or service; have a highly developed social conscience for the welfare of their employees and the public at large; are passionate espousers of environmental causes; have a heroic export record; maximise profits for the benefit of shareholders without ever exposing the unacceptable face of capitalism and are also fairly kind to animals.'

Get out of that.

29

Corporate advertising — the state of the art

In 1642, Rembrandt was asked to do a corporate advertisement. The client was a company of musketeers called the Kloveniersdolen. The chief executive was Captain Frans Banning Cocq. Traditionally, group portraits were dull representations of worthy people, likenesses in ordered ranks. Though ten years before Rembrandt's commission, another Dutchman, Frans Hals, was beginning to break the mould. Instead of painting people having their pictures painted he showed them behaving like human beings.

Rembrandt chose to depict the musketeers getting ready to march. The *Night Watch* (as it is still called even though cleaning has revealed the action isn't taking place in the dark), is an unorthodox solution to the problem of the group portrait. It shows no fewer than 29 figures yet these individual poses are completely subordinated to the bustle of the job in hand as the militiamen fall in behind their leader.

As one art critic has said about its composition:[1]

> Staffs, banners and muskets point in all directions, imbuing the company with a quality of disorganised vitality.

(How's that for corporate image—'disorganised vitality'?!) Rembrandt's accomplishment, he continues:

. . . is all the more remarkable given the staid tradition of the group portrait in Holland.

Twentieth-century corporate advertising is still waiting for its Rembrandt.

The chief fault of all advertising—product and corporate—is lack of identity. The work of our advertising grandfathers may today seem unsophisticated but at least it shows an understanding of the need to brand. Many early ads are indeed very little but brand names. (There often wasn't much room—on a horse bus—for much else.) Too many of our expensively produced commercial messages remind us of everything *except* the brand. One question, therefore, I ask of any ad I'm shown: 'IS BRAND EVIDENT?' Is the brand name—or the name of the company in the case of corporate advertising—inextricably linked to the promise of the ad, the message of the corporation? If the problem is serious in the day-to-day world of product advertising, in the world of corporate advertising it is absolutely *critical.*

Try this test. Here are twelve slogans, baselines of corporate ads. Try to guess, not the name of each company (though, if you can, splendid) but the type of *business* that company is in.

1 BECOMING A PART OF EVERYONE'S LIFE.
2 WHAT'S OURS IS YOURS.
3 THINK WHAT WE CAN DO FOR YOU.
4 WE GO OUT OF OUR WAY TO PLEASE YOU.
5 A POWERFUL PART OF YOUR LIFE.
6 A TRADITION OF PROGRESS.
7 WE HAVE CONNECTIONS.
8 IN BUSINESS TO SERVE YOU.
9 THERE'S NO STOPPING US.
10 WE'RE LOOKING FORWARD TO THE FUTURE.
11 JUST SLIGHTLY AHEAD OF OUR TIME.
12 BETTER IDEAS BEAUTIFULLY MADE.

Here are the answers.

1.	BECOMING A PART OF EVERYONE'S LIFE:	COLGATE.
2.	WHAT'S OURS IS YOURS:	BRS CONTRACT HIRE.
3.	THINK WHAT WE CAN DO FOR YOU:	BANK OF AMERICA.
4.	WE GO OUT OF OUR WAY TO PLEASE YOU:	MANILA.
5.	A POWERFUL PART OF YOUR LIFE:	WESTINGHOUSE.
6.	A TRADITION OF PROGRESS:	KRUPP.
7.	WE HAVE CONNECTIONS:	CABLE & WIRELESS.
8.	IN BUSINESS TO SERVE YOU:	THE POST OFFICE.
9.	THERE'S NO STOPPING US:	COMPUTER TECHNOLOGY LTD.

10. WE'RE LOOKING FORWARD TO
    THE FUTURE: SOUTH AFRICA.
11. JUST SLIGHTLY AHEAD OF OUR TIME: PANASONIC.
12. BETTER IDEAS BEAUTIFULLY MADE: SWAN

The interesting feature of this selection is not simply the interchangeability of the lines—or their vacuous quality—but the wide spread of the company activities involved.

This explains why I believe loss of identity has reached critical proportions in corporate advertising. In Chapter 27 we examined the reasons why some companies are unsure of what to say about themselves and the refuge they take in bland all-embracing lines. The effect is remarkable. It is not simply, as in product advertising, a matter of brands being confused within a product field, but of companies being confused in *totally different* fields.

Cases of mistaken identity extending beyond a product field into unrelated areas of activity are very common but generally unreported. Though any of us who has been involved in image research, tracking studies and the like, knows how totally unexpected competitors show up in respondent's minds. We may get angry, doubt their intelligence, but the fault isn't theirs. The onus is on the communicator.

Before it had been used, the line 'Simply Years Ahead' was attributed correctly to Philips by 2% of respondents. However, 17% attributed it to ICI. Why should this be? My theory is that ICI, being pioneers in corporate advertising, 'own the market'. Brand leaders in corporate advertising. It makes a kind of sense. Because we know and recognise a certain kind of animal called 'corporate advertisement'. However, we would never contemplate the idea of 'brand leaders in product advertising'. There are hundreds of product fields and countless brands. Yet when we come to the corporate advertising of the companies who labour in those fields and market those brands, somehow different considerations apply. The advertisements look and sound like each other. Hence, Bernstein's Law, (see page 185).

The disciplines in product advertising result in single-minded propositions which creative people transmute into unique ideas—'branded ideas'.[2] Companies find it difficult to arrive at a single-minded proposition (the company is too diverse and so are its audiences and the jobs the advertising has to do). So they select a cliché approach. They appropriate a thought. Unfortunately, it's equally appropriate to competitors and to companies in unrelated areas.

Here is a basic selection compiled by Graham Barnes of Colman RSCG:

a) How our products make life richer, more agreeable for the masses.

b) How we spend huge sums on, and are very successful in, technological development.
c) Despite our colossal size, we're terribly human really.
d) How concerned we are for the environment and other social/human relations problems.
e) How we are helping the country by exporting, exploiting North Sea oil/gas, etc.

Mushy propositions are the result of mushy thinking. Campaign objectives are normally very broad. The strategy, because it has to encompass so much, becomes vague. The target audience is ill-defined. And insufficient use is made of research either before (e.g. advertisement copy) or after (tracking studies) to assess respectively communication effectiveness and attainment of objectives.

Is it any wonder that the advertisements which result are imprecise? If the people responsible for the product advertising were responsible for corporate advertising, the situation would improve in two ways: a stricter discipline would be applied and the two forms of corporate communication would automatically be coordinated. I appreciate that a company executive might regard this solution as simplistic. 'Public affairs' and 'marketing' are separate territories. They are though presumably part of the same empire and if Rome could imprint identity in York 2,000 years ago it shouldn't be too difficult today to perform the same trick on the next floor. Coordination would at least guarantee that the departments learn from each other.

Meanwhile, back at the baseline, we discover all sorts of worthy utterances. The corporation is big, human, innovative, conscious of its duty, a setter of standards and, above all, a leader. Modesty may be difficult to convey. Panasonic though are 'just slightly ahead of our time'—unlike Data General who are 'a generation ahead'.

The future looms large in corporate ads. 'Computing for your future' (Triumph Adler). 'The future without the shock' (Exxon). 'A concern for the Future' (PPG). The trouble with the future is that it isn't now, which is where most of us live. So companies tell us that what they are futuristically about is really helping us, this minute.

Should you ever be called upon to compose a baseline for a company—any company—you could do worse than use my colleague Rex Audley's patent baseline kit. It consists of four components:

TODAY
TOMMORROW
NEEDS
SATISFYING

Rearrange and add your own seasoning of apostrophes, full stops, commas and (if they're not too rich for your blood) colons. Here are a few combinations to start you off.

SATISFYING TOMORROW'S NEEDS TODAY.
TODAY, TOMORROW. SATISFYING NEEDS.
SATISFYING TODAY TOMORROW'S NEEDS.
SATISFYING NEEDS: TODAY, TOMORROW.
TOMORROW NEEDS SATISFYING TODAY.

Toshiba, with oriental humility, are merely 'In touch with tomorrow'. (Fellow countrymen Hitachi are not even that: they are merely 'Touching your life'.) Alcoa are in a hurry 'We can't wait for tomorrow'. The Southern Company are 'Working towards tomorrow today'. RTZ offer 'Today's technology for tomorrow.' New York Life say 'We guarantee tomorrow today' (but they would, wouldn't they?). The University of Southern California is 'Meeting tomorrow's challenge today'. 'One company is helping tomorrow dawn twice in the same skies' (Grumman). And Rhône Poulenc, the French multidisciplined multinational, sums up its copy with the sentence:

> In more than 90 countries, Rhône Poulenc is finding today the answer to tomorrow's needs: in textiles, crop rotation and communication systems, as well as medicine.

(You can almost hear the copywriter sighing. 'There, I think I've got them all in. Just room for the baseline. "Rhône Poulenc. The creative chemical company worldwide".')

It's awe-inspiring really. 'Creating new markets for great ideas' (Alfa-Laval). 'One step ahead of a changing world' (Grace). 'Look to the leader' (Bank of America). 'A world of authority on light' (Thorn EMI). 'We work for America' (Internorth). (All of it? we ask, open-mouthed.) 'A world leader in electronics' (Motorola). 'Enterprise at work. Worldwide' (Pilkington). 'Serving people and nations everywhere' (ITT). The Corporation Bank of India on the other hand: 'Puts man where he belongs: at the centre of the universe.'

And where they are is where things happen. Things of import and wonder. 'Where science gets down to business' (Rockwell International). 'Where imagination become reality' (Textron). 'Where computer and control come together' (Honeywell).'Where the world comes for energy solutions' (McDermott International). I hope it forms a queue.

'We' is one of corporate man's favourite words. Though occasionally the companies admit customers may be necessary. 'Together we can find the answers' (Honeywell again). 'Partners in progress around the world' (First National City Bank).

Many realise the need to communicate and let you know *they* know. 'The listening bank' (Midland). '3M hears you'. 'We should be talking to each other' (ICL). 'When E F Hutton talks people listen.' 'We understand how important it is to listen' (Sperry). 'Expanding your ability to communicate' (Bell). 'We want you to be heard' (United Telecom).

Alas, clear and distinctive voices are submerged in noise. Maybe they listen too much to *each other?* You get the impression that a company doesn't sit down to tell us about why it does the things it does and how it can help us. *It sits down to write a corporate advertisement.* And that means a formal layout, a prestigious typeface, an important picture and a declamatory (or mock modest) baseline.

Occasionally the companies seem to be talking to each other *in* the advertisements. 'The listening bank' is answered by 'The action bank' (National Westminster). Whereas the Mellon Bank stays snootily on the sideline—'One of the banks that define banking.' (So there!) 'Quality in the best tradition' (Allen Bradley) is answered by 'Chemical takes you beyond tradition'. Others reveal their communications strategy and an identity crisis: 'Means more then metal' (IMI). 'Your Prudential agent knows a lot more than insurance.'

Maybe TRW has the right idea. It opts out of the promise business entirely and sums up its ads simply: 'A company called TRW.' It mentions the company name. Nothing else. And of course it's flexible. Besides, who in the company can knock it? The creative team faced with the usually boring task of cramming boring facts into a boring media schedule end up doing a boring ad. (With luck they can pass the chore to the juniors.) Or they jazz it up with acres of white space or colour or an intriguing headline or a piece of expensive abstract art and get back to product advertising where the briefs are clear and the disciplines themselves creative.

The greatest difference for the creative team between corporate and product advertising, according to Garbett,[3] is that the former needs:

> . . . a relatively deep understanding of business, finance and social issues and a patience to work with their complexities. Simple solutions and quick success are rare.

True. But it could be said also of product advertising. Superficiality, me-too approaches, hand-me-down solutions, lack of knowledge about the product, the market and the consumer and an impatience with complexities don't work there either. The creative person's job is to look at something and see it afresh and communicate that insight. He or she is rarely commissioned to promote a totally new product. Most often it's a product similar to the competition. The creative person's job then is either to communicate something new (10% of the time) or find a new way of communicating something (90% of the time).

The differences between corporate and product advertising are those of *degree*. The task is harder for the creative team because the proposition is too broadly expressed. Nevertheless the fundamental job is the same—to see something as if for the first time and communicate that insight. A cliché proposition is unfortunate but it is insufficient excuse for a cliché idea. 'Löwenbräu is the best quality beer you can buy' becomes 'When they run out of Löwenbräu order champagne.' Contrast the inspiration at work there with these flaccid statements originating (if that's the word) in corporate ads in one issue of *Forbes Magazine* (October 10th 1983).

> 'If there's one thing certain in the energy business today, it's that tomorrow will bring change . . . What Chemical has done yesterday, what we're doing today and what we're working towards for tomorrow are all part of the tradition of giving you the very best banking service.'
>
> (Chemical Bank)

> 'You can't know the whole picture if you're only able to see part of it.'
>
> (Citicorp)

> 'Creating useful products and services for you.'
>
> (Texas Instruments)

> 'Excellence is achieved only through consistency and innovation. And drive.'
>
> (Bankers Trust Co)

Creativity is not a substitute for facts. It uses facts and transmutes them. It is not a substitute for thinking. It is thinking made manifest. It is not a substitute for a corporate personality. It is a means of illuminating it.

When every product under the moon was busy associating itself with NASA's landing, Volkswagen showed a picture of the car and said: 'It's ugly but it gets you there.' An appropriate line in a style appropriate to Volkswagen.[4] Strictly speaking, it was not a corporate ad but it must have done wonders for the corporate reputation. The company personality shines through. Humour can help.

Hendrick Manufacturing Company is a 100-year-old perforated metal manufacturer in Carbondale Pennsylvania. Hendrick make holes in metal. Perforated metal is used in several industries (e.g. for car radio grilles and room dividers). Because people don't know where to go for holes, the company ran a series of corporate ads in publications like *Iron Age* and *Industry Week*. The theme was The Hole. Ads ran with headlines such as 'Meet the Hole Company', 'Meet the Hole Man', 'Meet the Hole Team', etc. Soon after the campaign several requests and unsolicited purchase orders for perforated metal came from people who had never bought holes before. They were marked for the attention of 'The Hole Man' or 'The Hole Team' or 'The Hole Company'. As the writers in the *Public Relations Journal*[5] point out:

> Sure Hendrick benefits . . . from this low cost corporate campaign. But . . . so has Carbondale, and so have Hendrick employees, stockholders, customers, suppliers and everybody else within shooting range of its advertising reach.

But humour is capable of blowing up in your face unless you check it out. Not

every audience finds the same thing as amusing as the company communicators do. Humour amplifies your message because it's noticeable and because
it promises reaction. Say something boring and nobody notices. Do
something you think funny and people not only notice, they laugh or tell you
it's not. Either way you get a reaction. Those who prefer not to know (the
majority) generally stay boring. Humour takes many forms. Not all are
suitable for corporate messages. Whereas the company's product ad can
indulge in fantasy it may be inappropriate for the communication of the
annual results. An animated corporate commercial could embarrass the staff.
A clever headline that nobody gets could put egg on the corporate face.

But if humour doesn't always pay, honesty surely does. The general public
is learning fast. It is suspicious of big business. It's time for the kidding to
stop. Deeds are more important than words. One 'off' deed can ruin a year of
promises. IBM can protest for all their worth about being British but one
maladroit decision from America to refer to the head office the transfer of
equipment by one British client to another, can make the protestations sound
hollow.

Platitudinous corporate baselines suggest there is nothing specific the
company wishes to communicate. Their seeming interchangeability confirms
the public in its view that all businesses are the same, faceless, even in league
with each other. As Joseph Kennedy is supposed to have said: 'Eventually
everybody does business with everybody.' The general public is suspicious
when a company acts out of character. It would much prefer it to 'tell it like it
is', explain what happens to the money it makes, why it has opened a factory
here and shut one there.

If a company departs from giving a straightforward story of its achievements, then the public asks that the subject be relevant. The International
Paper Company ran a programme called 'The Power of the Printed Word'. IP,
who produce more paper than the whole of Scandinavia, clearly have an
interest in literacy. They targeted 15–30 year olds with long copy ads: 'How
to read faster', 'How to write clearly', 'How to use a library' etc. Robert
Lauterborn, who was in charge of the project, claims that the company
received an average of nearly 1,000 letters a day for reprints over a period of
seven months. The Ogilvy and Mather campaigns merited many advertising
awards. More importantly there were more than 2,000 editorial versions in
newspapers in the US. Publicity is advertising you don't pay for.

But if IP 'owns' reading, Sperry 'owns' listening. That's no gimmick. They
have trained 25,000 of their employees at listening seminars. They have
distributed 500,000 copies of their programme. Research has shown that four
out of five people think that listening makes Sperry better at solving customer
problems. Seven out of ten think listening will make Sperry more innovative.

Pfizer Pharmaceuticals ran a series of relevant ads informing the public of
warning signs of major diseases. The success of the campaign was measured

by comparing samples' awareness of warning signs pre- and post-campaign. As *Ad Age* reported:[6]

> Pfizer found that before exposure to the angina messages 40% of those sampled correctly answered the true-false statement. 'There are no apparent symptoms of angina.' After exposure . . . 71% knew the answer.

Just as a good product ad is in some way a sample of the product so a corporate ad should be a sample of the corporation. Reading a print ad is a dialogue. It should resemble the dialogue the reader would have with the company itself. It should be person-to-person—with no pretence or wearing of masks. Each year *Fortune* polls US company executives to discover which companies *they* admire the most:

> The most admired companies believe that their ultimate success depends on how they are perceived by the public. 'Consumers trust certain companies,' says August Busch III, chairman of Anheuser Busch. 'Consumers trust IBM. Consumers trust an Anheuser Busch product. They trust a Boeing airplane.' Repeatedly corporations with first-class reputations are seen to put quality, integrity, and respect for the customer alongside profits on the bottom line.[7]

Trust has to be earned. You don't get it by claiming it, as Emery try with their line: 'We've earned the trust of American Business Worldwide.' Companies get to be admired *over time*. A good reputation cannot be made overnight. It can only be *lost* overnight.

Words must grow out of deeds. If they don't, they generate noise. The creative person must demand information—of deeds, actual events, examples of corporate belief in action. He must seek specifics—in what he is to say and to whom he is to say it.

A copywriter works best with the product in front of him on the desk. Not so easy with a corporation. But a company product could do, or the annual report, or the corporate image study. Maybe one of these could be the subject of the ad? Or maybe one of the company's employees. Or one of its customers. The customer may have a story which illustrates the theme of the brief. The writer should also have a newspaper on his desk. What headline would he like to see about the company? How would a reporter treat the story he's writing? What current newspaper story or public issue is (or could be) related to the theme?

The writer should do his own research, find out what his friends, family, the man in the corner shop think of the company and its products. What other company does it remind them of—and why? How does an employee feel about working there? What does the company do for his neighbour or aunt? And the answers should be written in concrete terms. It should avoid abstractions. It should move the reader towards action. Ideally it should get him to take some action immediately. If there's no annual report to send for or phone number to ring then at least he can get the reader to think, to compare, to remember, to imagine, to *participate* in the ad. Communication is best person-to-person and it's *two-way*. A corporate ad should reward the reader. It should start a dialogue but not conclude it. It should tell the reader what could happen next (e.g. what he could get by responding to the advertisement, by attending a seminar, by reading the employee report). If he needs to use figures, he should buttress them with facts. Equally he should supplement facts with key figures.

Corporate ads start with two strikes. Reader interest allegedly is ranked 35% below the norm for all advertising.[8] The ad has to look interesting—and *hold* interest. 'Soft' headlines do less well than hard headlines.[9] These truths apply also to product advertising. Some critics assert that there is no difference: every ad is a corporate ad. The reverse is also true.

'Every corporate ad is an ad.'

The best corporate ads are active rather than passive, concrete rather than abstract, specific rather than general. The personality is not so much described as revealed by performance. The words grow out of the deeds. And the ad grows out of the specific problem. So that it identifies the client and differentiates it from all others.

These are characteristics I like to think Rembrandt would have taken for granted.

30

Speaking up, speaking out

'There's no reason why you should have heard of us,' said the company executive to Bob Worcester. He ought to know. He was in charge of communications. In some companies the man in charge can control the flow. Maybe his job is to make sure nobody turns on the tap. It suits some companies to maintain the status quo. According to an International Advertising Association publication:

> Many companies feel that their products should maintain separate and unrelated dialogues with consumers, and a corporate identity should only be evident to shareholders, if at all.[1]

That view would be shared by many newspaper people who are opposed to companies occupying media space to push beliefs rather than products:

> The advertising director of one of the world's most important newspapers, in terms of its political and economic influence, stated during an interview, that he is 'opposed to corporate advertising entirely'.[2]

If it were in the media's power to ban corporate advertising, how many companies would lead a demonstration? Those who believe in the primacy of products over corporate reputation would carry on as before. Those who need to proclaim corporate virtues would do so via product advertising. Some good might come of the removal of barriers. Companies forced into corporate postures because of competitive activity would probably welcome a cease-fire: they would find other uses for their defence budget.

For corporate campaigns don't come cheap. Deciding what to say takes up time of expensive people. And speaking up takes place in important and expensive surroundings, large spaces in prestigious publications. Results are difficult to measure. At least in terms of tangibles like sales. When money is tight attitudes are expendable and the corporate campaign is the first to go. The result of that *is* tangible—in the bottom line.

There are other problems. Standing up and being counted is not unlike standing up and being shot at. Communication invites feedback, indeed dies without it. Declare yourself 'the listening bank' and the first time a customer has a complaint about an unsympathetic teller the otherwise ordinary event becomes news. Why? Because the advertiser has given the reporter an angle. News, remember is incongruity. If Japan Airlines say: 'To be prepared is everything,' then they had better be prepared next time something unexpected occurs. If the Prudential agent makes a mistake on a claim then the fact that he 'knows a lot more than insurance' suddenly has a new meaning. Maybe he should concentrate on insurance? Similarly, if Toshiba don't answer your call do you care if they're 'in touch with tomorrow'? When ICI were 'The Pathfinders' salesmen late for an appointment were met with comments like 'What was the matter—couldn't find the path?'

But these companies make their pronouncements, bravely and boldly. 'Hostages to performance.' If the company doesn't speak up for the company who else will? It's very defensive not to assert your strength on the chance that you may occasionally make a human error. (And anyway the Prudential could probably insure against it.)

The 'defence' budget analogy is apt. Most corporations regard corporate advertising as necessary in times of attack. Even those who aren't normally corporate advertisers. Maybe even more so—for the regulars have built up a fund of goodwill and have told their story before they needed to, and accordingly a point of view has been put across before it could be seen as part of a *debate*. Furthermore, the company's name would have been known whereas the company which hasn't advertised corporately may not be known and thus it makes its debut to a wider public in unfortunate circumstances and becomes identified with the problem. The media (like advertising people) resort to labels. The company is now known as 'acid rain' chemicals giant or 'mutant' multinational.

But the criticism is upon them and they have to respond—to a consumerist, environmentalist, politically changing, legislating and concerned society. The pressures are many and real (even if all the foundations for concern are not). There are industrial relations difficulties; union demands for more management consultation and participation; consumer watchdog activities; and pollution (physical and social) bodies; inquisitive governments (home and abroad); statutory authorities; individual Members of Parliament; feminists and many more. For the unprepared company, the only posture to adopt is defensive. David Kelley cogently defines the problem and reminds us that business as a whole is put in the dock:[3]

> Simply put, the critics of corporations have been allowed to set the terms of the debate in which everything concerning business is argued. Accepting the framework is a fundamental mistake. Philosophy has long taught that assumptions granted at the outset of any argument help determine the success or failure of a particular point of view. These assumptions set the framework for argument, and determine how the issue is stated, who has the burden of proof, what facts are relevant and how they are evaluated, which arguments seem convincing and which miss the point, what questions critics will ask and what they will accept as valid answers.

If for no other reason, corporate advertising should begin before defence is needed, at a time when it can be proactive rather than reactive. When a company says something about itself—proactively—in an advertisement, it does so on its own terms and the ad may even assume some of the stature of the publication thus aiding the communication of the message. On the other hand when a company is forced to use advertising space to puts its case, the fact that it's an *advertisement* in contradistinction to the opposite case which is put in the 'objective' publication proper reduces the integrity of the message and constitutes 'noise'. *Time* magazine[4] asserts that the:

> . . . differences between corporate reality and the public's perception have been further exaggerated by the public's appetite for news.

Not to mention the media's anxiety to create and satisfy that appetite. Either way the context of 'news' serves to dramatise the issue. A debate demands antagonists. Agreement isn't newsworthy. News is incongruity. Bishop marries sex-change organist. Pills kill. If journalists believe with Lord Northcliffe[5] that news is something somebody doesn't want to see printed, then the company's day-to-day task of communicating with the media is very difficult and the job of answering charges in the editorial columns positively heroic.

Charges, moreover, can't be contained. The industry will be vulnerable and all members will be tarred. The brush moreover, has a long handle. Philip Kleinman, examining oil company corporate advertising in 1982, wrote:[6]

> The companies, in bidding for North Sea drilling rights, were anxious to present themselves to politicians and publics as righteous, god-fearing citizens. Above all, they wanted to avoid a repetition of the American situation where Big Oil is widely regarded as a sinister conspiracy to put profit before patriotism.

Certainly UK oil companies and the British subsidiaries of US companies learned their lessons. The ads were proactive. McDonnell Douglas on the other hand couldn't help being reactive, despite the fact that it was no newcomer to corporate advertising. After the American Airlines DC–10 crash in May 1979 and the Air New Zealand crash in Antarctica in November the same year, it ran a series of commercials and print ads featuring ex-astronaut Peter Conrad, a McDonnell Douglas marketing vice president, to vouch for the plane's safety. Their total ad spend was about $6.9m. As the campaign opened airline officials questioned the timing. *Ad Age* correspondent Lois Kessler relates an analyst's comment:[7]

> People's propensity to forget is human nature. When a DC–10 crashes, nobody wants to fly in one for about a week. Then they forget. I don't think the campaign helped people forget, nor even helped them want to fly in a DC–10.

Conversely, other commentators congratulated McDonnell on fighting back. 'Perhaps it made sense,' said another analyst. 'Maybe it helped dispel the myths about the plane.'[8]

Potential take-over victims are naturally put into a defensive situation when they take the unaccustomed step of advertising to their shareholders who must be bemused by the attention, the huge expenditure and wonder if such a drain could have been avoided if just a fraction of it had been spent proactively. Increasing numbers of companies are on other companie hit lists. Before the talking is done solely with figures, some argument had better be put with facts. For a company this could be, literally, a matter of life and death.

Chemical companies and others who are seen as potential polluters (and accidents happen to the best regulated organisations) need to maintain a careful dialogue, steady and sober, about their doings. Then if an issue occurs, they can speak up in their natural voice, confidently argue their case and expect a reasonably good hearing.

Issue or controversy advertising began in the US (where corporate advertising expenditure is proportionately far greater) and spread to the UK and internationally.

The IAA notes two other developments.[9]

1. Evidence of social awareness introduced into advertising programmes, either in the texts and subjects chosen for product advertising, or in separate controversy campaigns to state overall corporate viewpoints.
2. Greatly increased emphasis on specific details and facts. (Comparative advertising where it is permitted or accepted, may owe its new strength to the effort to present the 'full competitive picture' in as straightforward a manner as possible.)

Another consequence of controversy advertising is that it forces companies to treat advertising more seriously, to use it as a means of determining corporate policy. Those who previously decorated the media now need to state a corporate position publicly and enter into dialogue. Those who previously said nothing are forced into utterance. Non-communication is negative communication. Besides if a company says nothing, the vacuum is filled by competitors and opponents.

During one period of concern in the boardrooms of America, the *Harvard Business Review*[10] surveyed chief executive officers of companies. One president, referring to the pressures his company was under, commented:

> We are forced back to emphasising product virtues.

How about that? 'Remember the good old days J G when we emphasised product vices?'

Threats have beneficient effects. Ralph Nader is not the universal bogeyman he may seem. Many US businessmen, I believe secretly welcome consumerism and the spotlight it throws upon them and their products' performance. As my colleague Peter Townsend argues, some of the leading packaged goods advertisers have trained consumers to be consumerists. Procter and Gamble for example were inviting housewives to examine the performance of their products—with comparisons before and after, torture tests, the incipient armoury of the consumerist.

Nader asks questions which responsible businessmen also ask. *A propos* of corporate advertising:[11]

> Are corporations spending their shareholders' money prudently?

> Should ads dealing with issues of public controversy be shown on TV or broadcast on radio? If so, should the Fairness Doctrine be made available routinely to critics for reply?[12]

Controversy advertising is not allowed on British broadcast media. But companies are free to state their case in the press. Do some of us share Nader's concern about:

> . . . buying corporate news machines to dominate the communication highways to the public about important political, economic and safety matters?[13]

Yet Nader appreciates that public utterances by a company put it *individually*—as opposed to putting the industry as a whole—at risk. Most US corporations prefer to act through their trade association on legislation. He questions the media's objectivity. They make large profits on corporate ads. Shouldn't they institutionalise citizen access to newspaper presses and air time?

> When the *New York Times* places full page ads in its newspaper soliciting image/issue corporate ads by indicating that the *Times'* integrity is wrapped around the message, it is time to ask its editors whether such integrity extends to expansion of space for reader opinion. Some newspapers place reader letters replying to corporate ads in a second-class category and rarely print them.[14]

But Nader is grateful to controversy advertising for the dialogue it generates.

> The flood of corporate image/issue advertisements, even more penetrating, timely and controversial, keeps the critical issues of corporate power and limited citizen access in the minds of more people.[15]

The company likewise can benefit from the airing of issues. Before it can articulate a policy it has to formulate it. Before it can formulate a policy it has to discuss it internally. Before it can discuss it, it has to understand it, analyse it, consider options. Changes will be necessary somewhere along the line—to corporate structure, to procedure. Controversy advertising, for all its adversarial quality, is just another form of corporate communication. And therefore a tool of management.

31

Research—the need to know

Anthony at our cocktail party is trying to impress Brian. Who knows if he is succeeding? Brian *knows*. Anthony *thinks* he knows. Feedback gives him some idea. Anthony looks for evidence. Cues are being sent continually by Brian. Anthony may, as a result of a gesture or remark from Brian, adjust his message or emphasis to reinforce a point (the vocal equivalent of italics) or omit it altogether. Without feedback we don't learn. The after-dinner speaker begins with a few jokes not simply to soften up his audience but to check, first, if he is on the audience's wavelength and, second, how quickly the signal bounces back. He regards the first couple of minutes as research. He will probably have conducted some research before he stood up—when invited to speak—into the size and nature of the audience, key members' backgrounds and idiosyncracies, the character of the gathering, etc. But unless he keeps on the *qui vive* during the speech he may lose his audience. Feedback helps you correct transmission in *real time.*

Social psychologists[1] would call Anthony a self-monitoring individual. He is sensitive to the expression and self-presentation of others. He uses their cues to monitor his own self-presentation, He is flexible and adaptive to the circumstances that confront him and to new situations as they arise.

Without feedback we don't learn. We are playing darts in the dark. The sound might tell us we were hitting the board. We might eventually learn to differentiate between the sound of the centre and the edge of the board but we would have no idea how many we had scored.

Corporate communication designed to affect the image of a company must employ research. If image is an impression perceived by the mind of a target respondent then the only way a company can also perceive it is when it is developed on the sensitised paper of a research report. If you believe in image you believe in research. In 1981 a survey by the US Association of National Advertisers revealed that 84% of corporate advertisers used research. Bob Worcester[2] estimates just over half of the top 100 UK companies use image research, whether or not they use corporate advertising. 'You can't,' he says, 'measure corporate image except by attitude research.'

After all, what else will tell a company if it is communicating what it hopes it is communicating? Encouraging sales figures don't tell it that its image is right (always presupposing that it knows what 'right' is). There are two tasks therefore for research: initially exploring the nature of the company's image and how it may have to be corrected—and measuring the success of the communications in reinforcing the image or, more probably, correcting it.

Simple non-research measures like sales or profit or market share might be sufficient for product advertising where communications provide a causal, though not unique link, but in the case of, say, corporate advertising the journey from attitude shift to purchase is long and intricate. Sales success following a corporate advertising campaign could occur *despite* the company's image or even as a result of a totally different image from the company's self-image! It is essential for a company to find out.

Image is intangible. It exists in a mind, a shifting picture. 'Image' is also a term which is used imprecisely. Research helps to bring some hard edges by making the company determine what the communications are meant to achieve and by providing a substantive word-picture of the received impression. Image—or reputation—is one of a company's key assets. A company needs to know if that asset is being utilised, wasting away or merely lying dormant.

Corporate advertising must be related to corporate image. Measurement of attitude change affecting the perceived impression of the company is paramount. Otherwise there is no tangible result of the campaign. And without such results corporate advertising is vulnerable, becomes easy to cancel or postpone. Unless of course there is a crisis. Corporate advertising is often undertaken to put out a fire, to 'correct' an image or 'replace' it with a fresh one.

Similarly research is often undertaken only when problems arise. The research company is expected to diagnose the patient with no access to his medical record—and do it in the ambulance on the way to the hospital, or ad agency, where the creative team stand ready with the coloured band aid. Research at this stage is nearly always too little and invariably too late. Research, like corporate communication, generally has to take place in good times before the bad. The good time research may warn a company of the bad times or prevent them. It will detect problem areas with audiences which the company doesn't suspect —and potential advantages too. It will provide norms against which targets can be set.

Having set the targets it is then comparatively easy to discover if they are being reached. In fact, as Garbett points out, it is:

> . . . easier to find out whether corporate advertising is achieving its objectives than to determine whether product advertising is achieving its sales objectives.[3]

Nor is it expensive. It costs approximately one-twentieth of the advertising budget to discover if the ads are communicating what you want them to. And when the alternative is not simply lack of understanding but negative and hurtful communication (e.g. disbelief of the company's case), the cost is sensible insurance.

Regular checks on corporate image (tracking studies), will graphically indicate changes in public perception of the company. One position or score is meaningless unless related to previous positions and scores, and more useful when seen in the context of similar scores for other companies with similar features (e.g. in the same industry, tackling the same problem area or exporting to the same market). Tracking studies take time. But then corporate advertising isn't direct response. And corporate identity works on a very long time scale. Wally Olins is realistic:[4]

> The corporate reputation is formed from the behaviour and performance of hundreds or thousands of people and products in an organisation. If a corporate identity is to be successful it will, over a considerable period of time, help to improve the performance of those thousands of people and products and to that extent, and only to that extent will its influence be measurable. Within this context research 'before' and 'after' the corporate identity programme is meaningless.

Nevertheless, on a broad scale, tracking study impressions will be made. And since the programme has been undertaken presumably in order to affect the image in some way, that movement must eventually become apparent to the powerful research lens. Provided, of course, there is benchmark data.

The company also needs normative data. If it discovers that the general public believes it makes 20% profit when it makes only 7% it may get worried until it learns that the general public has this inflated view of business profits in general. (In the US the figure is about five times higher than the actual level of profit margins in recent years.)

The purpose of research is to discover what the consumer thinks. Research should not be undertaken unless the company is prepared to be surprised. Research has a greater usefulness than mere checking out. It provides insights. It illuminates areas which were otherwise dark. It occasionally shocks. The question the company must ask itself is: 'Am I seeking confirmation—or information?' Too often it will see what it expects to see. And having seen, it will see no need to do further research. 'Why should I spend all that money when I can tell you here and now,' a client said to me over dinner, 'what the outcome will be?'

Perhaps he could—in the broadest terms. But could he quantify it? Could he compare that figure with a previous one? Could he compare one dimension of his company's image with another and therefore see which aspect of his communications message had to be emphasised at the expense of another?

The advertising business has swung violently away from research figures in the creative communication area since the barmy days of recall when a few percentage points determined the fate of a commercial (or even a writer). Qualitative research is—quite rightly—regarded as more helpful to creative people and planners. However, figures make opinions more tangible. For example, if two variants of an advertisement are prepared the choice in the agency could be totally subjective. The decision might be arbitrary. Simple communication research into the meaning of the advertisements could show that ad *A* was understood by twelve people out of twelve and ad *B* by three out of twelve. There is now a measurable gap between the two 'interchange-able' ads. The decision will still be judgemental (all decisions must be), but there will be some quantified evidence to support one view over the other.

Figures make *management's* opinions tangible too. Bob Worcester was invited by one company to discuss research into a forthcoming name change. The directors were convinced that their current name was hardly known. Therefore they felt there was no need to measure it. Worcester, on the other hand, needed a benchmark. He asked each of the directors to write down the percentage of the target audience who knew the company's name. The scores ranged from 2–18%. He pointed out that if the post-campaign research showed a score of 12%, 'Some of you would regard that as terrific, others as a reversal.' He got his benchmark study.

Surprise is a fact of life in communication research. Researchers need to remind potential clients of this fact. It will make company executives feel better about their mistakes—and will get the research companies more business from those who otherwise would be afraid of being shown up.

The Leo Burnett advertising agency in the US[5] worked for a farm organisation who were worried that their farmer members were being unfairly criticised by the general public for the rise in food prices. The agency wrote two ads to demonstrate that farmers were not making large profits from rising food prices but were being squeezed like everybody else by rising costs. The client approved the ads and was anxious to get started. The agency showed the layouts to several groups of consumers with the intention of making them more effective. They learned that the public was very concerned about retail food prices but that the farmer was not seen as the villain. Instead there was high awareness of the fact that thousands of farmers were struggling to get by. However, the ads needled the respondents who didn't want to know about farmers' troubles when they had enough of their own. The taped interviews were played to an astonished client. The campaign didn't run:

> Corporate advertising that is intended to change peoples' minds absolutely must be preceded by probing objective analysis of what people really think as opposed to what we *think* they think.[6]

The chairman of Westinghouse told a *Fortune* seminar in the early seventies about the hostility his company faced:[7]

> This hostility is real. College professors don't love us. The news media don't trust us. The government don't help us. Some special interest groups wish we weren't even around.

Opinions like this are expressed every day in boardrooms but unless there are figures to put beside them (and before them) and trends to observe they remain imprecise, and even though broadly true provide little basis for action. Research can provide basis for action. Indeed there is no purpose in research for its own sake. Reg Valin, chief executive of Valin Pollen, says:[8]

> Research not used as a guide to some positive action is simply research wasted: it should also go without saying that any action not tested by subsequent research is that much more likely to be less effective.

Research. Action. Research. Action. And so on. The time scales of corporate communications research are longer than those of product research. The serious corporate communicator must take the long view. BP believed at the outset of its corporate advertising campaign that it would be likely to span several years:[9]

> . . . and it was most important that the research should provide as much information as possible to aid management in planning.

But BP was anxious to measure not simply the effect the advertising had on the aspects of the company featured in the campaign but on the various dimensions of the company's image as a whole. Such research of course does not end when the campaign ends nor does new research have to be undertaken when a new campaign starts. Though various adjustments to the criteria may be necessary. The same criteria may be less relevant, measures may have to take into account changes in company philosophy or socioeconomic factors such as inflation or type of target audience, etc. Neverthe-less the basis for assessment remains the same and the tracking stays on track.

'Before' research concerns the context in which the communication will appear and in which the company operates. The company has to decide how broad this context dare be. Much will depend upon the nature of the communication. A corporate advertising campaign aimed at a specific audience may demand research which is narrow but deep (e.g. into industry or market) whereas a corporate identity change may demand research into society at large with special emphasis on, say, interested groups.

Some of this information already exists—in other data within the company. Research is rarely as discrete as its practitioners think it is. Background to one study (e.g. into new product development) will provide background information on, say, life-style or changing social habits. Further information is provided by syndicated studies, government bodies and industry associa-tions. The media themselves are generous (though self-interested) providers of data.

Desk research takes time but saves money. It receives scant attention at market research gatherings or in research publications. A research handbook of some 400 pages devotes two paragraphs to the subject. But desk research can't do it all, since corporate communication requires the company to find the answers to some specific questions concerning its image about which, unless of course a tracking study has already been commissioned, it can only hazard a guess. Group discussion—focus groups—with samples of relevant audiences can prepare the way, help determine how the company is seen and which aspects of the company's activities are known, understood, appreci-ated, ignored, supported, rejected, puzzled over.

This research must take place before—or at the latest simultaneously with—the determining of the corporate philosophy. Research is a manage-ment tool, a diagnostic instrument which can help the company to discover its strengths and weaknesses as perceived by its key audiences and analyse their cause. There may be very good and obvious reasons. As the psychiatrist says to his client in the cartoon, 'The reason you have an inferiority complex Mr Johnson is because you are clearly inferior.' On the other hand there may be aspects of the corporate character which the company has not communi-cated: the identity does not carry the personality. Again, there may be too many conflicting messages some of which are serving as noise. Then there may be a shock discovery—the company is invisible. Research is almost impossible because respondents don't know who the interviewer is talking about! In which case the purpose of the corporate communication becomes 'awareness'.

One particularly valuable diagnostic aid is research designed to 'map' the market-place. The company is seen in relation to other companies. Two axes (or sets of two axes) are drawn. For example, the respondent is asked to think of each company in, say, banking, on a spectrum from old-fashioned to modern and on a spectrum from personal service to computerised service. Where the axes cross is the mid-point of each spectrum. The banks are positioned on the map according to the average scores of the respondents. Bank *A* as a result sees how it is perceived, how that perception relates to its competitors and possibly where a new position (within achievable distance) could help it.

Many other techniques exist to help the company see itself as others see it. One is cluster analysis. Aspects of the company's personality are plotted. Certain aspects cluster. Attributes seem to go together naturally. Conversely incongruities may appear. It may depend upon the company being researched or the industry in which it operates. For example, it could happen that 'old-fashioned' and 'computerised' could cluster as desirable attributes for a bank whereas they would ill fit together for an airline.

During this period of deciding objectives for the corporate communications another form of research could take place—management meeting to 'hot-house' a corporate philosophy. In this intense think-session, the chief executive (or the corporate communications director) will act like the research moderator of a focus group. The individual members will be asked to measure the company's performance on various scales, map its position, draw its image by analogy . . . the sort of activities research respondents participate in and generally enjoy when asked to rate a packet of dessert mix. At the end of this period the company, thanks to its own deliberations and its dialogue with target audiences, will have determined its corporate position. It simply needs to test it out on the target group(s).

Garbett[10] warns that it may be difficult to locate 'respondents in government, finance and upper executive positions'. He also advises that the positioning be checked out with:

> . . . key middle management employees, selling agents or wholesalers, people closely related to the company who can provide a bridge between management's view of itself and the outside public's view.[11]

Because this research takes place within an organisation there is no reason why the procedures should be any less strict. Attitudes so close to home may polarise. Friends may tell you things they think you want to hear. Foes may express their personal antagonism. Professional research monitoring is essential.

There remains but one job to do and communication can start. The job, however, takes time. A goal has to be fixed. The overall objectives have already been set—in terms of awareness and attitude shift among key publics in order *ultimately* to affect a purchase. But, as we have seen, these long-term objectives form very imprecise and distant measures of communication. Furthermore, there may be other elements in the marketing mix. The success of corporate advertising (unlike product advertising) can be assessed primarily on awareness and attitude. Restricting it to these legitimate ends allows for possible cause and effect relationships to be analysed, provided a benchmark is set up immediately prior to the outset of the campaign.

The initial research will have given the company some idea of the way the company is regarded, though it is unlikely to be sufficient for the purpose of the benchmark study—especially since working out the company philosophy and message may have shifted the original criteria and altered the composition of the target groups. The company needs to know how well those groups know the company, what they know about its products, policies, type of service, size, management and/or financial skill, etc. How does the company score on the various attributes the company—and the key publics—regard as important? Come to that, how well do other companies in their industry perform?

Different research companies have perfected different techniques though the principles are roughly the same. Clients, of course, are encouraged to stay with the research company in order to be able to measure progress (meaningfully—in the same terms) and to assess their own performance against that of other companies within the industry, and other industries against the norms assembled over the years by that particular research outfit. In corporate communication everything is long term and decisions, accordingly, have to be carefully arrived at. We shall look in some detail in Chapter 32 at the MORI methodology. Meanwhile, to maintain balance, here is how the Opinion Research Corporation of the US describes its Image Measurement System.[12]

> The basis . . . is a list of statements, both favourable and unfavourable, from which the respondent chooses those which he feels best fit his idea or impressions of the company.
> He is free to choose as many or as few as he likes. Hence, only the items which stand out in someone's mind as primary characteristics of the company tend to be chosen.
> The statements cover various dimensions of a company's image such as product reputation, customer relations, corporate leadership, role as an employer, and civic responsibility.
> The statements are rotated so that possible bias, due to positioning in the list, can be minimised.
> Following this list of statements, overall image profiles are compared for the relevant companies under study.
> The data are presented in terms of the percentage of informants who selected each statement as characterising the company.

ORC rate an image selected by more than 40% of the public as an extremely strong element of a company's reputation. Between 20% and 40% may be regarded as stronger than average.

Whichever of the reputable systems is chosen, the company ends up with a good idea of how well known the company is and for what—*plus* a photograph of the company taken at one particular period of time. Analysis of the picture, the words and the figures, will give the company enough data from which to set the goals the communications programme is to achieve.

In Chapter 32 we shall examine some goals—scored and missed.

32

Research—the how

Bob Worcester's attitude to corporate image research is like the Irishman's response to the motorist seeking directions: 'If I were you I wouldn't start from here.'

Images have been forming and changing as long as the company has been in existence. Research should have begun ages ago. Other influences, extraneous to the company but impinging on it, need to be measured. But then MORI have a battery of trend measurements—over a decade's worth—which enables them:[1]

> . . . to give early warning of danger in the expectations and concerns felt by the public towards large companies in general.[1]

MORI research how key sub-groups feel about the ethics, profitability, practices, etc. of business in general and of industries in particular. The inner ring on our wheel is a special concern of Worcester:[2]

> In some industries (such as oil, banking and insurance) individual company images are significantly affected by attitudes generic to the industry, and it is essential to understand them as such. For other companies, research can point out areas of operation which are well regarded, but in which the company has failed to project its involvement—or conversely, poorly regarded sectors with which the company is disproportionately, and damagingly associated.

Having set the context, MORI then look at the specific company and, like ORC, measure the strength of the image. They use five-point scales of familiarity and favourability. The respondent is given a board and some cards (bearing the name of the company under scrutiny and its competitors). The respondent places each card along each scale indicating how well it knows it and how highly it regards it. Overall ratings are then obtained for a number of companies and mean familiarity is plotted against mean favourability on a 'scatter' chart.

The next step is what MORI call the 'cafeteria' technique. The respondent is handed a list of image statements and selects any—as many or as few as he wishes—which fit his opinions or impressions of the company in question.

The company thus gets a good idea not only of which attributes it is associated with but how deeply those opinions are held. On display in the cafeteria are statements like these:

. Their products are leaders in their field.
. Their products give real value for money.
. Treat customers fairly on complaints.
. Honest in the conduct of their business.
. You can believe their advertising.
. One of the most research-minded companies.
. Maintain a high standard on safety.
. Good company to work for.
. Deal fairly with trade unions.
. One of the best companies to own shares in.
. A company with international operations.
. Too big for the good of the country.
. Make too big a profit.
. Their prices are too high.
. Have too many labour disputes.
. Not concerned enough about important social problems.
. An old-fashioned and backward company.

Clearly this list and the ORC technique allow the company to set specific goals for the corporate communication programme. For example, though the overall purpose of the advertising might be to improve all favourable measures and reduce the negative ones—and obviously nobody is going to knock such an achievement—a more realistic aim would be to shift attitude on key attributes by a specific amount over a specific time period. This applies especially when the communication is addressed to a specific sub-group. Two dozen attributes may have been chosen by the total sample but as far as, say, MPs are concerned there is a serious misconception about the contribution the company is making to the UK economy. The goal can then be set in the numerical terms, e.g. to increase the 'contributes significantly to UK economy' image dimension from 20 to 45.

Nevertheless, a meaningful picture can emerge from a composite analysis of the attributes. For example, in Autumn 1979 and Autumn 1980, MORI measured the image profiles of four major oil companies in Britain, all of which were engaged in corporate advertising during the year. They also measured advertising recall. The two measures are plotted on a matrix, (see page 216).

Worcester maintains that a company landing in Sector *A* is in real trouble. 'The advertising has sunk without trace.'[3] Sector *B* isn't much better since the advertising is recalled but not much about the company. Sector *C* is

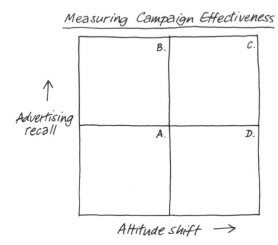

Measuring Campaign Effectiveness

satisfying—the advertising has penetrated and, particularly, shifted attitudes. But Sector *D* is Worcester's ideal territory:[4]

> Significant attitude shift being achieved without high awareness of the advertising or a feeling that the public are 'being got at' or that the company's expenditure on advertising is unnecessarily high.

Each oil company was measured on 34 positive image dimensions and an average increase calculated:[5]

> Figures for advertising recall largely reflected expenditure—yet the table recalls striking differences in the extent of the attitude shift, the real measure of the effectiveness of the advertising. Note the difference in achievement between companies 1 and 2, double the positive shift for similar recall (and expenditure). Oil company 4 though gets Worcester's accolade for 'achieving a strengthened image with relatively low media expenditure'.

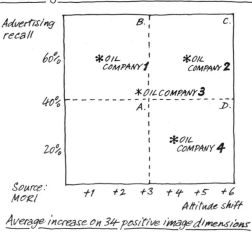

Advertising Awareness and Attitude Shift 1979–1980

Average increase on 34 positive image dimensions

Yankelovich, Skelly and White researched the effect of corporate advertising by taking a selection of image dimensions and relating them to ten companies. Half of them did no corporate advertising, half of them did. Respondents were asked which of these traits described each company very well. They calculated average scores for the five companies for each trait. The scores were higher on all traits for those companies who did corporate advertising. The percentage difference between the scores was termed the 'lift' factor. On the trait 'pays good dividends', the lift was 35%; on 'good stock to buy/own'—31%; on advanced technology/R&D—25%.

Yankelovich has done further research which has refined but confirmed these results. Tracking of corporate advertising—*en masse* or for a single advertisement—must be conducted consistently and regularly. The intervals of course will depend upon the nature and purpose of the campaign. There may be a deadline of a year. In which case it would be necessary to monitor progress at quarterly intervals. A five-year deadline would suggest a yearly review. The same time each year eliminates seasonal variations.

The BP campaign noted in the previous chapter had the following main objectives:[6]

1 To improve the public level of awareness of BP and its activities.
2 To improve BP's corporate image, in particular to: sharpen the company's identity as a successful British company; inform the public that BP is not just an oil company;
3 To improve the public's attitude to BP as an employer.
4 To improve the public's attitude towards BP as a source of information.
5 To support staff in their endeavours and boost morale.

The campaign was researched in 'waves'. Each wave used the same questionnaire. It comprised indices such as:

> awareness, familiarity, image, both in relation to other large companies and
> . . . to other oil companies, knowledge of the company's other activities, and
> . . . goodwill.[7]

There were also measures connected with advertising (spontaneous and prompted awareness, content, recall, slogan identification, etc.) and questions:

> . . . designed to explore the effect of other variables, unrelated to advertising
> . . . general background attitudes to the oil industry and large corporations.[8]

The benefits of the campaign decayed rather quickly. It was therefore resumed after about six months (earlier than planned) 'in order to consolidate the position gained'.

Research indicated that television was more effective than press in achieving BP's objectives. Subsequent advertising used television alone. The result in 1982, after three years of the campaign, was that when asked to mention the name of the first oil company they could remember 48% said BP compared with a figure of 20% in the mid–1970s. 50% of respondents regarded BP as successful compared with 22% at the start of the campaign.

Tracking studies serve to remind us of the tennis volleys of genuine communication. Feedback must be fed into the communications programme. The lessons learned from the respondents' reaction to the campaign form the basis for the company's next stage: the ads are adjusted, as are the emphases of the study itself. Some feedback may be critical or even hostile. The company should not over-react. The only safe advertising is bland advertising, the sort which elicits no response at all. People interested enough to write are people who are interested. Again, some of these comments can lead to copy revision or even new ads. And further research can check if these or any other new concepts ring bells with the key audiences (very much in the manner of product advertisement development research).

Phillips Petroleum's dialogue with their customers in the US revealed an indifference to stories of performance. 'They say it's our job,' said the corporate advertising director. 'They wanted to know what we were doing for the country and how responsible we are.'[9] The resulting ads increased awareness and strengthened the Phillips image. More telling, the company received requests for information which amplified the material presented in the advertising.

Oil companies are heavy corporate advertisers and researchers. When Esso UK realised in 1974 how important it was to be identified with exploration and production in the North Sea they briefed their agency McCann-Erickson and a then small creative outfit called The Creative Business. We answered the brief in our own way, suggesting that the company make news rather than ads and assume a brand leader role. Quite simply we recommended that they sponsor entertainment for the men on the oil rigs and the coastal bases. A troupe called Esso North Sea Artistes—with a distinctive, nostalgic and newsworthy acronym. We enjoyed ourselves putting the presentation together and watching the reaction in the Esso boardroom but we could feel the hot breath of the tiger on our backs. Sure enough a superb series of six forty-five second films appeared on television highlighting:

> . . . the significance of North Sea oil in everyday life, dramatising the difficulty of finding and bringing it ashore . . . and drawing attention to Esso's involvement . . . By the end of the first two weeks (October 1975) the public's awareness of Esso's involvement had more than doubled and was comparable with BP and Shell.[10]

The oil companies seem to be playing rather elaborate musical chairs, taking over each other's position in the awareness race. Even assuming each other's identities.

It's surprising how often the public muddle up just who says and who does what within an industry. When researching oil company advertising, we often find ourselves listening to 'recall' of the Shell (sic) Tiger.[11]

Shell, who are traditionally one of the country's predominant corporate advertisers, discovered from opinion research in 1980 that it had a considerable number of positive attributes (quality, elegance, reliability and a powerful emblem) and that certain subjects should be carried in the ads (information about Shell's contribution to the UK economy, its involvement in the North Sea—of course—and the Britishness of Shell). However, there was concern that Shell's profits were too large, its prices too high and that they did not show sufficient care for the environment. Hugh Wickham, head of marketing communications, commented:[12]

> We believed that our new campaign should give the public a better understanding of our aims and objectives and show that we are concerned with people; emphasise our authority to maintain (our) quality reputation . . . demonstrate our responsibility with the country.

Whilst Shell were researching themes for their new campaign, BP—who had access to the same research and came to a similar conclusion—somewhat pre-empted Shell with a heavy television campaign (referred to earlier). As a result BP showed a commanding lead on all dimensions in that year's MORI research. Shell's new campaign aimed to recover their lead.

As we go to press BP and Shell are battling it out, with Esso a clear third. The following figures for 1983 track moves over eight months on seven attributes.[13]

'Top of' Mind awareness (which company do you think of?)

	Feb	July	August	Sept
BP	22	45	38	38
Shell	31	23	26	28
Esso	24	17	19	17

Makes a valuable contribution to Britain's economy

	Feb	July	August	Sept
BP	64	73	74	71
Shell	43	37	33	42
Esso	24	17	17	20

Involving North Sea oil

	Feb	July	August	Sept
BP	65	72	70	71
Shell	52	49	50	50
Esso	31	25	24	22

Helping to develop industry

	Feb	July	August	Sept
BP	63	70	73	68
Shell	32	37	38	47
Esso	24	13	14	17

Good job for British motoring

	Feb	July	August	Sept
BP	40	36	37	43
Shell	41	35	38	45
Esso	32	26	28	30

Responsible attitude to the environment

	Feb	July	August	Sept
BP	49	45	43	40
Shell	33	38	38	39
Esso	23	21	19	18

Socially responsible

	Feb	July	August	Sept
BP	35	41	44	40
Shell	32	27	27	33
Esso	16	12	15	12

Lloyds Bank, realising that all banks seem very much the same to ordinary people, felt the need for a positioning and identity for Lloyds which related more clearly with the feelings, needs and ambitions of customers. The identity chosen was the logo made living—the Black Horse. After four bursts of advertising, spontaneous awareness increased over five times. Symbol recognition increased by a factor of more than six. Nevertheless one respondent, asked what animal Lloyds Bank suggested, replied instantly, 'a sheepdog'. (It was like Lassie, it wagged its tail. It was always pleased to see you. The respondent, it transpired, had been well treated as a student. However, when asked what animal another Bank suggested he said 'a vulture').

Here is how Hoechst UK, the chemical giant, tracked its image over three years (1976–9).[14]

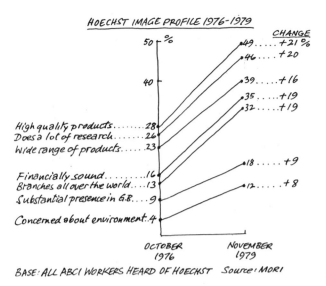

HOECHST IMAGE PROFILE 1976-1979

BASE: ALL ABC1 WORKERS HEARD OF HOECHST   Source: MORI

The table below shows how familiarity of Hoechst progressed over the same period against two competitors Bayer and CIBA-Geigy.

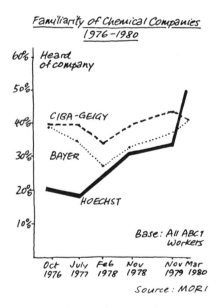

Familiarity of Chemical Companies 1976-1980

Source: MORI

Often, however, comparison is made outside a company's own industry. ITT Europe, for example, has tracked itself against IBM and Philips. These companies are only partially in the same industry as ITT, and were chosen primarily as American and European multinationals respectively. Despite all these important names and the years of hard labour put in by Worcester and others:

> There has been no extensive research on the impact of corporate advertising anywhere in Europe.[15]

So says Neil Ryder, until recently corporate advertising manager of the *Financial Times*. Which could be either a reason or a tailer for the *FT/RSL* survey. Comments Gillian Hall, *FT*'s market research manager:[16]

> The main objectives are to measure the relationships between corporate advertising and corporate image, and where such relationships exist to try to describe the factors that influence the relationship. The research should also help us to look at the relationship between the image of a company and the image of its industry.
>
> The research consists of two parts. The first is a continuous study with 1600 interviews being carried out over the first 12 months of the research [which monitors] movements in familiarity and image of individual companies against their advertising activities and of events such as involvements in take-overs, mergers, or indeed any newsworthy events.
>
> The second stage . . . is a point-in-time study in 4–6 weeks after the end of the 12 month continuous study [which] will examine the statistical relationship between image and advertising, both product and corporate.

A shortlist was formed of 120 companies. The research then drew up the following guidelines:

1 The image/awareness/contact questions must be answerable for all companies.
2 At least 10% of our sample should be likely to have heard of any company that we include on our list.
3 We excluded banks, airlines and car manufacturers as it is often very difficult to distinguish between product and corporate advertising.
4 A company could only be included if the list included a sufficient number of other companies in the same industry, so that analysis of the data by industrial sector would be meaningful.
5 The company must be prepared to provide us with regular analysis of their product and corporate advertising, PR and sponsorship activities, financial and other corporate announcements etc.

As a result, 54 companies formed the final list. Respondents are asked first of all how much they know about a company. Companies which a respondent knows nothing about are excluded from *all* further questions. Of the remainder the respondent is asked if he/she has had any contact and if so of what type (e.g. seen advertising, reported in media, interests in company, used products). The respondent is asked to name the company's main product category. The fourth question on the agenda is an old friend, the attribute list. In this case a relatively short one.

. A well managed company.
. Known for the high quality of its products and services.
. A leader in technological development.
. A company that contributes greatly to the British economy.
. I would recommend working for this company if a friend were to ask my advice.
. I would recommend investing in this company.
. Keeps the public well informed about its activities.
. I would defend this company in public if I heard it being criticised.

Early indications show that the sample knows a lot about 20% of all 54 companies, but, not surprisingly, the figure rises to 25% of British companies and, somewhat surprisingly, 25% also of US companies. In the oil, pharmaceutical and engineering section the figure is 31%. Advertisements are the chief source of information (40%), with 'reported in media' sharing second spot with 'used products' at about 28%. Hardly any of the companies were invested in. Only 20% of the companies are regarded as being well managed and 25% as having high quality products. Only 6% would the respondents defend in public. Of British companies 28% 'contribute greatly to the British economy'.

The participating companies will quite probably learn more from this survey than the rest of us. Corporate advertising has followed a lap or two behind product advertising in applying the disciplines and techniques of advertising planning and research. But there's none so devout as your late convert. The progress in the past decade (*pace* Mr Ryder) has been impressive. Advertisers are quick to learn where the blame for failure lies—in inadequate formulation of objectives, lack of specificity in targeting, poor media selection.

Research can help. To repeat, if you believe in image you must believe in research. Research helps a company get to grips with its image in no fewer than seven ways.[17] It shows changes over time; compares a company's image with those of other companies; it quantifies an anticipated outcome and a desired outcome; it provides internal comparisons (i.e. sub-groups within the company); it compares the ideal with the actual; and it points up international differences. The last word belongs, of course, to Worcester:[18]

> Properly used, research can contribute to the formation of advertising objectives and strategy, and to the evaluation of its success in changing perceptions and attitudes.

33

Crisis management

Nothing tests a person like a crisis. Nothing better tests a management or communications management. This is the time when 'corporate relations' stands up and gets counted. Or discounted.

> A spokesman for the company which manufactures thousands of paracetamol tablets a week said: 'I think these tablets are safe. I can't believe that these granules could kill anybody in this way unless they were in poor health.'[1]

Here is PR man in his familiar and uncomfortable role of defender. The situation is controlling him. The story is telling itself. To someone who probably can't grasp all the facts. Lord Northcliffe said that journalism is:[2]

> A profession whose business it is to explain to others what it personally does not understand.

Nevertheless, the reporter senses that the story won't go away. The PR man prefers to keep his hand on the tap controlling the flow of information from the company. The role of mass communications in society, say some sociologists, is to contain conflict and maintain the status quo. Business wants to tell the media things in its own time and at its own discretion. Instead it more often than not finds that the only occasions when the media are really interested find it unprepared and in a defensive mood.

> A spokesman for a petrol company said 'if all other petrol companies ceased giving gifts we would be the first to stop. As it is we must reluctantly continue.'[3]

News is incongruity. The PR man doesn't go out of his way to make himself or his company appear ludicrous. Maybe the journalist just hears it that way. Maybe he doesn't like 'spokespersons'. To him, Nixon's Ron Ziegler is the archetypal spokesman. When a real story happens and the journalist wants the facts 'the higher you get the better your chances for candour'.[4] The information the public relations department distributes is, according to the journalist, usually run-of-the-mill but the fault is believed to lie with management. Says a city bureau chief at the *Wall Street Journal*:[5]

> It's a rare corporation that fills in a public relations person. Some of them have a tendency to stonewall reporters, which is frustrating because of our deadlines. In general we go to the public relations department for non-controversial, non-investigative information. For other types of information we go to the inside sources.

PR departments—in time of crisis—are regarded by the investigative journalist as providers not of message but of noise. They protect the company, fillet the truth and predigest the communication. Occasionally they delude themselves by achieving favourable headlines in the more friendly publications.

> Lack of understanding is the reason for Britain's drug industry's bad image.[6]

That's all right then—seems to be the intended reaction—we're just misunderstood. (Though, to be fair, the article points out that misunderstanding, like communication, is two-way.) But three drug disasters in a generation are more than mere 'misunderstanding'. Thalidomide, Practolol and Opren are genuine causes for public concern and media scepticism. Nor can it be denied that public relations and advertising skills were used to cloud issues, obscure and avoid as much as inform.

What makes a crisis so dangerous for a company is precisely what makes it meat and drink for the investigative journalist—one problem will inevitably lead to at least one more. The story will be related backwards and forwards in time. The initial incident or effect (e.g. a death), will generate an enquiry into the cause (e.g. a fault), which will spawn a subsequent further effect (e.g. a retraction or correction or resignation). The PR defence mechanism may put the story on hold for a short time but delaying tactics will create the suspicion not only that the 'facts' aren't what they seem, but that the origin of the incident was itself attended by dubious communication. 'PR exercises'—in this pejorative sense—are less common than the detractors would claim. The problem is that (as any PR man knows) one bad story will be remembered while 100 good stories are paid scant attention.

The US PR community is still trying to live down the Potlach Industries scandal of the late 1960s. The lumber company wanted to demonstrate its pollution control sensitivity. It showed a clean flowing river. The ad in *Time* said: 'It cost us a bundle but the Clearwater River still runs clear.' The *Wall Street Journal* discovered that the photograph had been taken more than 50 miles upstream from the factory.[7]

> Downstream, (they pointed out), the Clearwater isn't so clear. Fishermen say foam and the smell, both products of the Potlach plant, are sometimes evident 60 miles downstream.

Westinghouse Electric Corporation is the world's largest maker of nuclear reactors. After the Three Mile Island accident they decided to be aggressive. They issued a statement saying that the plant's safety features had been tested by the incident proving just how safe nuclear power was. A day later the danger increased. Pregnant women and children were evacuated. How did Westinghouse react? They refused to comment further and said its earlier statement 'doesn't apply anymore'.[8]

Three Mile Island, cigarettes and health, the recall of a car, Tylenol, Opren, asbestos—crises generally affect large numbers of people, can seriously damage the company's reputation, can cost the company heavily and, as we have seen, are of continuing interest to the media because there are vibrations both backwards and forwards in time.

A crisis is a critical situation, the outcome of which will be of great importance to the company. Strictly speaking it is a decisive or crucial time, a point when forces come together, a 'crunch'. However, it may *last* any length of time. It could be over in hours or carry on for years. Often crises aren't recognised. Sometimes time bombs are spotted and defused. Some remain hidden—in bills slowly working their way through the legislature or embryonic issues growing in the warmth of debate among interested groups.

Special interest, segmentation within society and media response to social change—each of these factors will contribute to the germination of crisis. As could specific EEC legislation in the areas of disclosure requirement, protection, economic nationalism, trade union power and industrial democracy. Special interest groups are no longer unprofessional idealists with a second-hand Roneo machine. As Peter Ryan, director of Public Affairs for the drug company Sterling-Europa said:[9]

> The media expansion has been better understood and better exploited by the questioning radical elements in our society than by the unquestioning reactionaries who still inhabit even the most successful and forward thinking parts of our establishment.

In case that sounds a particularly British view here's the director of corporate communications, Dow Chemical Canada Inc. describing typical management as:[10]

> . . . hard-nosed, profit oriented . . . people who, in the majority, lacked any well developed sensitivity to the world outside the plant gate, except insofar as their interest in customers went, who were petrified by the television medium, and who viewed the PR function as little more than the producers of an employee house magazine of dubious distinction.

The government may set up a Committee on the Safety of Medicines (CSM), but an independent pressure group keeps an eye on them. Drug Watch has brought together various consumer organisations and members from community health councils, the universities and the law.

A company may not suspect a time bomb is there—it may not hear the ticking. It cannot, however, avoid the explosion. Most 'crisis management' takes place in the midst of debris. The company dares not say anything. It has to speak with one voice. The issue is clear. The chief executive is closely involved. The act of communicating concentrates the corporate mind on the corporate policy. The company must wherever possible take the initiative.

These, you will note, are precisely the courses of action we have been advocating for normal corporate communication. This is *not* to imply that communication procedures which don't work well in normal times suddenly click into place the moment a disaster erupts. In fact the well rehearsed procedures give a company in a crisis a head start. But crisis focuses activity. Questions of territory and personal authority become irrelevant. The company's affairs are more efficiently coordinated and directed.

Hygrade Food Products,[11] a Detroit company, make Ball Park frankfurters, second biggest seller in the US, and accounting for over half of the company's $200m sales.

In November 1982 a housewife rang the *Detroit News* to say she had found a razor blade in a Ball Park frankfurter. The newspaper ran the story and thirteen other people claimed they had found blades, nails and other foreign objects. The president stopped all production, recalled 350,000 pounds of frankfurters and put all employees at the Livonia plant to work over the weekend inspecting thousands of cases of Ball Parks with metal detectors. The company set up a media information centre, gave the press full cooperation and facilities and named Chuck Ledgerwood as spokesman. Ledgerwood told the media what it was doing. He also visited the home of the woman who had brought the complaint and discovered that her husband used the same sort of blade (Gillette Blue) which she had alleged she had found in the frankfurter. Under police questioning she and her husband and the other claimants admitted to having lied in order to claim big company settlements. When the media realised that the company had been victimised it rallied to the company's cause. So did the mayor who proclaimed: 'Livonia loves Hygrade week'.

The $1m in lost sales was virtually recovered. Originally the disgruntled plant personnel had been suspected. Ledgerwood spoke in front of all of them and apologised. The crisis, says Ledgerwood, pulled the company together and productivity has risen considerably. The PR effort cost $30,000.

But then public relations need not be an expensive exercise. It is wrong to compare it with advertising. It is usually far more focused than advertising and the media space it occupies does not itself have to be paid for. The time and manpower expounded, estimates Traverse-Healy,[12] equates with that of a lawsuit, government investigation or public boycott.

> Putting it at its lowest, public relations will have more than earned its keep if these and similar disputes have been avoided.

Seven people died in Chicago after swallowing Tylenol capsules. The event put J&J's $450m sales in jeopardy and cast doubt over the efficiency of the company's entire operation. The news quotient was sensational—e.g. half a million press cuttings. But J&J were well disciplined. They had a corporate philosophy, clear lines of authority and a procedure. The chairman ran a working group which contained the president and four other top executives. It met twice daily for six weeks. It took the initiative. A flash alert went to the public. Airlines were alerted. The medical profession was informed at once. The company spent $100m, in recall. The product was introduced in a triple-seal pack within six weeks (instead of what would have normally taken a year) and a press conference mounted via satellite in 30 cities. The culprit who had added cyanide to the tablets was caught. Eight bottles had been tampered with. A total of 31 million bottles were destroyed. J&J regained over 85% of previous sales in six months and secured fifth place in *Fortune*'s survey of most admired companies but first place in the 'Community and Environmental Responsibility' section. J&J would probably endorse the International Association of Business Communications' four principles for dealing with emergencies: preparation, candour (even if it hurts), action and initiative.

Norwest Bank in Minneapolis was the victim of the biggest blaze in the city's history. They had a contingency PR plan to ensure customers that their funds were safe and business would continue as usual:

> They provided for the location of visual back-up records, numbers of key executives to be notified and the availability of office space in the event departments would have to be relocated at short notice.[13]

The president went on television. A 'war room' was put up in the building opposite. The press was given unlimited access to bank executives. When Norwest reopened for business bank executives, wearing red and white T-shirts with the message 'NW Bank Info', directed customers to bank locations.

Preparation, candour, action and initiative. They seemed sadly lacking at Three Mile Island. The *Wall Street Journal*[14] pictured the plant's 'beleaguered public relations officers huddled in a nearby motel room'. The press was getting hostile, the public was getting nervous and the rest of the nuclear power industry was getting its head down. Ideas were suggested—according to the *Wall Street Journal*—involving the Metropolitan Edison Company who were to hold a press conference with so-called experts who would show that the accident wasn't serious; reporters would be 'placated with "press kits"'; and the media could be given a special list of Met Ed communication numbers to call for official information—only the phones would be off the hook.

As it happens, none of these suggestions was used. As it also happens, two *Philadelphia Inquiry* reporters heard the discussion and a full report appeared the following Sunday headed: 'A Secret Utility Meeting about Public Relations'.

The team ended up getting the sort of publicity they sought to avoid. In fact it was considerably worse—on two counts: first, it detailed steps which were never taken; second, it ensured that *any* subsequent action would be unlikely to be believed. The older you get the more you appreciate the old sayings. 'Don't cry wolf.' 'Honesty is the best policy.' 'Oh what a tangled web we weave . . . '

At Three Mile Island they wove jargon. The Nuclear Regulatory Commission and other officials resorted to abstract words. Abstractions don't hurt as much. Abstractions can hide facts from the public. Perhaps from your colleagues, even from yourself.

> The great enemy of clear language is insincerity. When there is a gap between one's real and one's declared aims, one turns, as it were, instinctively to long words and exhausted idioms, like a cuttlefish squirting out ink.[15]

What was going on in the reactor building? One official discounted the possibility of a reactor melt-down and consequent hasty evacuation of the public as 'a failure mode that has never been studied'. We know what noise does to the integrity of the communication. It doesn't do much good either to the integrity of the communicator.

One lie, one piece of verbal dexterity to confuse or to hide, and the issue which till then could have been reasonably debated becomes polarised. The company's credibility is severely damaged. The issue is seen in strictly black and white terms. All previous goodwill has been hurt. What had previously been accepted as fact is now reinterpreted for the 'real' meaning (i.e. for the purpose behind the statement or the fact that the company is presumed to have wanted to hide).

I should imagine that any company involved in a crisis, particularly one which fermented gradually, regrets actions which weren't taken as a matter of course some time before. The need to communicate is not always felt. More's the pity. As we have seen, the writing of a leaflet or booklet forces the company to examine its principles and operating procedures.

Today sophisticated companies pre-empt not criticism, but prejudiced reporting, by making known their involvement in societal issues. By openly communicating when they don't have to they make their position known and their right to a voice, if and when an issue arises, will be recognised by the media and the public. Sometimes it is the industry's rather than the individual company's voice which is heard. The individual company may not be able to afford the cost of an advertising campaign and the industry can also bear the brunt of hostility better. Industries, more and more, are telling their story—proactively—to more and more publics.

Study of these crises suggests certain guidelines.

1.   Take the initiative

A company must not try to maintain a low profile. The incident will be subject to speculation in the media long before any official or semi-official enquiry gets going. Accordingly how a company behaves in the initial period is vital to goodwill—and business.

A company must take the initiative. No news (and 'no comment') will be interpreted as bad news. Silence will imply guilt.

2.   Keep in contact with the media

Dialogue must start when times are good. This can pre-empt a crisis—or at least mitigate its effect. It will put any bad news in context. It will provide favourable background for the good news.

3.   Speak the truth

Journalists are better at detecting lying than company spokespersons are at lying. And anyway telling the truth is always easier.

4.   Treat the media with respect

The incident is a genuine news item. It probably irks the company to realise it will get more coverage from this than it achieved in total in the past three years. Nevertheless it must realise that the journalist has a job to do and should not assume that he is antagonistic. (Furthermore, relationships forged in fire might well last.) A US company advises its executives:

> The reporter on the scene or on the phone only wants to report the facts, not to pass judgement on our company. The quicker we give him what he needs, the quicker he will move on to another story and permit you to get on with your work.
> Keep a list of news media handy so that you can call them with details if they're not on the scene.
> If you have a camera, shoot pictures.

As reporters arrive, give them all pertinent information, and advise them regarding photographs.

5. Do not speculate

A company must deal in facts. It must assume that everything it says will be quoted. Thus speculation—in the belief that it is 'off the record'—should be avoided.

6. Do not ask for a retraction

Misquoting will frequently happen. By then the damage is done. Retraction generally adds to the story's development.

7. Make sure internal communications are good

Good internal communications generally indicate good external communications. (This was certainly the case with Johnson & Johnson during the Tylenol crisis.)

8. Keep your communications simple

The media don't know as much about the company as the company does. A company should say as much as necessary and no more. A spokesperson should not answer questions that aren't asked. (J&J restricted the discussion to Tylenol, did not discuss other products and guarded the corporate reputation.)

Jargon must be avoided. The journalist a company deals with in a crisis may not be the industry or business journalist the company is usually in touch with. The company can't assume knowledge.

9. Think of the headline

This concentrates the mind and condenses the message. The main facts must be communicated first. As with all communication the sender must put himself in the position of the receiver.

10 Think about the questions

Similarly, the spokesperson must consider the questions a good, trained journalist will ask—who, what, when, why, where, how? The release must also answer these questions.

11. Think in terms of people

News is about people. Facts, statistics, and stories must be personalised.

12. Monitor all media coverage

Only by keeping tabs on every release, every phone conversation, every report, article, comment and news item can the company hope to retain some control of the story. When the media makes a factual error they should report it at once. Communication is continuous dialogue. Keeping tabs teaches the company how media relations works and what works better.

13. Follow up

The story isn't over when the crisis ends. The company should write and thank the media, provide follow-up information, maintain the dialogue.

To any good PR man or company communications executive none of this is new. To the rest of us it all sounds common sense. The sad fact is that common sense is a rare commodity in the world of company communications. The companies who succeed in crisis management keep things simple: the policy is one of short lines of communication, single-minded messages and direct contact. The issues are clear. The action is straightforward.

People look back on war as a time when everything somehow was simple and clear cut. They knew what had to be done and set about doing it. It's the same with crisis communications. A company pulls together. But coordination of effort—in communications as with everything else—should not be a crisis necessity but a basic operational policy.

34

Dimensions of image

Image is a representation in the mind. But it is very powerful. It is a 'true reality'. It affects attitudes which in turn affect behaviour. No company can afford to ignore image. The impression it creates—consciously or unconsciously, whether it wishes to or not—inevitably affects the people who do business with it. No wonder that companies are deluded into a belief that impression management is *their* true reality, that the appearance of, say, efficiency or social concern will be an adequate and less expensive substitute for the real thing. The gains are short term. Impression management is successful only when the image reflects the reality, when the aspects of identity which the company chooses to emphasise are congruent with its personality. A company may decide to change its personality. This is perfectly possible—but difficult. No wonder that some companies choose the softer option of 'changing their image'. Changing a personality to fit a new desirable image requires a change of heart to match the change of face. Company beliefs and behaviour will need to be modified.

The impetus for a personality change, no matter how small, is often research of some sort. Bad financial results or loss of custom will tell a company that it is doing something wrong. Remedial behaviour can be effected here, of course, without recourse to research. However, when the problem isn't that cut and dried, when the company begins to worry about how it is perceived, then research is essential. It is the only means of delivering a picture of how the company is seen by the audience it wants to impress. The techniques we examined (see Chapters 31 and 32) will provide answers on which the company can base its action.

One advantage of such investigation is that it makes an image *tangible* and therefore a tool of management. Impressions become quantified. Research is generally of more use to the executive when numbers are attached. But numbers are meaningless unless seen in context. Is this figure higher than it was? Is this figure less than it should be? Is this figure on a par with the figure for the industry? Management uses simple mathematics throughout its working day to run the enterprise. When it comes to image, however, it is thrown back on hunch, subjective impression, conflicting views and prejudice, couched in a language of unbusinesslike imprecision.

If image is a company asset then any decision which affects the external perception of the company must be carefully examined. If image is a reflection of the company's personality then it is conceivable that change (for better or worse) in corporate thinking or behaviour will be detected impressionistically. Indeed, an executive's first awareness of the importance of any change may consist of a chance remark overheard or a casual observation from a friend. 'I see your lot's got a second wind.' 'You're getting hard-nosed in your old age.' If image is this important there must be a means of giving it tangible shape, not simply in occasional research reports, but in the day-to-day running of the business.

There is. It happens like this. The chief executive or the director of communications calls a meeting of the board of management. They agree a list of long-term corporate values, those important attributes which they jointly believe have been institutional in building the company and/or will be instrumental in the future growth. They must be scrupulously fair. They must include values which they believe are necessary whether or not they are currently held with as much fervour as they once were. Reaching a decision could take the morning but, as with so much communication work the activity itself is almost as important as the end product.

Let us suppose that the team decides on these corporate values.

1 INTEGRITY
2 VALUE FOR MONEY
3 TECHNICAL INNOVATION
4 SOCIAL RESPONSIBILITY
5 SERVICE
6 RELIABILITY
7 IMAGINATION
8 QUALITY

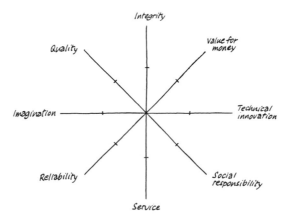

The eight values are charted. They form the spokes of a wheel. Each spoke is a nine point scale—zero at the centre, nine at the end of the spoke. The team is then asked to score the company's *perceived* performance on each dimension. The chairman of the session then asks each person to score individually and privately. He then reveals the individual variations on each dimension.

The exercise may stop at this point. There may be considerable disagreement over the company's image, its performance, its priorities. It is not unusual for otherwise tacit internal disagreement to surface in this way or the extent of personal differences to be revealed. Though this may not be the first time such differences have been aired, it is probably the first time they have been measured.

If the exercise stops it will still have served some purpose. If it goes ahead, then on the basis of the scores an average mark is plotted on each of the spokes. The dots are joined up.

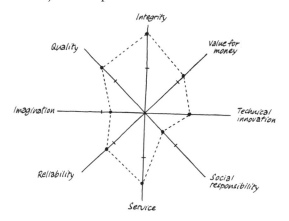

This is the pattern the company is thought to project. This is a print of the image. The team looks at it. Is it the image it *wants* to project? How far does it differ from the reality? Separate patterns are jointly created. If an overhead projector is available the patterns are drawn with coloured pens on acetate sheets. The reality is laid upon the image. The desired image is laid upon both. The team may decide to subdivide the audience, to look at the company through the eyes of specific markets. It may wish to involve more people in the exercise (e.g. divisional executives who specialise in the market under review).

How congruent are the various patterns? Is the company perceived very differently by the financial community or the trade? Is the local community's view different from that of the general public? Are there problems? Are the variables in perception a cause for concern or indifference? For example, it may not matter that the social responsibility score is less and the technical innovation higher among the trade than the local community. A reverse finding might cause headaches. Remember, these are as yet only internal guesses. The scores may be mutually arrived at but the team may be suffering mass self-delusion.

Professional research will no doubt be instigated to check internal accuracy and the validity of the measures themselves. However, even without this the exercise is useful in that it articulates and quantifies what have been up till then half-formed impressions, and by so doing allows management to check, if nothing else, the *consistency* of its actions. Apart from providing general guidelines for corporate behaviour, it can give practical help in three specific areas—branding, new product development and acquisition.

Let us suppose that the desired (and attainable) image pattern has been determined. Let us suppose also that the corporate name is the brand name and that therefore the identities of company and brand are largely similar. If all company products carry the identical mark and name then it is worth attempting a dimensional image study of each of the main products. If the patterns are reasonably similar then the company's communications will act synergistically (each product's communications will help the others), and a corporate advertising campaign, say, will function on all cylinders. Conversely, if the pattern shows wild dissimilarities then the company has seriously to consider its branding policy.

For example, the (imaginary) Monarch Oil Corporation stamps every product or service with its sign. It has come to represent technical superiority and imagination above everything else. Its lubricants, aviation fuels, specialist racing oils are unmatched and its standard of service is noted, not for its speed, but for the calibre and qualifications of its consultant technicians. Monarch's industrial division sells a bituminous compound to contractors. The product is virtually a commodity and the market is ruled by price. Here Monarch is forced to compete by means of price-cutting deals. The image pattern to that audience of Monarch's industrial division and its products would in no way coincide with that of Monarch's corporate image pattern. In fact the two images might be considered mutually damaging. Specific experience in the industrial context could give the lie to the grander image of the corporation: the added values of corporate reputation might seem irrelevant to the industrial customer, indeed could appear a hidden cost. In the first communication the mismatch of appearance and reality, and in the second the mismatch of offering and need—constitute noise. It could be worth Monarch considering hiving off its industrial division under a separate trading name.

Similarly, a consumer goods company could examine image patterns to find congruity between products, and as a result decide to institute a sub-brand (or sub-brands) for those which don't fit and/or could damage the company image. Conversely, a company with a multi-brand policy could use image patterns for the reverse purpose—i.e. to rationalise brands and assemble diverse products under a few key names.

In new product development there are at least two important and interrelating questions to be asked. First, what will this extension of the business do to the image of the company? Second, does the existing image affect the company's credibility in this new area? Internal attempts at delineating the image dimensions of the company and the new product will give some guidance, but professional help should be sought to ensure product compatibility. Compatibility is crucial in merger situations. British Leyland had its share of problems which research might have signposted. According to Jaguar's John Egan, BL:[1]

> ' . . . thought if they showed the Jaguar in their showrooms it would rub off on them. Instead, BL rubbed off on us.'

Two acetate sheets would have told them that. Similarly, what congruity—if any—would exist between the image dimensions of 'Austin' and 'Rover' now shot-gunned into Austin Rover?

The company's need to assess compatibility is even more pressing in the case of acquisition and diversification. The image pattern of the company to be acquired should be compared to the company's own before the final decision is taken. There are four options:

1. Swallow up.
2. Run the acquisition as a division or separate brand.
3. Treat the acquisition as an autonomous unit.
4. Decide against acquisition.

Research is crucial to the final decision in cases of acquisition. It is also important when a company contemplates diversification. Research, as we have seen, reveals a company to itself and helps a company decide who it is and what it is about. Diversification by definition will alter the personality of the company and the perceived image. It is not sufficient that the new enterprise can be contained within the company's sphere of operations.

A client of Le Creative Business in Paris makes metallic tubes. They decided to diversify. The diversification strictly speaking was only technological. However, the technological link was not as important as the image gap between their normal and new activities. Manufacturing congruity was subordinate to consistency of personality. LCB Paris conducted an audit of their products, analysed the company's image and assessed its relevance to each present and anticipated product area. They defined the company's *domaine de compétence*—'equipment for the practice of outdoor activities'. This can include everything from rucksacks to camping stools, from tents to outdoor games. But 'practice of' means that the activity must be seriously undertaken. If a new venture does not fit the personality of *professional application* it is not considered. However, the company had previously been doing considerable business in lounge chairs for television, a profitable use of metallic tube technology. Naturally they did not want to give this up. They continue making them under a different brand name.

The company obviously should also seek information on customer perception of its competitors. Here again, the views of its own people—at senior and at operational level—will be useful, not only as a base for the professional research study, but as a marketing discipline for management.

'Image' can be a vaporous concept. Imprecise language, superficial thinking and self-styled 'image makers' contribute to the insubstantiality. But the reality of image cannot be denied. It is a result of actuality—experience, and knowledge—plus the feelings, beliefs and impressions which that actuality engenders. If only a company could hold it, run a rule over it and assess its value. This book—and especially this chapter—has attempted to make that possible.

35

Prologue

This book pleads the case for a total view of company communications; for their integration and coordination; for a better understanding of the subject in order that its importance may be truly recognised within the company.

Recognition is the exception in British companies. The responsibility rests with the chief executive. It is a responsibility he is only too willing to delegate if indeed he regards it as worth bothering about at all.

I have drawn heavily on US material, not simply because the Americans have written more about corporate communications or because US companies spend a greater proportion of their promotional budgets on corporate advertising, but because the subject is treated more seriously and in greater depth across the Atlantic. The typical British managing director is reticent. His idea of communication is one-way (pea-shooter) and he regards dialogue as an inconvenience or a threat. Staff should speak when they are spoken to. Consumers are there to consume: why don't they get on with it? He is put out when an American opposite number on meeting him for the first time calls him by his first name. He is equally tongue-tied when a New York waitress hands him the check and says 'Have a nice day!' People are supposed to know their place. And besides he's never been good at small talk.

In Search of Excellence is subtitled *Lessons from America's Best Run Companies*. One of those lessons is 'Intense Communication'. In the best companies communications are informal, barriers are removed, meetings happen without formal agendas:

> The flow is free; everyone is involved. Nobody hesitates to cut off the Chairman, the President, a Board member.[1]

Such behaviour would not occur if the chief executive did not positively encourage it. The communication policy of a company is dictated by the boss: in some cases actively, in most cases passively. The passive communicator regards the subject as low priority and is then surprised when the company's image fails to match what he believes is the company's reality. He finds the company has been summed up by a journalist as, shall we say, 'a sleeping giant'. Whereas he knows the intensity of effort which has gone into retooling and export initiatives etc. His dozen years of hard labour controlling the company are as nothing compared to a phrase which is the outcome of, what, five days of investigation. ('And half of that was spent talking to our competitors.')

But if the image doesn't fit the reality whose fault is it? The journalist may have been unprofessional, selective in his sources or anxious to reinforce a previously held belief. But had the company been paying attention to its communications the image could have taken better care of itself. And had it conducted tracking studies the company would have seen where its potential strengths and weaknesses lay.

Only too often, however, the image *does* fit the reality. If the company has not managed successfully to communicate its activities then the title sleeping giant may be merited. Certainly the communications department has been caught napping.

Journalists aren't the only people who sum up companies. Remember, all our nine audiences do the same, piecing together their mosaics. A lady in a group discussion looked at a press advertisement for a supermarket. The full page was crowded with offers. She said she wouldn't shop there. 'The gangways would be too narrow.' The untidy ad suggested a messy store. The ad is a sample of the product.

Images are powerful. A company is what people feel it is, believe it is, as much as what they know it is. The company has to know how it is perceived. It has to be in charge of its image.

A Scottish engineering company thought it knew what it was and decided to run a series of corporate advertisements to tell the financial world about its size, development, profits and successful labour relations. Within six months it had ceased trading. Why? The labour force (who had not been consulted) read the ad, saw the reference to profits, put in a heavy wage demand which was refused, went on strike . . . Communication begins where clarity begins—at home. A major bank advertises in twenty countries. The campaign is planned in London. The *Financial Times* ran a supplement on Canada. Sure enough the bank took an advertisement. Not head office but the Canadian branch. Unfortunately it hadn't alerted London, let alone sought its approval, with the result that the bank was seen to be taking two different stances in the same publication in the course of a week. A bank which simultaneously projects two differing images may find that both have been subsumed by a third, namely that of a disorganised company. 'How can I trust them to transfer my money internationally when they can't even manage their own communications?'

Image and reputation reflect performance. It's the same for a company as for an individual. And the more company communicators think of themselves as people—and their audiences as people—the better will they understand and carry out communications. A company communicates whether it wants to or not. An image will be perceived whether it likes it or not. A company can't really be in charge of its image unless it knows what it's doing, has articulated that knowledge and communicated it internally first and externally. A company can't improve its image without reference to its personality. Nor can it *directly* alter its image. It can only adjust its identity properly to express its personality; or, if necessary, re-examine its personality. To attempt an 'image change' by means of a new logo, slogan and colour scheme unrelated to the character of the company can bring at best only short-term success. Painting the privy won't cure the plumbing.

On the other hand, understanding the image can help the company diagnose the problem. And the techniques of communication management by which image is made tangible—whether creative (writing a for-instance ad or concept board) or research (tracking study or dimensions of image) or both (role playing or Chinese portrait)—are pretty good diagnostic tools. They help a company discover its soul and express its philosophy, its *raison d'être*. With patience, effort and inspiration the company may manage to convey its personality in a sentence.

To the chief executive, suspicious of cheap slogans and simplistic solutions, I say this: other people will sum you up in a few words. The least you can do is try to do it for them. Besides, not all slogans are cheap slogans.

And once the philosophy and the message have been determined the company has to know how best to communicate it. Face-to-face is the model. Companies are people and so are audiences. How do people communicate? They transmit formally and informally. They use codes. They decode. They create and counteract noise. Logics are accompanied by 'psychologics'. Communication is exchange. Feedback is sought and interpreted. Action. Reaction. And reaction acted upon. Tennis volleys. Not a pea-shooter. Newton's Balls (see Chapter 6). Judge any piece of communication by the criterion of face-to-face. 'Would I actually say these words if the audience was sitting opposite me?' 'Does this invite response or simply dumb action?' 'Will sending this message by telex create more noise than sound?' 'What do I want him to think, feel, believe . . . do? And then what?'

If all forms of communication take face-to-face as the model then how much easier to coordinate them. For coordinated they must be. Even if the company decides against transmitting identical messages, a decision has been made and the consequences considered. All nine audiences will also need to be considered, because all nine will receive impressions, whether or not they are directly addressed. No communication is discrete. And of all nine audiences the staff is the most important. And of all nine media the *product* is the most important.

Nine times nine is 81. The wheel is a checklist, a thought starter, a reminder of the breadth and interrelationship of communications. A company good at internal communications is nearly always good at external communications.

The public relations department and the marketing department work for the same company and must contribute to a common communications policy. Product and corporate are related. As Nick Winkfield says:[2]

> Each product is marketed in the context of the company as a whole.

The press release and the television commercial, the packaging and the service engineer, the mailshot and the product performance—all, as far as the audience is concerned, emanate from the same source: the company.

The Copernican view of company communication puts the company at the centre. And at that centre's centre must be one person: the chief executive. It cannot of course be his full-time role, but whoever is in charge must have authority and the ear of the chief executive. It makes no sense to have him report to the financial director or the personnel officer or the sales department.

But does the person with the role have the authority? Bob Worcester estimates that 80% of the executives with the corporate affairs portfolio are no more than middle-rank executives responsible for the implementation of policy, of corporate projection, made by the chief executive or the Board. Instead of appointing a strong personality to take an active part in shaping policy and advising management they employ a gatekeeper. Instead of risking internal conflict between a communications director and other board members jealous of their territory, the chief executive chooses a mouthpiece. And very often that mouth is instructed to remain shut. A good example of chief executive/communications director partnership was that of Michael Edwardes and John McKay at BL.[3]

> McKay looked at his subject as being far wider than public relations, and reported direct to the Chairman and Chief Executive: therefore he knew exactly what was going on at the higher levels. He was fully in the picture, and to do the job properly, this was the only way to play it.

The attention paid by British management to advertising (whether for the company or its products) is significantly less than that of its US counterparts. Nevertheless, the expenditure of time and money on advertising is considerable when compared with the expenditure on internal communication. And internal communication is where the problem begins and where the solution must start.

Reticence has been regarded as natural, as peculiarly British, as an admirable quality. If we have achieved our ends we must not brag about it and if as a result we thereby do not teach others some secret of our success, so be it. If we have failed, then to talk about it is embarrassing to both listener and talker. Once more lessons stay unlearned.

Modesty is a virtue. Non-communication, however, is a commercial sin. And British understatement, dislike of the limelight, diffidence—no more than a convenient excuse for inaction. Because—and this is the truth of the matter—the average British chief executive hates to communicate. It makes him feel uncomfortable. He has got where he is without too much communication. Why should he have to put up with it now? He will pay lip service to the idea of employee communication and give it a low priority.

He may—possibly—genuinely believe that his employees need to know how the company is doing, what management's plans are and how they can help. But he will not stand up and say so, let alone enter into dialogue. He will find alternative media—personal or impersonal. He will assume that essential information is seeping down—rather than making sure that essential information is moving across and back again. Communication to him means crossing social and cultural barriers and adopting unaccustomed roles. 'The Ruling Class,' says communication consultant Douglas Haines, 'is raucous in the hunting field, noisy in bed and reticent everywhere else.'[4] Reticence in the office is a brake on efficiency. Non-communication is negative communication. Internally as well as externally. Successful companies make communication part of the job specification of senior personnel.

Walk into any executive's office in Novo's Copenhagen headquarters and you will find a white board and a stock of felt pens. (An IBM executive would recognise that. How else do you talk and exchange ideas?) Danes are not nature's extroverts. They're rather like us. But Novo Danes are different. Novo has an image of a successful research-based company, innovators in bio-technology. And the reality matches the image not because they worry about their image but because they concern themselves with communication.

If the image is wrong the fault is that of the company and the onus is on the chief executive. If that's you, what do you do? How do you start? Here are ten 'action points'. Only two (items 2 and 6) need involve you in outside costs.

1. Choose eight *image dimensions* by which you believe (honestly) your company should be judged. Form them into spokes (zero at the centre, nine at the edge) and plot:

   (i) *Your* assessment of company performance.
   (ii) Your idea of the image perceived by your most important audience.
   (iii) Your ideal image pattern.

   Invite colleagues to do the same. Discuss. If necessary. . .

2. Commission *benchmark image research* as the start point of a tracking study. Examine it to decide which image dimensions of the study need correcting. Set measurable goals.
3. If you have a *philosophy* set it against the image revealed in 2 above or your internal assessment, 1 above.
4. If you don't have a *philosophy*, then you and/or your colleagues must write one. If possible also sum it up in one line.

5. Examine your *identity*. Is it a true reflection of your personality (as defined in your philosophy)? If not ask a consultant to help you correct it.
6. List the *nine audiences* and check how—and how well—you communicate with each. Are the communications planned or accidental, direct or indirect?
7. List the nine *channels*. How many are being used? 'Rotate the Wheel.' Are there unusual means of contacting your audiences?
8. Assess the quality of *face-to-face communications*. Especially your own. Check it for noise. How good is the feedback? (Is it pea-shooter or Newton's Balls?) What is it doing to relationships?
9. Use *face-to-face* as a model for all communication.
10. Check the *coordination* and integration of all communications—internal/external; corporate/product; advertising/PR etc. Who is responsible? And to whom?

Corporate communications must happen by design not by default. Ralph P Davidson,[5] chairman of the board at Time Inc., puts the case most forcefully:

> Time and again, we've seen companies ignore that lesson. They keep their communciations professionals on the fringe of the organisation; they ignore planning; they regard outside opinion as only something to manipulate; they hoard secrets and refuse to co-operate with reporters, employees and community leaders; and then they're totally unprepared when the unexpected happens.

Amen.

Image is a reality.
It is the result of our actions.

If the image is false and our performance is good, it's our fault for being bad communicators.

If the image is true and reflects our bad performance, it's our fault for being bad managers.

Unless we know our image we can neither communicate nor manage.

References

Chapter 1
1. Peters, T. J. and Waterman, R. H. jnr., (quote), *In Search of Excellence*, New York: Harper and Row, 1982.
2. Galli, A., 'Corporate advertising: more than just a nice warm feeling all over', *Public Relations Journal*, November 1971.

Chapter 2
1. Ways, M., 'Business needs to do a better job of explaining itself', *Fortune*, September 1972.
2. Martan, K. and Boddewyn, J. J., *Journal of Advertising Research*, August 1978, quoted in Garbett, T. F., *Corporate Advertising. The What, the Why and the How*, New York: McGraw Hill, 1981.
3. Harriman, B., (quote), 'Up and down the communications ladder', *Harvard Business Review*, September/October 1974.
4. Kindre, T. A. and Callanan, P. W., 'Facing the issues: corporate advertising's greatest challenge', *Public Relations Journal*, November 1973.
5. Davidson, R. P., (quote), 'Total corporate communications—by design or default?', *Cross Currents in Corporate Communications*, New York: Fortune, **12**, 1983.
6. Kemp, G., *The Company Speaks*, London: Longman, 1973.
7. Traverse-Healy, T., 'The state of the art', a paper presented at the IPRA Congress, Bombay, January 1982.
8. McLaughlin, N., 'Shall we put the chairman on the box?', *Corporate Communications*, supplement to *CBI News*, 11 November 1983.
9. Cordtz, D., 'Business and television', *Cross Currents in Corporate Communications*, New York: Fortune, **5**, 1976.
10. Burdus, A. 'Communicating confidence. Will the big corporations please speak up?', *Advertising Magazine*, Summer 1980.
11. Ways, M., *Cross Currents in Corporate Communications*, (Introduction), New York: Fortune, **1**, 1972.

Chapter 3
1. Rogers, C., *Theory of Personality and Behaviour*.
2. McGinniss, J., *The Selling of the President*, London: Andre Deutsch, 1970.

3. Boorstin, D., *The Image*, London: Weidenfeld and Nicolson, 1962.
4. Stridsberg, A. (ed.), *Controversy Advertising*, New York: International Advertising Association/Hastings House, 1977.
5. O'Sullivan, T. *et al*, *Key Concepts in Communication*, London: Methuen, 1983.
6. Windt de, E. N., 'Corporate communications—top management perspective', *Cross Currents in Corporate Communications*, New York: Fortune, **4**, 1975.
7. Ways, M., 'Business needs to do a better job of explaining itself', *op. cit.*
8. McFadyen, E., 'How to achieve successful regeneration', *Retail and Distribution Management*, November/December 1983. (My italics.)
9. Kemp, G., *The Company Speaks, op. cit.*

Chapter 4

1. Priestley, J. B., *Saturn over the Water*, London: Heinemann, 1961.
2. Goodpaster, K. E., and Matthews, J. B. jnr., 'Can a corporation have a conscience?', *Harvard Business Review*, January/February 1982.
3. Johnson, D., 'Corporate communications and the consumer', *Cross Currents in Corporate Communications*, New York: Fortune, **4**, 1975.
4. Olins, W., *The Corporate Personality*, London: The Design Council, 1978.

Chapter 5

1. Martin, N. H. and Simms, J. H., 'Power tactics', *Harvard Business Review*, November/December 1956.
2. *Encyclopaedia Britannica*, definition of *personality*.

Chapter 6

1. Goethe, W., *Elective Affinities*, 1809.
2. *Webster's New World Dictionary*, definition of *communication*.
3. *Ibid*.
4. *Webster's New Collegiate Dictionary*, definition of *communication*.
5. Shannon, C. and Weaver, W., *The Mathematical Theory of Communication*, University of Illinois, 1982.
6. In common with most writers on this subject I owe a debt to Shannon and Weaver whose construct this is.
7. Gordon, G. N., *The Languages of Communication: A Logical and Psychological Examination*, New York: Hastings House, 1969.
8. Churchill, W. S., from a speech delivered in the House of Commons, 4 June 1940, quoted in *The Second World War*, **2**, *Their Finest Hour*, London: Cassell, 9th edition, 1983.

Chapter 7

1. Wrightsman, L. S., and Deaux, K., *Social Psychology in the 80s*, Monterey, California: Brooks/Cole, 3rd edition, 1971.
2. Lannon, J. and Cooper, P., 'Humanistic advertising. A cultural perspective', *International Journal of Advertising*, London: Holt, Rinehart and Winston, **2**, July-September 1983.

3. Cantril, H., 'Perception and interpersonal relations', *American Journal of Psychiatry* **CXIV**, 1957.
4. Zalkind, S. S. and Costello, T. W., 'Perception: implications for administration', *Administrative Science Quarterly*, September 1962.
5. Wrightsman, L. S. and Deaux, K. (quote) *op. cit.*
6. Kotler, P., *Principles of Marketing*, Englewood Cliffs, New Jersey: Prentice Hall, 1980.
7. Gordon, G. N., *The Languages of Communication: A Logical and Psychological Examination*, *op. cit.*
8. See, for example, O'Sullivan *et al*, *Key Concepts in Communication*, *op. cit.*
9. Gordon G. N., *op. cit.*
10. O'Sullivan *et al*, *op. cit.*
11. Gibb, J. R., 'Defensive communication', *Journal of Communication*, **X**, September 1961.
12. *Ibid.*

Chapter 8

1. The definition is adapted from Tawney.
2. Olins, W., *The Corporate Personality*, *op. cit.*
3. *Ibid.*
4. *Ibid.*
5. *Ibid.*
6. *Ibid.*
7. Bevis, J. C., 'How corporate image research is used', a paper presented at the ESOMAR Wapor Congress, Vienna, 1967.
8. Lippman, W., *Public Opinion*, New York: Macmillan, 1949.

Chapter 9

1. Gordon, G. N., *The Languages of Communication: A Logical and Psychological Examination*, *op. cit.*

Chapter 10

1. French, D. and Saward, H. *Dictionary of Management*, London: Pan, 1977.
2. Olins, W., *The Wolff Olins Guide to Corporate Identity*, London: ISBA/The Design Council/The Design Management Institute, 1983.
3. Garbett, T.F., *Corporate Advertising. The What the Why and the How*, New York: McGraw Hill, 1981.
4. Olins, W., *The Corporate Personality*, *op. cit.*
5. *Ibid.*
6. Zabel, R. P., 'Accountability in corporate communications', *Cross Currents in Corporate Communications*, New York: Fortune, **5**, 1976. (My italics.)
7. They distribute Omega watches in the UK.
8. Olins, W., *The Corporate Personality*, *op. cit.*

Chapter 11

1. Drucker, P., *The Practice of Management*, London: Heinemann, 1955.

2. 'Working it out', *The Guardian*, 1 September 1982.
3. Zabel, R. P., (quote), 'Accountability in corporate communications', *op. cit.*
4. Stridsberg, A., (ed.), *Controversy Advertising*, New York: International Advertising Association/Hastings House, 1977.
5. Allen, A., (quote) 'Corporate advertising—out of the ivory tower, into marketing', *Public Relations Journal*, November 1974.
6. 'The will to win', CBI document, London: CBI, 5 March 1981.
7. Olins, W., *The Corporate Personality*, *op. cit.*

Chapter 12

1. Bavelas, A. 'Leadership: man and function', *Administrative Science Quarterly*, **IV**, no. 4, 1960.
2. *Encyclopaedia Britannica*, definition of *personality*.
3. Bavelas, A., *op. cit.*
4. 'The regulation of corporate image advertising', *Minnesota Law Review*, **59**, 1974.
5. Weiss, E. B., 'Don't kid the public with those noble ads', *Advertising Age*, 3 August 1970.
6. Curtin, D. J., 'A new basis for corporate communications', *Cross Currents in Corporate Communications*, New York: Fortune, **1**, 1972.
7. Plummer, Dr. J. T., 'Lifestyle analysis and corporate communications', *Cross Currents in Corporate Communications*, New York: Fortune, **3**, 1974.
8. Worcester, R., in conversation with the author.

Chapter 13

1. Margulies, W. P., 'Make the most of your corporate identity', *Harvard Business Review*, July/August 1977.
2. See Bernstein, D., *Creative Advertising: For this you went to Oxford?*, London: Longman, 1974.
3. O'Toole, J., 'Advocacy advertising shows the flag', *Public Relations Journal*, November 1975.
4. McFadyen, E., (quote), 'How to achieve successful regeneration', *op. cit.*
5. Harriman, B., 'Up and down the communications ladder', *op. cit.*
6. Murray, I., 'Sir Terence's grand design', *Money Observer*, November 1983.
7. *Ibid*, (quote).
8. Hume, S., 'Stars are lacking lustre as ad presenters', *Advertising Age*, 7 November, 1983.
9. McGinniss, J., *The Selling of the President*, *op. cit.*
10. Hume, S., *op. cit.*
11. 'Chrysler tries to sharpen its brand identity', *International Business Week*, 21 November 1983.
12. *Ibid.*
13. *Ibid.*
14. *Ibid.*
15. King, S., 'Has marketing failed?' a paper presented at the 15th Annual Conference of the Marketing Education Group, University of Lancaster, 1982.

Chapter 14

1. *Shorter Oxford English Dictionary*, definition of *philosophy*.
2. *Ibid.*
3. Peters, T. J. and Waterman, R. H. jnr., *In Search of Excellence, op. cit.*
4. Kemp, G., *The Company Speaks, op. cit.*
5. Garbett, T. J., *Corporate Advertising. The What, the Why and the How, op. cit.*
6. Kotler, P., *Principles of Marketing, op. cit.*
7. *Ibid.*
8. Kemp, G., *op. cit.*
9. Watson, Thomas, Snr., (IBM), quoted by Baker, E.L., 'Managing organisations culture', *McKinsey Quarterly*, Autumn 1980.

Chapter 15

1. Andrews, R. V., 'Crisis communication: the Tylenol story', a paper presented at the Corporate Communications Seminar, Amsterdam, November 1983.
2. MacNeil, R., *The Right Place at the Right Time*, Boston: Little, Brown and Co., 1982.
3. Bono de, E., *Wordpower*, London: Penguin, 1979.
4. MacEwan, E. C., 'Corporate advertising—the advancing state of the art', introduction to ANA Conference, New York, October 1982.
5. Gordon, G. N., (quote), *The Languages of Communication: A Logical and Psychological Examination, op. cit.*
6. ⋆Novo uses the term *rationale*.

Chapter 16

1. *Workplace Communications Advisory Booklet No. 8*, ACAS, July 1983.
2. *Ibid.*
3. Howell, R. G., 'Research in communications media based on an attitudinal survey in a major subsidiary of a world ranking European multi-national', a paper presented at the 2nd AMA/ESOMAR Conference, Paris, March 1981.
4. *Ibid.*
5. Pratt, K., 'Internal communications within Dunlop', a paper presented at the 2nd AMA/ESOMAR Conference, Paris, March 1981.
6. Howell, R. G., *op. cit.*
7. Cairncross, F. 'Big is no longer best', *The Guardian*, 26 January 1976.
8. *Ibid.* (quote), Bolton Committee Report, 1971.
9. 'The case for quality', prepared by the Department of Trade and Industry and the C.O.I., London: HMSO, 1983.
10. Harriman, B., 'Up and down the communications ladder', *op. cit.*

Chapter 17

1. 'Shell reaffirm confidence in corporate advertising on television', *Viewpoint*, London, Independent Television Contractors Association, 1984.
2. Parkinson, C. N. and Rowe, N. *Communicate*, London: Prentice Hall, 1977.

3. *Ibid.*
4. Kirby, R. E., 'Adversity, hostility and corporate communications' *Cross Currents in Corporate Communications*, New York: Fortune, 6, 1977.
5. Galli, A., 'Corporate advertising: more than just a nice warm feeling all over' *op. cit.*
6. Garbett, T. F., *Corporate Advertising. The What, the Why, and the How*, *op. cit.*
7. Hart, N., *Industrial Publicity*, London: Cassell/Associated Business Programmes, 1971.
8. Hall, G., Internal Memorandum, *The Financial Times*, 1984.
9. Traverse-Healy, T., 'The state of the art', *op. cit.*

Chapter 18
1. Traverse-Healy, T., 'The state of the art', *op. cit.*
2. Ways, M., 'Business needs to do a better job of explaining itself', *op. cit.*
3. Worcester, R., 'Corporate image research reviewed', a paper presented at the ESOMAR conference, Helsinki, 1971.
4. Gettig, B. R., 'Alcoa: focusing on the issues', *Public Relations Journal*, November 1974.
5. Levitt, T., quoted by Garbett, T. F., *Corporate Advertising. The What, the Why and the How, op. cit.*
6. Worcester, R., 'The role of research in evaluating public relations programmes', *IPRA Review*, November 1973.
7. Ways, M., *op. cit.*
8. Batchelor, C., 'B.E.T. gets its message through to a sceptical city', *The Financial Times*, 12 January, 1984.
9. Valin, R., 'What publics think about the company', *Management Today*, September 1982.
10. Parkinson, C. N. and Rowe, N., *Communicate, op. cit.*
11. Worcester, R., quoted by McLaughlin, N., 'The image is the message', *Corporate Communications*, supplement to *CBI News*, 11 November 1983.
12. Garbett, T. F., (quote), *op. cit.*

Chapter 19
1. Burdus, A., (quote), 'Communicating confidence. Will the big corporations please speak up?', *op. cit.*
2. Valin, R., (quote), 'What publics think about the company', *op. cit.*
3. Francis, C. G., (quote), 'Corporate advertising—the advancing state of the art', a paper presented at the ANA Conference, New York, October 1982.
4. Kemp, G., *The Company Speaks, op. cit.*
5. Edwardes, M., *Back From The Brink*, London: William Collins, 1983.
6. Workplace Communications Advisory Booklet No. 5, ACAS, *op. cit.*
7. McLaughlin, N., 'Changing the face of the house journal', *Corporate Communications*, supplement to *CBI News*, 11 November 1983.
8. Workplace Communications Advisory Booklet No. 8, ACAS, *op. cit.*
9. In conversation with the author.
10. See Ways, M., Keynote address (question and answer period), *Cross*

Currents in Corporate Communications, New York: Fortune, **2**, 1973.
11. Stridsberg, A., (ed), *Controversy Advertising, op. cit.*

Chapter 20

1. Edwardes, M., *Back From The Brink, op. cit.*

Chapter 21

1. Bevis, J. C., 'How corporate image research is used', *op. cit.*
2. Ladd, D. W. jnr., 'Mirror, mirror on the wall', *Cross Currents in Corporate Communications*, New York: Fortune, **6**, 1977.
3. Winkfield, N., 'International corporate image research', a paper presented at ESOMAR Conference, Budapest, October 1981.
4. *Morning Advertiser*, 25 September 1982.
5. Ries, A., quoted by Allen, A., 'Corporate advertising—out of the ivory tower, into marketing', *Public Relations Journal*, November 1974.
6. James, W., *The Principles of Psychology*, New York: Henry Holt and Co, **1**, 1890.
7. Friedlich, B., 'Communicating with the financial community', *Cross Currents in Corporate Communications*, New York: Fortune, **1**, 1972.
8. Olins, W., *The Corporate Personality, op. cit.*
9. McCormick, J., 'Ford draws up a new identity—in triplicate', *Advertising Age*, 24 January, 1983.
10. Fitch, R., in conversation with the author.
11. Boorstin, D., *The Image, op. cit.*
12. Allied Breweries Annual Report, 1981.

Chapter 22

1. Worcester, R., 'Around the conferences', *Advertising and Marketing Magazine*, Autumn 1979.
2. Bradshaw, D., quoted by Gould, P., 'Whitbreads's sales to new markets', *Marketing Magazine*, 5 August 1981.
3. *Ibid.*
4. Parkinson, C. N. and Rowe, N., (quote), *Communicate, op. cit.*
5. Research report, quoted by Vedder, B., at satellite conference, London, December 1982.
6. Walker, B., 'A colourful matter of taste', *CBI News*, 17 July 1981.
7. Willenkin, B., 'Brand advertising confronted with satellite television', a paper presented at the ADMAP Conference, Rome, April 1982.
8. Boorstin, D., (quote), *The Image, op. cit.*
9. Winkfield, N., 'International corporate image research', *op. cit.*

Chapter 23

1. Erdman, L. A.
2. Garbett, T. F., *Corporate Advertising. The What, the Why, and the How, op. cit.*
3. Burdus, A., 'Communicating confidence. Will the big corporations please speak up?', *op. cit.*

4. Atkinson, B., *Once Around The Sun, 1951*.
5. Attributed to Lord Northcliffe.
6. Barraclough, S., (quote), *The Headline Business*, London: CBI, 1981.
7. Traverse-Healy, T., 'The state of the art', *op. cit.*
8. Kelley, D., 'Critical issues for issue ads', *Harvard Business Review*, July/August 1982.
9. *Encyclopaedia Britannica* definition of *communication*.
10. Carnegie, D., *How to Win Friends and Influence People*, New York: Simon and Schuster, 1936.
11. O'Neill, H., 'The research behind a corporate campaign', *Cross Currents in Corporate Communications*, New York: Fortune, **7**, 1978.

Chapter 24

1. Margulies, W. P., 'Why, why, why? A step-sister to consumer', *Advertising Age*, 6 July 1981.
2. Olins, W., *The Corporate Personality*, *op. cit.*
3. Barnard, C., quoted by Peters, T. J. and Waterman, R. H. jnr., *In Search Of Excellence, op. cit.*
4. Ladd, D. W. jnr., (quote), 'Getting approval', *Cross Currents in Corporate Communications*, New York: Fortune, **12**, 1983.
5. Margulies, W. P., *op. cit.*
6. Edwardes, M., *Back From The Brink, op. cit.*
7. Margulies, W. P., *op. cit.*
8. Lyet, J. P., 'Corporate communications—the management view', *Cross Currents in Corporate Communications*, New York: Fortune, **3**, 1974.
9. Kirby, R. E., 'Adversity, hostility and corporate communications', *Cross Currents in Corporate Communications*, New York: Fortune, **6**, 1977.
10, Margulies, W. P., *op. cit.*
11. Sharp, J. T., 'Making it all work for you', *Advertising Age*, 6 July 1981.
12. Ogilvy, D., *Confessions of an Advertising Man*, London: Longman, 1964.
13. Harvey-Jones, J., quoted by Marckus, M., 'The human face of ICI', *The Observer*, 26 February 1984.
14. Olins, W., *The Corporate Personality, op. cit.*
15. Curtin, D., 'A new basis for corporate communication', *op. cit.*
16. Falk, R., *The Business of Management*, 2nd edition, London: Penguin, 1961.
17. Redhead, H. M., 'The second six sins of corporate advertising', *Cross Currents in Corporate Communications*, New York: Fortune, **4**, 1975.
18. *Ibid.*
19. Kotler, P., *Principles of Marketing, op. cit.*
20. *Ibid.*
21. *Ibid.*
22. Allen, A., 'Corporate advertising—out of the ivory tower, into marketing' *op. cit.*
23. Worcester, R., in conversation with the author.

Chapter 25

1. Tschoepke, E. T., 'A corporate identity for a service industry', a paper presented at the Corporate Communications and Corporate Advertising Seminar, Amsterdam, November 1982.

2. Lorenz, C., (quote), 'The revolution at SAS', *The Financial Times*, 31 October 1983.
3. Margulies, W. P., 'Make the most of your corporate identity', *op. cit.*
4. *Ibid.*
5. Tschoepke, E. T., *op. cit.*
6. The aim study referred to by Garbett, T. F., *Corporate Advertising. The What, the Why and the How, op cit.*
7. Tschoepke, E. T., *op. cit.*

Chapter 26

1. Williams, H. M., 'Corporate conduct and the bicentennial', *Cross Currents in Corporate Communications*, New York: Fortune, **5**, 1976.
2. Huxley, A., *Themes and Variations*, London: Chatto and Windus, 1950.
3. Falls, C.B.
4. Page, A., quoted by Galli, A., 'Corporate advertising: more than just a nice warm feeling all over', *op. cit.*
5. McLaughlin, N., 'Avoiding the identity crisis', *Corporate Communications, supplement to CBI News*, 11 November 1983.
6. Peters, M., quoted by Olins, W., *The Corporate Personality, op. cit.*

Chapter 27

1. Worcester, R., 'Measuring the impact of corporate advertising', *ADMAP*, September 1983.
2. Kleinman, P., 'Pushing the principles instead of the petrol', *The Guardian*, 28 October 1982.
3. Ogilvy, D., promotional piece for Ogilvy and Mather.
4. Research Services Ltd., 'Corporate image in Britain', guidelines to research programme, December 1982.
5. Margulies, W.P., 'Why, why, why? A step-sister to consumer', *op. cit.*
6. Graves, J., quoted by Allen, A., 'Corporate advertising—out of the ivory tower, into marketing', *op. cit.*
7. 'The regulation of corporate image advertising', *Minnesota Law Review 189*, **59**, 1974.
8. Worcester, R., 'Corporate advertising', *ADMAP*, September 1983.
9. Worcester, R., in conversation with the author.
10. Garbett, T. F., *Corporate Advertising. The What, the Why and the How, op. cit.*
11. *Ibid.*
12. Sachs, W. S. and Chasin, J., 'How top executives view corporate advertising', *Public Relations Journal*, November 1976.
13. Wreford, A., in conversation with the author.
14. Wreford, A., reproduced by kind permission of McAvoy Wreford.
15. Association of National Advertisers, 1983. Biennial study of trends in corporate advertising.
16. Research Services Limited, figures provided by *The Financial Times*/RSL.
17. Orthwein, J. B., 'What are you trying to do to whom?, *Cross Currents in Corporate Communications*, New York: Fortune, **6**, 1977.
18. Burdus, A., 'Communicating confidence. Will the big corporations please speak up', *op. cit.*

19. Garbett, T. F., *op. cit.*
20. *Ibid.*
21. *Ibid.*
22. 'Advertisers express belief in values of continued advertising', *Printers'
    Ink*, 8 September 1950.

Chapter 28

1. Wreford, A., in conversation with the author.
2. Lutos, M., quoted by Hood, M., 'Banks change advertising balance',
   Marketing Week, 4 November 1973.
3. *Ibid.*
4. Johnson, S., *The Idler*, 1758–60, ('Promise, large promise, is the soul of an
   advertisement.')
5. Yankelovich, P., 'A study of corporate effectiveness', a research
   document commissioned by *Time*, 1977.
6. *Ibid.*
7. Worcester, R., in conversation with the author.
8. Garbett, T. F., *Corporate Advertising:. The What, the Why and the How*,
   op. cit.
9. Starkey, R., in conversation with the author.
10. Margulies, W. P., 'Make the most of your corporate identity', *op. cit.*
11. Kelley, D., 'Critical issues for issue ads', *op. cit.*

Chapter 29

1. Turner, R. A., *Colliers Encyclopedia*, New York: Macmillan, **19**, 1976.
2. See Bernstein, D., *Creative Advertising*, *op. cit.*
3. Garbett, T. F., *Corporate Advertising. The What, the Why and the How*,
   op. cit.
4. *Ibid*, (quote).
5. Hewens, F. and Poppe, F., 'New impressions for an old device', *Public
   Relations Journal*, November 1972.
6. Giges, N., 'Pfizer boosts informational series of ads', *Advertising Age*,
   October 1983.
7. Ferry, N. J., 'America's most advanced corporations', *Fortune*, 9 January
   1984.
8. Gallup and Robinson quoted in 'Corporate image advertising', *Advertising
   Age*, 14 January 1983.
9. Gallup and Robinson quoted in 'Making it all work for you', *Advertising
   Age*, 6 July 1983.

Chapter 30

1. Stridsberg, A., (ed.), *Controversy Advertising*, *op. cit.*
2. *Ibid.*
3. Kelley, D., 'Critical issues for issue ads', *op. cit.*
4. 'Why corporate advertising?' a marketing report commissioned by *Time*.
5. Attributed to Lord Northcliffe.
6. Kleinman, P., 'Pushing the principles instead of the petrol', *op. cit.*

7. Kessler, L., 'Defense giant goes on offense—sometimes', *Advertising Age*, 24 January 1983.
8. *Ibid.*
9. Stridsberg, A., (ed.), *op. cit.*
10. *Harvard Business Review*
11. Nader, R., 'Challenging the corporate ad', *Advertising Age*, 24 January 1984.
12. *Ibid.*
13. *Ibid.*
14. *Ibid.*
15. *Ibid.*

Chapter 31

1. Wrightsman, L. S. and Deaux, K., *Social Psychology in the 80s, op. cit.*
2. Worcester, R., in conversation with the author.
3. Garbett, T.F., *Corporate Advertising. The What, the Why and the How, op. cit.*
4. Olins, W., *The Corporate Personality, op. cit.*
5. Matthews, L., 'Corporate advertising—a worthwhile use of a corporation's resources?', *Cross Currents in Corporate Communications*, New York: Fortune, **2**, 1973.
6. *Ibid.*
7. Kirby, R., 'Adversity, hostility and corporate communications', *op. cit.*
8. Valin, R., 'What publics think about the company', *op. cit.*
9. Drake, P., Penny, J. and Samuels, J., 'BP—Britain at its best', *Advertising Magazine*, Autumn 1981.
10. Garbett, T. F., 'Researching corporate advertising . . . in six stages', *Journal of Advertising Research*, February/March 1983.
11. *Ibid.*
12. Opinion Research Corporation literature.

Chapter 32

1. Worcester, R. and Lewis, S., 'Mirror, mirror on the wall', *MRS Survey Magazine*, 1 June 1983.
2. *Ibid.*
3. *Ibid.*
4. *Ibid.*
5. *Ibid.*
6. Drake, P., Penny, J. and Samuels, J., 'BP—Britain at its best' *op. cit.*
7. *Ibid.*
8. *Ibid.*
9. Gage, T. J., 'Grooming the image for a real impression', *Advertising Age*, 14 June 1982.
10. 'Esso corporate live tiger campaign', McCann Erickson document, 1976.
11. Worcester, R. and Lewis, S., *op. cit.*
12. 'Shell reaffirm confidence in corporate advertising on television', *op. cit.*
13. *Ibid.*
14. Worcester, R., 'Measuring the impact of corporate advertising' *op. cit.*
15. Milmo, S., (quote), 'The empire cuts fat', *Advertising Age*, 24 January 1983.

16. Hall, G., *The Financial Times, op. cit.*
17. Worcester, R., from an article in preparation.
18. Worcester, R., Measuring the impact of corporate advertising', *op. cit.*

Chapter 33

1. Parsons, D., *Funny Ha Ha and Funny Peculiar*, London: Pan Books, 1965, quote from *Daily Mail*.
2. Attributed to Lord Northcliffe.
3. Parsons, D., *op. cit.* quote from *Daily Express*.
4. Zalaznick, S., quoted by Cooper, M., 'Crisis public relations', *Public Relations Journal*, November 1981.
5. Revzin, P., quoted by Cooper, M., *ibid*
6. *Pharmaceutical Business News*, 6 July 1983.
7. Allen, A., 'Corporate advertising—its new look', *Public Relations Journal* November 1971.
8. Petzinger, T. jnr., 'When disaster comes, public relations men won't be far behind', *Wall Street Journal*, 23 August 1979.
9. *Pharmaceutical Business News, op. cit.*
10. Stephenson, D. R., 'Crisis situations. Opportunities in work clothes', a paper delivered to the Business and Professional Advertising Association of Dallas/Fort Worth, 31 January 1983.
11. Adapted from Levy, R., 'Crisis public relations', August 1983 (journal unknown).
12. Traverse-Healy, T., 'The state of the art', *op. cit.*
13. Levy, R., *op. cit.*
14. Petzinger, T. jnr., *op. cit.*
15. Orwell, G., *Shooting an Elephant and Other Essays*, London: Secker and Warburg, 1950.

Chapter 34

1. Berss, M., (quote), 'Jaguar Johnny', *Forbes Magazine*, 27 February 1984.

Chapter 35

1. Peters, T. J. and Waterman, R. H. jnr., *In Search of Excellence, op. cit.*
2. Winkfield, N., 'Developing and protecting international corporate, product and brand image', RSL document, June 1981.
3. Edwardes, M., *Back From The Brink, op. cit.*
4. Haines, D., in conversation with the author.
5. Davidson, R. P., 'Total corporate communications—by design or default?, *op. cit.*

Index